MONTGOMERY CLIFT, QUEER STAR

Contemporary Approaches to Film and Media Series

A complete listing of the books in this series can be found online at wsupress.wayne.edu

General Editor
Barry Keith Grant
Brock University

Advisory Editors
Robert J. Burgoyne
University of St. Andrews

Caren J. Deming
University of Arizona

Patricia B. Erens
School of the Art Institute of Chicago

Peter X. Feng
University of Delaware

Lucy Fischer
University of Pittsburgh

Frances Gateward
California State University, Northridge

Tom Gunning
University of Chicago

Thomas Leitch
University of Delaware

Walter Metz
Southern Illinois University

Montgomery Clift, Queer Star

Elisabetta Girelli

Wayne State University Press
Detroit

© 2014 by Wayne State University Press, Detroit, Michigan 48201.

All rights reserved. No part of this book may be reproduced without formal permission.

18 17 16 15 14   5 4 3 2 1

Library of Congress Cataloging-in-Publication Data

Girelli, Elisabetta.

Montgomery Clift, queer star / Elisabetta Girelli.

pages cm. — (Contemporary approaches to film and media series)

Includes bibliographical references and index.

Includes filmography.

ISBN 978-0-8143-3514-7 (pbk. . alk. paper) — ISBN 978-0-8143-3924-4 (e-book)

1. Clift, Montgomery—Criticism and interpretation. 2. Gay motion picture actors and actresses—United States. 3. Homosexuality and motion pictures—United States. 4. Queer theory. I. Title.

PN2287.C545G57 2013

791.43086'64—dc23

2013018444

Composed in Dante MT

To my mother,
Marialuisa Macchia:

"What a queer thing life is!
So unlike anything else,
don't you know, if you
see what I mean."

CONTENTS

Acknowledgments ix

Introduction 1

1. Montgomery Clift and Queer Theory 11

2. Irruption in Hollywood: The Beautiful Boy 33

3. The Peak of Stardom: Desire, Multiplicity, Deviancy 77

4. The 1956 Car Accident and a New Queerness 121

5. The Final Period: "Abnormality," Asexuality, Asynchrony 175

Epilogue 221

Notes 225
Filmography 237
Bibliography 239
Index 243

ACKNOWLEDGMENTS

A great number of people helped, supported, and inspired me while writing this book, and my debt to them is incalculable. First among all is Will Brown, who on a now-distant bus journey, from Leuchars Station to St. Andrews, suggested I should work on Montgomery Clift: I'll be grateful to him for the rest of my life. Many other friends and colleagues gave me vital encouragement at the start of this project. I cannot thank Alisdair Gibson enough for pointing me in the direction of disability studies, and thus helping me shape my ideas for what became chapter 4; but I'm equally grateful for his friendship and amazing patience, especially when bombarded by my messages at the height of many Clift-related crises. Robert Burgoyne and Dina Iordanova provided much-needed support at the initial stage of my writing, and I am very thankful for their crucial help. Heartfelt thanks to all my long-suffering colleagues at the University of St. Andrews, past and present ones, for graciously putting up with my Montgomery Clift obsession, and for their moral support at each stage of my work on this book. A special "thank you" to the fabulous Karen Drysdale and Rhona Paterson, departmental secretaries but also friends, counselors, and all-around rescuers. Thanks to Mike Arrowsmith for helping me with film clips and images throughout this project, and for displaying the patience of a saint while solving my technical issues.

Outside my immediate work environment, I am greatly indebted to people who have believed in my research and validated my ideas, even when I myself felt lost. Thanks to Pauline Small for her enduring support, through years of London-based and then long-distance friendship, and for discussing Montgomery Clift over many postfilm dinners at the South Bank. I am grateful to Mark Glancy for inviting me to share my work on Clift at his Film History Seminar, and for his friendly encouragement over a period of many years. Thanks to Kylie Rodier for enthusiastically listening to my Clift-related musings, and for lovely coffee sessions at the Royal Festival Hall. I am very grateful to Alice Black for celebrating Montgomery Clift and Elizabeth Taylor at Dundee Contemporary Arts, and for inviting me to give a talk about them. Cheers to the incomparable Fredrik Gustafsson for coming to my rescue during last-minute revisions!

As my work on Montgomery Clift progressed, I was incredibly lucky in gaining the help of people I had never met before, who generously shared their time and knowledge of Clift, and provided me with invaluable practical assistance. Words cannot express my gratitude to Deanna Waddell for her friendship and extraordinary kindness, for putting me up in Boston, and for sharing a memorable day in New York City. A million thanks to Steve Allen for sending me his precious material on Montgomery Clift, and for being such a friendly supporter of my work from afar. Thanks to John Demsey and Simon Forgette for kindly allowing me to visit 217 East Sixty-First Street, Montgomery Clift's last residence in New York.

Grateful thanks to the Carnegie Trust for the Universities of Scotland, who helped fund my trip to New York to consult the Montgomery Clift Papers, and thanks to the wonderful staff at the Billy Rose Theater Division of the New York Public Library, who made my two weeks there so pleasant and productive.

A special note of thanks to all my Facebook friends, for their tolerance, humor, and endless goodwill in the face of my barrage of "Monty" status updates (not to mention photos and film clips): I feel you've shared my daily struggles and achievements, and I know you helped me to get through it all. Thanks to the Taste coffee shop in North Street, whose wonderful crew kept me going with the best coffee in St Andrews and lovely chats, during the long weekends when I was writing in my office.

Finally, to my partner, Tony, and my mother, Marialuisa: thanks for absolutely everything!

Some of the material covered in this book was published in an article called "Man and Boy: Montgomery Clift as a Queer Star in *Wild River*," in the *Journal of Popular Film and Television* 39, no. 3 (2011).

Introduction

"I don't want to be labeled as either a pansy or a heterosexual. Labeling is so self-limiting. We are what we do, not what we say we are."[1] Montgomery Clift challenged prescribed models of identity throughout his life and career; his legacy as a film star stands out as a continuous, creative act of transgression, defying the cultural dominancy of sexual and gender "normality." Clift is a major figure in postwar Hollywood; his place in film history rests not only on his outstanding talent and the range of his work, but also, and arguably more, on his crucial role in the development of representations of masculinity. The first of a crop of young male actors who subverted conventions, Clift was a strikingly beautiful man, combining on-screen erotic ambiguity with real-life sexual nonconformity. He epitomized the shift from monolithically heterosexual models of virility (such as, for example, the image John Wayne projected, with whom Clift starred in *Red River*, 1948) to a greatly more nuanced, complicated portrayal of male identity. Clift was also a hugely talented actor, trained on stage since he was thirteen, and who collected Oscar nominations since his first screen appearance, in *The Search* in 1948. Worshipped by critics and audiences, he remained one of Hollywood's most marketable leading

INTRODUCTION

men until 1956, when a devastating car accident nearly destroyed his face. Clift never recovered from the trauma, as the accident brought to a head his history of alcoholism, drug addiction, and mental fragility; it also robbed him of his exceptional beauty, revoking his heartthrob status overnight. Visibly burdened by physical and mental pain, with part of his face paralyzed, and afflicted by spiraling ill health, Clift was turned into a tragic, disturbing figure by the press; his worsening condition was greatly sensationalized and openly held against him by an increasingly hostile Hollywood. Yet Clift continued to make films, crafting a series of unorthodox performances that have been too often overlooked; while the first phase of his career was defined by an ambivalent though palpable sexual presence, his post-1956 work shows him as a socially alienated subject, engaged in unusual and often nonsexual relationships. Montgomery Clift died in 1966, aged forty-five; the body of work he left behind consists of seventeen films and a range of male characters that, in their disruption of normative structures, are astoundingly modern. As issues of sexual and gender representation move at the core of critical inquiry, and the very concept of a fixed identity is questioned, the exploration of Clift's subversive legacy is more topical, and more exciting, than ever.

Film stars are actors who achieve a privileged, iconic status in the public imagination. More than other performers, stars generate their own discourse about themselves, in which screen appearances merge with biography and publicity. In Montgomery Clift's case, a single event in his life not only affected his celebrity aura but also brought factual changes to his looks and health, impacting his work as an actor: the event was, of course, the 1956 car crash, which effectively gave rise to two visibly different figures, the pre- and the postaccident Clift. As a result, his career path falls almost too neatly in two separate halves, yet as Richard Dyer points out, a star's image "is a *complex totality* and it does have a *chronological dimension*"[2] (Dyer's emphasis). Clift's 1956 accident gives structure to his chronology by being an obvious turning point, yet it does not alter his total signification as a star: beautiful or damaged, healthy or dramatically ill, young or prematurely aged, Clift maintained an essential disruptive function, against conventions of the male, the lover, and the Hollywood leading man. His image had been replete with ambiguity from the start, since *The Search* and *Red River* had rocketed him to stardom in 1948; a few months later his face graced the cover of *Life* magazine. Such meteoric fame was largely based on his quality of dissonance, and his disorienting erotic charge. *The Search* cast him as a US Army engineer in postwar Germany: looking radiant and sexy in a landscape of devastation, he was not involved in a conventional romance plot but in an extraordinarily close relationship with a young boy, whom he loved and nurtured at the exclusion of any other interest. As John Wayne's young foil in *Red River*, Clift gave a highly erotic yet ambivalent performance, appearing as a willing object of desire for both the male and the female gaze; the unresolved tension between his sexual directions was shocking. Both films showcased Clift's groundbreaking persona, defined by vulnerability, emotive intensity, and a self-displaying emphasis on his body. Even his beauty strayed from canons of male attractiveness, as he looked exquisite and nearly perfect, beautiful rather than handsome; together with his youth, ambiguous sexual persona, and stunning performances, Clift emerged as an immensely attractive yet unsettling figure in postwar Hollywood. Film reviewers were ecstatic: "Montgomery Clift is superb" was the verdict of *The Tribune* on *The Search*, and *Time* found Clift in *Red River* to be "that rare bird—with both screen personality and acting talent." Fan literature was even more extravagant: "The hottest actor since Valentino" announced *Look*, while celebrity guru Louella Parsons felt that Clift "sort of insinuates himself into your mind." The fans were stunned and emotional, as photographer Richard Avedon recalled years later when he confessed, "the minute Monty came on screen I cried";[3] Caryl Rivers thought that Clift's beauty "was so sensual and at the same time so vulnerable it was almost blinding."[4] In 1949, *Movie Life* published a piece on Clift simply titled "Tall, Dark and Different." These reactions reflected the extraordinary impact of Clift's looks and style, which were strikingly unusual yet at the same time suited to a cultural context fraught with the expectation of change. The immediate postwar had ushered in an era in which many cardinal values, which had until then defined American society, would be challenged and redefined. Dominant assumptions about gender roles, the family, and the authority of the Establishment were no longer unassailable, and the following two decades would witness an increasing opposition to traditional ideologies. Specifically, the late 1940s and the 1950s were characterized by a

INTRODUCTION

crisis about the meaning and function of masculinity, and by the emergence of youth culture; at the same time, the McCarthy anticommunist witch hunt, with its broad antidissidence agenda, reflected the strength of a punitive social order that remained hegemonic. Sexual activity was the target of control and repression, and alternative sexual orientations would be criminalized well into the 1960s, yet the Kinsey reports on sexual behavior, published in 1948 and 1953 amid huge sensation, had coolly announced that 10 percent of American males were homosexual, and that homosexuality was part of an erotic continuum that denied rigid divisions. In this transitional age, Montgomery Clift embodied a new, unorthodox brand of man, who dared to be sexually ambiguous and distinctly "unmasculine." While Clift's innovative presence would soon be echoed by a pack of young actors, from Marlon Brando and James Dean to Anthony Perkins and Paul Newman, Clift was the first, and arguably the most deviant male star of his generation. Moreover, though usually linked to Clift by the media, these other stars' relation to filmmaking was not the same as his: they tended to rely on a system, be it the newly trendy Method school of acting (which Clift never practically embraced, and later in life would flatly deny of even knowing[5]), or the structure of the Hollywood studios, which Clift both defied and manipulated. With unheard-of independence, Clift rose to the top of stardom while being virtually never under studio contract; the only time he was, with Paramount in 1948, he was signed on astonishingly liberal terms, with the freedom to refuse any part or director, and to terminate the agreement at any time.[6] This contract ended abruptly in 1949 when Clift, with typically baffling selectiveness, refused the lead role in Billy Wilder's *Sunset Boulevard* and chose instead *The Big Lift*, a film about the Berlin airlift shot on location in Germany. Clift's legendary fussiness in accepting roles, the huge number of sure hits he rejected, and the total freedom he had in his choices, increase the significance of each film he made; in addition, Clift vastly changed his scripts, often deleting whole chunks of dialogue and drastically rewording his remaining lines. The result is a series of screen roles utterly shaped by Clift's intervention, acquiring their deeper meaning from his unique commitment to character and performance. From the beginning, the men Clift portrayed were conflicted, ambivalent, and socially dissenting; when this was not explicit in the script, Clift weaved a thread of subversion into his characters, complicating their erotic desire and adherence to gender or even national patterns. In *The Big Lift*, for instance, an overtly propagandistic film celebrating the strength of the US Army, Clift spends key scenes out of his American uniform, trying to pass for a local; he also assumes a feminized, victimized, and sexually uncertain role in his affair with a German woman. If Clift's screen roles constructed a disorienting male identity, oozing sex appeal yet not unequivocally heterosexual, rumors about his life and his perennial bachelorhood amply contributed to his ambiguous image. Sexually and romantically involved with men and women, Clift lived in the open secret of the closet; the press was alternately suspicious of his lack of girlfriends, disparaging of those he did have, or adamant that he was madly in love with his favorite costars, Elizabeth Taylor and Marilyn Monroe. "His love life has everyone guessing," complained *Photoplay* in 1949, declaring in a later article that Clift was "that rarest of all Hollywood paradoxes—a young actor who isn't excited about his appeal for feminine movie-goers." That same year, the *Hollywood Reporter* suggestively asked, "Is It True What They Say About Monty?" while Clift himself, in reply to the question of what special girl he liked, assured journalists, "I like 'em all." In November 1951, the caption under an image of Clift and Taylor on the cover of *Silver Screen* said, "Here's Why Our Marriage Will Last," a few months after *A Place in the Sun* had made them Hollywood's hottest screen couple; Clift's denials did not stop news of their impending wedding from recurring throughout his life. Meantime, Clift shocked public opinion with his on-and-off relationship with Libby Holman, fourteen years his senior and not especially good looking. Labeled "an enigma" by the press, Clift was also the target of blackmailers, who spotted him cruising in gay bars and were quietly dealt with by his lawyers; nonetheless, gossip about his sex life would at times surface and be swiftly silenced, as early as in 1948 when powerful columnist Hedda Hopper phoned his agent, asking if it was true that Clift had been charged with pederasty (it wasn't, though a week later Clift was arrested for trying to pick up a youth, and the incident was hushed up).[7]

While Clift's erotic appeal was imbued with sexual ambiguity, it was also firmly based on his dazzling beauty; the 1956 accident literally tore apart Clift's image, which then reassembled itself into a hybrid

INTRODUCTION

mix of past and present. Constantly measured against his former looks, Clift now appeared out of sync with himself; this rupture became part of his total meaning as a star, as difference and continuity were held in tension by his increasingly aberrant presence. Although Clift's health fluctuated, his ever-worsening addictions hastened his deterioration; aged and often ill, he brought to the screen his pain and disquieting looks, informing his roles with a suffered alien quality. He could appear almost freakish, as in *The Young Lions* (1958); or wrecked by anguish and sexual dilemmas, as in *Lonelyhearts* (1958); or, in *Judgment at Nuremberg* (1961), in radical breach of bodily and mental "normality." Clift's perfectionist approach to acting never changed, nor did his emotional intensity, or his stress on nonverbal communication; however, there had always been an absent side to his eroticism, a hint of remoteness in the midst of enticement, and this aspect now turned into an increasingly asexual quality. In roles defined by social disruption, or by alienized physicality, Clift's defiance of a "normal" sex drive completed his subversive function. *Freud* (1962) was Clift's last big role, a memorable portrayal of a culturally dissident Sigmund Freud; the film was followed by some desperate years for Clift, who found himself blacklisted by Hollywood because he was deemed too ill to be insurable. *The Defector* (1966) showed him frail and worn out, oscillating between ghostliness and random flashes of intensity; it was to be his last screen appearance, as he died before the film was released.

This book covers Montgomery Clift's whole career, tracing his trajectory of subversion; in doing so, it means to challenge the reductive approach that has defined most studies of Clift, often limited to his preaccident films, and to the identification of gay or bisexual subtexts in his performance. This book offers instead a full exploration of Clift's disruptive presence, which can best be approached as a complex structure of queer significations. Recent developments in queer theory have expanded the scope of "queer" to include a range of identities and social practices not confined to same-sex relations, indeed not confined to sexuality. These configurations, however, express a fundamental challenge to "normality." This book assesses Montgomery Clift by applying queer theory to his star persona, film roles, and performances, examining the range of oppositional meanings he brought to the screen.

The book is divided into five chapters. Chapter 1 reviews the exist-

INTRODUCTION

Icon: Preaccident Montgomery Clift, at the peak of his fame in A Place in the Sun.

ing scholarship on Montgomery Clift, discussing its emphasis on youth and beauty and its tendency to pose a fixed sexual identity; the need for a new, radical approach to Clift is identified. The book's methodology is established by introducing queer theory; through a brief history of the development of queer criticism, the case is made for its appropriateness to a study of Montgomery Clift. Chapter 2 examines the stunning beginning of Clift's career, tracing the emergence of key elements in his persona. It starts with an analysis of *Red River*, considering the impact and implications of Clift's erotic spectacle. Drawing on Eve Kosofsky Sedgwick's theory of homosocial desire, Clift's disruptive masculinity is located at the center of a multiple sexual structure, in excess of both patriarchy and homosexuality. *The Heiress* (1949) sees Clift again as an object of desire, yet expressing an enigmatic sexual identity. In a role informed by the queer archetype of the Dandy, and through a self-displaying performance based on the clash between appearance and essence, Clift emerges as an ambiguous and closeted subject. The chapter then discusses *The Search* and *The Big Lift* (1950), two

INTRODUCTION

films shot on location in postwar Germany; a US soldier in both roles, Clift heavily destabilizes notions of gendered Americanness. In the light of queer criticism of intergenerational love, Clift's obsessive relationship with a boy in *The Search* is read as a strong platonic bond, reverberating with displaced notions of mother-and-child sensuality. *The Big Lift* is a Cold War propaganda feature, turned upside down by Clift's de-virilized, de-sexualized, and partly de-Americanized presence. With reference to Judith Butler's theory of performative gender formation, Clift is shown as a disruptive agent in the incessant reconstruction of militarized Americanness. Chapter 3 focuses on Montgomery Clift at the peak of his fame, in 1951–53; it argues that this period sees the crystallization of Clift's complex persona, expressed through an astounding range of queer identities. *A Place in the Sun* and *I Confess* see Clift caught in narratives of deception, ambiguity, and excessive desire, linked through the powerful structure of the closet. *A Place in the Sun* marks the beginning of Clift's personal and professional relationship with Elizabeth Taylor. Producing some of Clift's most iconic images, the film places him in the untenable position of all-desiring subjectivity. Subversively wanting too much, Clift here inhabits at once what Sedgwick calls "the viewpoint of the closet" and "the spectacle of the closet." *I Confess* shows Clift at his most verbally reticent, in an astonishing performance centered on facial expression, body language, and the refusal to talk. As a priest keeping the secret of the confessional, while being equally secretive about his own motives, Clift is trapped in a web constructed by his own silence, through a muted speech act that sexualizes both knowledge and ignorance. The chapter concludes by discussing *From Here to Eternity*, the film that crowns this stage of Clift's career, providing him with a role that has remained powerfully linked to his star image. As the rebellious US soldier Prewitt, Clift presents an unorthodox yet committed military identity, disrupting established notions of the American soldier. By applying Judith Butler's discussion of "Don't Ask, Don't Tell" to Clift's presence in the film, *From Here to Eternity* is analyzed as a queer text, charting Prewitt's struggle for self-determination. Chapter 4 starts by discussing Clift's 1956 car accident, with its dramatic and far-reaching implications; it considers the devastating effect of the crash on Clift himself, the changes it brought to his star image, and the repercussions for his career. Happening halfway

INTRODUCTION

through the shooting of *Raintree County* (1957), a sweeping Civil War drama, Clift's accident inevitably shapes the film into a narrative of personal chaos. The chapter moves on to examine Clift's first film after the car crash, *The Young Lions*, where Clift took the extraordinary decision of altering his already-battered looks for the worst. In the light of Robert McRuer's "crip theory," Clift's self-alienizing move is assessed as a deliberate queer strategy, highlighting deviancy from his former self and from canons of physical norm. The chapter next focuses on *Lonelyhearts* and *Suddenly, Last Summer* (1959), whose plots center on social and sexual perversion. With reference to Sally R. Munt's work on the queer reclamation of shame, *Lonelyhearts* is read as a conflictive text, whose normative trajectory is compromised by Clift's immersion in pleasurable sexual disgrace. Miraculously avoiding censorship, *Suddenly, Last Summer* sees Clift as the master of a complex aberrant structure, in a film whose veneer of queer horror belies the vindication of sexual difference. Drawing on Leo Bersani's classic essay *Is the Rectum a Grave?*, Clift's character is seen as the rescuer of queer identities from oppressive representations. Chapter 5 looks at the final period of Montgomery Clift's career, when his increasingly deviant image challenged expectations of "normal" adult sexuality; clashing more than ever with heteronormative structures, Clift also subverted socially accepted time progressions. The chapter first discusses Clift's "straight queer" presence in *Wild River* and *The Misfits*. Projecting a hybrid man/boy identity suggestive of asexuality, in *Wild River* Clift turns heterosexual romance into queer kinship. *The Misfits* is heavily shaped by Clift's special affinity with Marilyn Monroe, as their roles blur the boundaries of screen and real life; linked by what Leo Bersani theorizes as queer near-sameness, Clift and Monroe here meet in a transgressive space outside patriarchy. The chapter then turns to Clift's alignment with queer temporality, as his image became more and more defined by the asynchrony inscribed in his body. In *Judgment at Nuremberg*, as a man sterilized by the Nazis, Clift gives a devastating portrayal of a temporally hybrid subject, forever meeting past horrors in the present. *Freud* is the apt conclusion of Clift's career: asserting a sexually and temporally hybrid identity, Clift's performance disrupts Freud's own radical thinking, challenging epistemologies of sex and time.

ONE

Montgomery Clift and Queer Theory

The Need for a New Critical Approach

The existing scholarship on Montgomery Clift presents many valid and enlightening arguments; at the same time, it appears limited in scope, and often shortsighted in its analysis. Clift's subversive function was vastly more complex and spanned a much longer period of his career than is usually acknowledged. Critical analyses of his star persona and performances have been inadequate on three major points. Firstly, their general indifference to Clift's films made after 1956, films that are replete with oppositional meanings. This indifference effectively equates sexual and gender subversion to youth, beauty, and overt erotic display. Secondly, Clift's disruptive screen presence has been narrowly explained, in terms of fixed notions of homosexuality and bisexuality. Thirdly, the qualities and articulation of Clift's sexuality have been acknowledged only in terms of passive self-offering and overt sexual drive. There are far-reaching implications in this critical stance. To identify social subversion in Clift only when young and sexy means, ultimately, to endorse an extremely conservative view of dissent: any deviant identity linked to age, to a less-than-perfect face and body, and to ill health and pain, has been cast out or censored, because of its uncomfortable connotations. This process of elimination points to an alarming hierarchy of subversion, and to such a limited appreciation of social and human possibilities—not to mention cinematic material—as to amount to critical bigotry. Montgomery Clift's career continued into the 1960s, and these films amply reward the scrutiny for textual and subtextual disruptions of dominant cultural codes; despite being and looking older, and having lost much of his beauty, Clift radically challenges normative notions of masculinity and heterosexuality. His entire career, therefore, can be seen as the continuous, though varied, articulation of the same disruptive function.

The only academic monograph on Clift to date is Amy Lawrence's *The Passion of Montgomery Clift*, an impressively researched work that explores the cultish appeal of Clift's life and star persona.[1] Lawrence's project is concerned with the making of the Clift legend, which is significantly based on notions of tragedy and undeserved suffering; she interestingly compares it to religious discourse, and to the narrative and visual iconography of sainthood and martyrdom. Lawrence's book is remarkably informative and originally argued; it offers insightful, close analyses of Clift's performances, which are brought to inform her general thesis. While she necessarily considers the often-made claim that Clift was a subversive figure, her approach is rather aimed at debunking this notion: she strives to expose the fan discourse grown around him, and its ramifications, as semimythological constructs. Indeed, her critical take on Clift strips him of significations that may appear exceptional, apart from the recognition of his superb skills as an actor; the book uses this solid approach fruitfully, although it does not foster a full exploration of the meanings inherent in Clift's work. Overall, Lawrence's book marks an important acknowledgment of Montgomery Clift's place in film and cultural history; as a critical text, it locates itself firmly on the side of deconstruction, concerned with revealing the structure of Clift fandom. The majority of the other scholars working on Clift have, on the whole, focused on his subversive impact and function; while there is a consensus on the essential factors that make up the star's disruptive image, the scope of these analyses has been strikingly limited. Most of these critical accounts focus, almost overwhelmingly, on Clift's preaccident career, covering his films up to and including *From Here to Eternity*. Clift's ambiguity is always read as expressing a homosexual or bisexual meaning; however, even when the term "bisexual" is used, Clift's engagement with female characters is rarely discussed or deemed relevant.

Steven Cohan has provided a notable contribution, devoting to Clift a significant section of his book *Masked Men: Masculinity and the Movies in the Fifties*.[2] Cohan's perceptive assessment, largely based on textual analysis and contextual references, can be seen as the prototype of accounts of Montgomery Clift as "the beautiful boy."[3] Indeed, the concept of the "boy" is absolutely central to Cohan's examination of Clift as a performer and signifier. Beginning his discussion by quoting an article by the columnist Sidney Skolsky in 1957, Cohan highlights a conservative critical perception of Clift, and of some of his contemporaries such as Marlon Brando, James Dean, and others, as being "a boy who'd like to be a man"; Cohan turns this scathing term upside down by reclaiming it as "the boy who is not a man," and using it to denote an unsettling new figure in postwar Hollywood. Cohan thus makes a primary generational identification between Clift and his peers, approaching the star as a young rebel; this identification, which Cohan explores in its subversive implications, is effectively used as a total "explanation" of Montgomery Clift. Through explicit links to the (young) Brando, and the (forever young) Dean, Cohan articulates his concept of the "boy who is not a man" by relating it to notions of bisexual desire, to Clift's offering of himself to the male and the female gaze, and to the denaturalization of established gender and sexual roles. Clift's disruptive presence, he argues, was characterized by an erotic appeal based in spectacle: unlike traditional "manly" actors, Clift reveled in a self-display that was ambiguously targeted, resulting in a dynamic of desiring and being desired that Cohan labels "bisexual." Like most scholars discussing Clift as a subversive figure, Cohan concentrates on the actor's first film, *Red River*, and on the iconic *A Place in the Sun*. With its generational conflict, assorted homoerotic subtexts, and the big and brutal John Wayne as Clift's counterpart, *Red River* is seen by Cohan as the blueprint for Clift's persona. Drawing attention to the performative quality of Clift's portrayal of his character, Matthew, who is mostly occupied by competing with Wayne and other males, Cohan leaps to see Matthew's sexuality as also performative. As a product of Clift's intense acting style, with its emphasis on nonverbal communication, this per-

CHAPTER I

formativity is also found key to Clift's bisexual connotations. The same notion is applied to *A Place in the Sun*, where Clift's character, George, exhibits a self-reflexive desire in his obsession for Angela, and a closeted attachment for Alice. Clift's distinctive style and physical appearance, Cohan concludes, constructed the star as "a desirable boy by revealing the ground of his masculinity in performativity and bisexuality."[4]

While Cohan's analysis is very useful and insightful, it presents several problems that typify critical approaches to Clift. To begin with, to apply any sexual label to Clift's persona, whether "homosexual" or "bisexual," effectively minimizes or deletes ambiguity, rather than highlights it. The scope of Clift's sexually informed performances, and the possibilities that can be derived from them, vastly exceed the available meanings of "bisexual." If Clift's sexual image is unsettlingly ambiguous—and it most certainly, consistently is—it is because it *remains* ambiguous; that is, it remains undetermined, rather than neatly split into a fifty-fifty allocation, or into any other combination of sexual percentages. Presenting important variations from one film to another, which makes sexual labeling inappropriate, Clift's erotic performance is impossible to pin down. The Clift spectacle is aberrant not because it is directed at two targets, the male and the female gaze, but because its direction stays profoundly unclear. In *The Search*, for example, Clift's erotic charge is not aimed at anyone in particular, yet it bears significantly on the film's negotiation of its central relationship, that between Clift and a child; at the same time, Clift's character, Steve, displays a striking lack of overt sex drive, and sexual narratives are conspicuously absent from the plot. This multiplicity of meanings, rather than a mere "swinging both ways," defines the ambiguity of Clift's persona, and therefore its shock and excitement. Nor is Clift always articulating sexuality as a spectacle; on the contrary, some of Clift's films directly challenge the very presence and nature of sexuality, bringing notions of celibacy and asexuality to the fore. In his discussion of Montgomery Clift, Steven Cohan never specifies the exact meaning of "performativity," although it would readily suggest a nod to Judith Butler's theorization of gender formation;[5] he does, however, refer it to Marjorie Garber's exploration of bisexuality,[6] and uses it to reconfirm Clift's persona as bisexual. Even bisexuality, however, is not adequately accounted for in Cohan's text, which ignores Clift's interaction with female characters as, indeed, female characters. The heterosexual liaison in *Red River* is seen as a poorly disguised resolution for an implied homosexual love story, while the complex tension between George and two women in *A Place in the Sun* is brought to bear on a closeted gay subtext. While there is considerable interest to be found in these readings, Cohan uses them at the expense of a closer look at Clift's heterosexual performances. The concentration on male-to-male eroticism is a feature of most studies of Clift; in practice, this approach ignores not only the strength of some of his heterosexual love scenes but also the extraordinarily complex relationships he often builds with women on screen. It is remarkable that Cohan's chosen examples, *Red River* and *A Place in the Sun*, contain two of the most sexually charged scenes of Clift's entire career, both involving women. Toward the end of the first film, Matthew/Clift is unexpectedly reunited with his love interest, Tess (Joanne Dru), as she surprises him in his hotel room. The two embrace, and Tess starts talking to him, but all the while Matthew is caressing her face, hair, and shoulders, seemingly unaware of her words; his eyes are fixed on her with barely repressed desire, his touch is slow and intimate. It is a strikingly erotic performance on Clift's part, heavily suggesting sex in a film that does not actually show any; similarly, in *A Place in the Sun*, George/Clift exudes sexual energy when he seduces Alice (Shelley Winters), by insinuating himself into her bedroom after she has half-heartedly told him to leave. Although the scene turns to darkness and we only hear the couple's murmurs, heavy sexual overtones have been clearly built up by Clift's prior behavior, which is physically insistent and erotically charged.

Most importantly, Cohan totally ignores Clift's career after the 1956 car accident; his analysis conflates Clift, as a star and performer, with the young Clift, an exceptionally beautiful man never past his early thirties. Apart from a passing mention of *The Young Lions*, Cohan does not elaborate on how Clift's inherent "boyishness," with its disruptive implications, was both maintained and transformed when the star ceased, in terms of age and looks, to be a boy. While Cohan focuses on Clift's "deviant body as a beautiful, bisexual young male,"[7] he does not engage with the profoundly deviant connotations of Clift's body after 1956. Finally, the insistence on fitting Clift into a narrow generational slot elides key differences between him and his peers; it also risks ascrib-

CHAPTER I

ing to Clift's persona characteristics it never had. For example, Cohan refers to both Clift and Brando as figures suggesting a "lack of formal education" and a "working-class identity,"[8] ignoring Clift's evidently educated, upper-class roots, as well as his established status as an intellectual actor.[9]

The fascination with Montgomery Clift as an icon of youthful rebellion, which is shared by scholars and fans, points to a craving for categorization that lies at the root of stardom. While stars are seen as uniquely different, they are also made to fit into recognizable "types"; Cohan's account of Clift as a subversive "boy" is consistent with Richard Dyer's description of the "rebel" type of star, in which Dyer includes Clift. This type is characterized by youth, and therefore by the equation of subversion with a certain age: "youth is the ideal material term on which to displace social discontent, since young people always get older (and 'grow up')."[10] Graham McCann is another scholar who has approached Montgomery Clift from the "young rebel" angle, in *Rebel Males: Clift, Brando, and Dean*. McCann pointedly locates Clift in the context of the Method school of acting, highlighting the generational and stylistic affinities between him, Brando, and Dean. However, while McCann's analysis is somewhat diluted by this method, and not particularly helped by constant references to Clift's biography, his book is noteworthy for at least mentioning aspects of Clift's career and performance that Cohan conspicuously ignores. Discussing Clift's sexual orientation, McCann fairly randomly shifts to Clift's screen persona and back, yet he accurately remarks that although some of Clift's characters suggest overt eroticism, others are defined by a timid or absent sexual expression. Instead of acting on his desire, in the predictable fashion of Hollywood leading men, Clift often retires into himself by showing only the feeling of that desire; at times his sexuality comes across as "latent" or "almost presexual."[11] Clift's ambiguity is partly built on his sexual nonperformance, which greatly problematizes his male identity and motivations. Having recognized this essential factor, however, McCann is then led to the extravagant conclusion that Clift acts this way because "he is a romantic rebel."[12] Likewise, although McCann is one of the rare scholars to survey Clift's later career, however briefly, he evades any in-depth analyses of Clift's postaccident films, merely linking them back to the star's "rebelliousness."

Montgomery Clift and Queer Theory

A related but separate strand of criticism has dealt with Montgomery Clift's appeal to gay audiences; it has produced some interesting analyses, yet it has also conformed to some of the customary limitations of Clift scholarship. Accounts of gay spectators' investment in Clift mostly focus on strictly homosexual meanings, reducing his ambiguous persona to that of a varyingly successfully masked gay man. Kylo-Patrick R. Hart offers a valid starting point by highlighting homosexual subtexts in many of Clift's early films; however, he not only entirely avoids the films made after 1956 but also explicitly declares them uninteresting. Hart's contention is that Clift is relevant to gay spectators as long as he is "sexually or homoerotically enticing," something that is seen as being dependent on his preaccident appearance.[13] Brett Farmer has offered a more nuanced contribution to the gay spectatorship issue in his book *Spectacular Passions: Cinema, Fantasy, Gay Spectatorship*.[14] Farmer has produced one of the most thought-provoking readings of Clift as a star through a psychoanalytically informed analysis. He is the only scholar to venture, however limitedly, into notions of "queerness" rather than just "gayness" by stressing the complex oppositional quality of Clift's sexual and gender identity, and by actually making use of the term "queer." Although not immune to the bias toward a generational reading, Farmer makes a welcome distinction between Clift and the two actors traditionally associated with him, Marlon Brando and James Dean. He points out how Clift's performance, unlike his two peers', is devoid of "masculine" traits such as aggression and violence. Farmer sees Clift's softer, more vulnerable style as a sign of his "dephallicized masculinity," and rightly identifies it as subversive of orthodox male behavior; his essential argument, however, is based on the assessment of Clift as a "masochist." Starting with "Freud's assertion that masochism prototypically entails the assumption of a psychic position of passive femininity,"[15] Farmer reclaims the term as potentially liberating; given that male masochism is radically at odds with patriarchal power, a masochistic male suggests deviancy and social disruption. Farmer then applies a masochistic reading to virtually the whole of Clift's career, arguing that it provides gay spectators with an identification that is not only pleasurable but also empowering through its meaning of resistance. This is an interesting interpretation, as it locates Clift on a much wider spectrum of difference than is usually acknowledged; by allowing the possibility of radical disruption in psychic and social terms, Farmer presents Clift as a deeply deviant figure, opposing heteronormative masculinity through a range of strategies. However, there are obvious problems in labeling Clift a "castrated" male,[16] or a "self-debasing masochist."[17] First of all, while Farmer's defense of masochism is coherently argued, it cannot delete the disempowering connotations that the concept, or term, certainly still conveys: while opposition to patriarchy is good, the willing acceptance of physical and mental suffering may be much less good, and surely does not automatically grant a positive weight to Clift as a star or role model. Second, a masochistic reading of Clift's film roles is suggestive yet highly subjective, arguably going directly against the most likely reactions to Clift's performances. The characters Farmer insists on calling masochists, such as Matthew in *Red River*, for example, Prewitt in *From Here to Eternity*, or Noah in *The Young Lions*, can be very easily read as fearless men, stubbornly resisting the status quo through a heightened sense of dignity and defiance. Notions of being a "willing victim" are effortlessly denied by these characters' narrative role, as well as by Clift's performance. Likewise, Farmer's analysis is enriched by the inclusion of Clift's later films in his discussion; however, he not only blankets them with the same "masochistic" interpretation, he also insists on their uniformly homosexual meaning. This is all the more disappointing as Farmer acknowledges the multiple queer possibilities offered by Clift's heterosexual scenes, yet he entirely glosses over them, linking them to an unfounded biographical interpretation that strips Clift's relationships with women of any sexual content. Curiously ignoring the mass of evidence for Clift's heterosexual experiences, he ultimately reads each of Clift's relationships with females—on and off screen—as between "siblings."

The scope of Clift's ambiguity includes situation and identities that are defined by uncertainty, but not simply in the sense of a basic erotic indecision between men and women. Clift's performance shows a constant process of sexual renegotiation, which points to a dynamic state of noncompletion; sexual identity is always in the process of recasting itself. This constant shift, with its inherent doubts and multiplicity, forms the core of Clift's ambiguous sexuality; its refusal to be pinned down, labeled, and accordingly filed is what makes it truly subversive.

Clift's erotic persona also varies dramatically from film to film and is certainly not uniformly passive. *Red River, A Place in the Sun,* and *Stazione Termini* (1953) contain his most erotically charged scenes, where Clift actively expresses and acts on sexual desire, notably with women; on the other hand, Clift's character in *From Here to Eternity,* for example, entirely lacks any heterosexual drive, and his erotic attachments, only implied and hinted at, are passive and forged with men. At the same time, at each stage of his career Clift produced performances that verged on the asexual, insofar as "asexual" may connote an absence of sexual initiative or openly expressed desire. These performances may still reveal a self-reflexive eroticism and physical self-display, as in *The Search* and *The Big Lift;* or they may show Clift as a totally passive yet self-aware object of someone else's desire, as in *I Confess.* In some films, Clift's ambiguity is defined by the possible absence, or mere suspension, of his sexual desire, such as in *Wild River* and *Freud;* at other times, his sexuality actively transgresses social boundaries yet remains directed by others and finally mysterious, as in *The Heiress* and *Lonelyhearts.*

This book challenges the reductive scholarly approach applied to Montgomery Clift so far and seeks to examine the ways in which he functioned as a sign of difference and disruption throughout his career. By bringing to the screen sexual and gender subversion, nonnormative social structures, and the perceived abnormality of pain and illness, Clift constructed a coherent series of oppositional characters. Any criticism hoping to explore his work in its fullness must employ an inclusive strategy, allowing for Clift's multiple directions, representations, and meanings to be appropriately read. Queer theory is the obvious critical tool for such an exploration.

Queer Theory: Indeterminacy, Fluidity, and a Challenge to "Normality"

The scope and boundaries of queer theory are still far from being indisputably established; if, on one hand, it is possible to trace a history and a working model of queer criticism, there is also a marked resistance to categorically state what "queer" describes. This conceptual fluidity befits a critical approach born out of what is known as poststructuralism, a term summarizing the intellectual drive that has dominated critical thinking since the late twentieth century. Poststructuralism is characterized by the challenge to the previous assumptions of humanism, in particular to the notion of identity as a stable, unified, complete expression of a prior self. Poststructuralist thought challenges fixed social categories and definitions, seeking instead to uncover the ongoing formative process underlying the production of identity. Queer theory is firmly located in this critical project; specifically, queer is symptomatic of a shift in focus that has also significantly affected feminist and postcolonial theory. The concept at the center of this shift is that identities are culturally produced; rather than being the expression of something already there, they are constructed and acquired and constantly in the process of being constituted and reconstituted. Individual identity, therefore, is not innate or coherent, but rather assumed, multiple, and fragmented. This new take on identity did not, of course, occur out of nowhere: the ground for it was prepared since the early 1900s, through Sigmund Freud's revolutionary theorization of the unconscious. Freud's claim that human behavior is largely directed by forces outside individual control, indeed beyond subjective knowledge, precipitated the end of previous assumptions about identity; notions of the self became associated with unknown desires and motives, and with the illusory coherence of the mind. Similarly crucial for developments in critical thought has been the work of the linguist Ferdinand de Saussure, which also appeared in the first part of the twentieth century. Saussure argued that language, far from being a mere tool to describe reality, is in fact constitutive of reality; understood as a signifying system that precedes the subject, language shapes human beings' experience, directing and limiting what it was erroneously believed only to express. Later on in the 1900s, Marxist criticism stressed the importance of ideology in the molding of social identities, and the systemically predetermined nature of an individual's sense of self. While poststructuralist thought was made possible because of these major influences, queer theory has been especially influenced by the work of Michel Foucault, most notably his monumental *History of Sexuality*.[18] Foucault introduced the notion of discourse, which refers to the often-conflictive sum of ideas associated with a particular notion at a given historical and cultural junction. Identity, according to Foucault, is created by discourse; sexual identities are thus unstable, as much as culturally specific, and concepts of "heterosexuality" and "homosexuality" are wholly relative. Crucially, Foucault also argued that sexual categories are potentially oppressive, insofar as they can be the instruments of regulatory regimes. In this light, ontological definitions, explaining who and what an individual supposedly is, and epistemological narratives used to recognize and label identities, become intrinsically suspicious. Within these parameters queer theory makes its entry.

Although "queer" as a term had been used since the 1800s to describe male same-sex relationships, it did not enter its current usage until the early 1990s. In both its theoretical and political implications, queer places itself after "gay and lesbian," which in turn had been deliberately adopted to replace "homosexual." Just as gay and lesbian were seen as progressive terms, dispelling the pathological connotations of homosexual, queer has been adopted as a more productive, liberating notion than its predecessors. This chronology, however, is far from enjoying a consensus, either among academics or political activists; gay and lesbian continue to be widely used, and even preferred to queer, to connote different viewpoints and strategies regarding sexual identities.

In political terms queer signals a turning point, arriving after the identity politics of the liberationist gay movement of the late 1960s and '70s. The model of gay activism based on the reiteration of strongly defined identities, such as gay and lesbian, started to raise questions and dissatisfaction from those who felt an affinity with the movement yet were excluded from it because of a variety of factors. It was pointed out that an individual's sexual identity, rather than rigidly fit into categories of gay or heterosexual, was vastly complicated by other elements: class, race, age, the presence or absence of disability, personal experience, history, and practices. A new way of looking at sexual categories was to acknowledge that in themselves they did not guarantee any specificity. With increasing urgency, it was felt that established sexual labels were not useful, indeed that they were damaging: they were exclusive of countless individuals that, however, shared a common liberationist attitude toward alternative sexual orientations. The cultural impact of these ideas coincided with the crystallization of activism around the AIDS and HIV crisis of the mid-1980s; the focus on safe sex meant a shift in emphasis from sexual identities to sexual practices. The virus, rather than being a "gay disease" as the media had labeled it, could infect anyone, and people of different sexual orientations were placed in the same relation to it, and consequently to each other. While the gay community had rallied into action to provide AIDS- and HIV-related help, their effort was being crucially supported by people who did not fit the "gay" label: HIV-positive individuals of every sexual orientation, as well as their friends, relatives, and caregivers. This situation accelerated a move to the "politics of difference": the deceptively simple idea that people are different from each other, and that these differences should be highlighted, yet not divisively employed.

In critical terms, the introduction of queer marked a similar change, even a rupture, from the identity emphasis of lesbian and gay theory; the preoccupation to delimit and defend specific sexual categories was replaced by the effort to free the undetermined, the multiple and the possible from the perceived dogma of "homosexual," "heterosexual," and even "bisexual." As Mark Norris Lance and Alessandra Tanesini write: "to say that one is of a given identity is to say that one *ought* to take that identity to be part of one's script for one's life, that one ought to allow an associated script to demand coherence with one's other scripts, that one ought to assign social priority to facilitating one's living according to the resulting narrative unity of the various scripts."[19] Notwithstanding the ongoing academic debate about its exact signification, queer can be understood as a term and a practice that aims at denaturalizing sexual and gender categories; by drawing attention to the inconsistencies and contradictions underlying allegedly "normal" configurations, queer challenges the legitimacy of a whole spectrum of rigidly constituted identities. As Annamarie Jagose writes, "queer is less an identity than a *critique* of identity."[20] Queer thus questions all compulsory patterns of sexual and gender behavior, rather than just signaling the forced dominance of heterosexuality; it consequently asks for a revision of socially sanctioned models of relationships. At the same time, queer also seeks to destabilize traditional notions of bodily normality and desirability. To effect a queer reading of any given text, situation, or performance, or "to queer" it as a critical practice, means to highlight the inherent dissonances and possibilities of its production of sexual and gender identities; in turn, this demands to call attention to the constructed, prescriptive nature of representations of normality.

Montgomery Clift and Queer Theory

A growing number of scholars have explored the possibilities of queer theory, giving rise to one of the most prolific and dynamic fields in contemporary academia; Eve Kosofsky Sedgwick and Judith Butler have been especially influential. In fact, queer theory is virtually unthinkable without Sedgwick's pioneering writing; she charted new ground with her literary-based analyses of male same-sex discourse in *Between Men: English Literature and Male Homosocial Desire*[21] and *Epistemology of the Closet*.[22] Sedgwick's oeuvre reads like a concerted, formidable attack against the oppression of fixed sexual and gender identities. In exemplary queer fashion, she demonstrates how the dogma of exclusion and opposition, central to the sustaining of the homo/hetero structure, has informed a whole system of denotation and connotation that posits the "naturalness" of polar differences, such as private/public, masculine/feminine, natural/artificial, innocence/initiation, or health/illness. Similarly, her discussion of the closet problematizes the opposition silence/speech, and what she calls "the relations of the closet—the relations of the known and the unknown, the explicit and the inexplicit."[23] Alongside Sedgwick, Judith Butler has radicalized notions of gender and sexual identity. While writing primarily from a feminist perspective, Butler has provided a critique of gender formation that has proved invaluable for queer criticism; specifically, her book *Gender Trouble*[24] formulated a set of ideas that continue to inform queer scholarship and are creatively reapplied to a variety of contexts. Butler's most productive intervention is her discussion of performativity, understood as the psychic and social process by which gender is created and assumed: rather than being the expression of a prior, innate "essence," the effect of femininity or masculinity is the result of a repetitive impersonation of the qualities supposedly defining it. Crucially, gender is not only performatively derived but also heterosexually determined, indissolubly linked to patterns of sexual behavior that posit a "natural" desire for the opposite sex. This leads to two major considerations: First, that gender and sexual identity are not innate but socially constructed and enforced through compulsory repetition. Second, that heterosexuality is not an original "norm" from which other sexual orientations have deviated; on the contrary, it is an imitation itself, "nothing other than a parody of the *idea* of the natural and the original."[25] It follows that gender and sexual identities are fragile, contingent, and unstable; normative repetition is thus made necessary by the ever-present threat of their dissolution. As a visible example of the way gender can be deconstructed, Butler points to drag, referring to the work of the anthropologist Esther Newton, who suggests that drag exemplifies the process by which every social identity is assumed.[26] This set of ideas has clear implications for the body, seen as the surface on which gender production is dramatized. Butler highlights the way bodies are forced into expressions of "femininity" "and masculinity" and constantly fail to fulfill the gender ideal. An important qualification, which Butler carefully makes but which her critics often forget, is that performative gender formation is not consciously undertaken; it is rather an internalized action whose successful repetition is the object of regulation and punishment by normative societies. As a strategy, Butler advocates the awareness and unmasking of the performativity behind identity, or, in other words, the denaturalization of supposedly natural configurations.

The work of Eve Kosofsky Sedgwick and Judith Butler is especially suited to an analysis of Montgomery Clift. According to an often-invoked passage by Sedgwick, "queer" points to "the open mesh of possibilities, gaps, overlaps, dissonances, and resonances, lapses and excesses of meaning when the constituent elements of anyone's gender, or anyone's sexuality aren't made (or *can't* be made) to signify monolithically."[27] Indeed, Clift's sexual persona is not reducible to neat labels or descriptions, being articulated through a wide reaching, conflicting, and constantly shifting range of configurations. As Clift's private and professional trajectory encompasses a vast gamut of identifications, his star persona is built on the cumulative, disorienting effect of these discordant images. The "enigmatic" aura the press ascribed to Clift was produced by a multiplicity of meanings that, then as now, defied the comfort of easy categorization: "Monty was open—he was hidden—he was gay—he was straight; in essence he seemed to represent a new kind of man—a man who refuses to make judgments on sexual preference."[28] From the beginning of his career, Clift presented a multifaceted image that, in order to be explored, presupposes the abandonment of binary systems of classifications; this analytical process must be based on the deconstruction of sexual stereotypes, including those of recent, gay-affirmative assessments and bisexual labelings. The words of Patrick Califia, another queer scholar who challenges the usefulness of "gay" and "lesbian," are readily applicable to Clift's resistance to categorization: "Our actual behaviour (as opposed to the ideology that says homosexuality means being sexual only with members of the same sex) leads me to ask questions about the nature of sexual orientation, how people (especially gay people) define it, and how they choose to let those definitions control and limit their lives."[29] A queer man living in an era before queer theory, Clift is an ideal subject for revisionist assessment, a critical practice queer scholars fruitfully embrace. The work of Alexander Doty has provided a crucial template for this approach to film criticism, uncovering the latent queerness of previously unquestioned texts and personalities and paving the way for a queer reassessment of popular culture. In Doty's view, queer marks "a flexible space for the expression of all aspects of non-(anti, contra-) straight cultural production and reception."[30]

Against the oppressiveness of social categories, a queer identity is specifically advocated by Mark Norris Lance and Alessandra Tanesini in their article "Identity, Judgements, Queer Politics." They argue that the assumption of any identity can effectively be a political endorsement of what that identity is commonly expected to entail; consequently, an ideal hierarchy of identities would see "heterosexual" as a wholly inappropriate one, being irretrievably tainted by the implicitness of its homophobic privileges. While "gay" and "lesbian" are seen as potentially empowering in certain situations, "queer" emerges as the identity of choice, by intrinsically avoiding the pitfalls of social acquiescence: "when people claim 'We're here, we're queer, get used to it,' they are not implicitly accepting what society takes to be proper for queers."[31] Although intentionally polemic in its denial of straight identities, Lance and Tanesini's text shows the appeal of queer in the face of the perceived limitations of other terms. Conversely, scholars who choose to retain the use of "homosexual," or of gay and lesbian, have adopted a queer approach, rather than a queer terminology. Sheila Jeffreys, for example, recuperates "homosexual" by effectively queering it, defining as homosexual desire simply a desire that "is based upon sameness instead of difference of power, desire which is about mutuality."[32] Likewise, Leo Bersani's theory of "homo-ness" employs the homo suffix to posit a nonjudgmental model of human relationships, which is not necessarily dependent on same-sex desire. While Bersani is adamant that gay and lesbian identities have a valid part to play in the construction of an antihomophobic culture, he also sees that ideal culture of homo-ness as one shared by people of every sexual orientation, including straights. In what is, essentially, a queer reference to the obliqueness of human interconnection, he claims that "the most varied, even antagonistic, identities, meet transversely."[33] Queer can validate relationships that are considered abnormal or wrong: these may be cross generational, or not monogamous, or exclusive yet not based on sex. In a profound way, queer seeks to expand the terms of what is considered meaningful human contact and to widen cultural understandings of sexual and emotional bonds between people. Indeed, for all its impeccably poststructuralist credentials, queer is not so far from humanism in its concern with people's entitlement to whatever makes them human: "in the midst of the craziness, hostility, ignorance, and angst that plague human relations and sexuality, I feel entitled to whatever comfort or gratitude I can find."[34]

These developments lead to the concept of "straight queerness," probably the most striking break from the previous assumptions of lesbian and gay theory. In opening up "queer" to "straights," queer scholars formally recognize the contradictions, deviations, and potential subversion in the sex lives of many ostensibly heterosexual people. The whole work of Eve Kosofsky Sedgwick is, among many other things, an endorsement of straight queerness, relentlessly exposing the sexual nonconformity, indeed the *impossibility* of conformity underlying even the most apparently linear configurations. Alexander Doty talks of "cases of straight queerness, and of other forms of queerness that might not be contained within existing categories."[35] Nikki Sullivan, reflecting on what Lynne Segal has called the existence of "many heterosexualities,"[36] argues that queering straight sex "can allow the possibility of moving away from stabilized notions of gender and sexuality as the assumed foundations of identity and social relations."[37] A similar view is expressed by Clyde Smith, a heterosexual man and a participant in the mostly gay dance scene in San Francisco: "I claim the identity of queer heterosexual to further my own desires for a world of multiple possibilities."[38] Calvin Thomas sees queerness as the key to unlock the contradictions and possibilities underlying straightness, and, like Sedgwick, highlights the fallacy of homo/hetero distinctions: "straightness, like all identity-formation, is an effect of constitutive exclusion and thus never ceases to depend on the excluded, the *part maudit*, the abjected itself—the recognition and acknowledgement that all along one has needed 'the queer' that one really is(n't) to be 'the straight' that (no)one (ever) really is."[39] A straight queer, therefore, will not only challenge the imperative to desire exclusively members of the opposite sex but also the compulsory translation of that desire into a pattern of sexual activity of 2.5 sexual encounters per week. The notion of straight queerness is suggestive when applied to Montgomery Clift, given his intense, highly unorthodox relationships with women, and the fact that in most of his films he is heterosexually paired. This is obviously not to dismiss readings of Clift's performance that identify gay or homoerotic subtexts in his films. On the contrary, this book proposes to examine how multiple sexual directions overlap and coexist in Clift's work, producing a range of meanings that elude, exceed, or contradict traditional expectations. As queer theory challenges the unimaginative models of human relationships society endorses, it can provide valuable insights into the cluster of identifications Clift held in tension.

Notions of queerness have been fruitfully linked to developments in disability studies. As critical strategies aimed at deconstructing dominant cultural forms, both "queering" and "cripping" ask for a rethinking of "representations of bodily normality" and seek to "expose the arbitrary delineation between normal and defective."[40] According to Eli Clare, "the construction of gender depends not only upon the male body and the female body, but also upon the nondisabled body,"[41] while Robert McRuer argues that able-bodiedness and heterosexuality are "mutually constitutive."[42] The cultural hegemony of able-bodied heteronormativity rests on narrow definitions of desirability, beauty, physical and mental health, and on equally rigid divisions between masculine and feminine traits; it is also necessarily based on a series of absences, or denials. By definition, the "normal" body is linked to the "normal" mind, with "normality" understood as the lack of deviant shapes and behaviors, illness, pain, pleasure derived from "wrong" sources or conditions, or anything that may unsettle established notions of balance and harmony. Hegemonic normality often denies the reality and valid-ity of subjective experience: this may be the experience of well-being, should this happen within an "abnormal" context, or of pain, which is likewise relegated to the "abnormal" regions of human existence. The antiheteronormative project of queer theory exposes the arbitrariness of bodily normality and its wider ramifications for the classification of human beings into "right" and "wrong." In *Gender Trouble,* Judith Butler refers to gender normativity when addressing "the ontological field in which bodies may be given legitimate expression."[43] This regulatory field clearly also comprises, and depends on, fixed notions of sexual behavior. In the light of the queer commitment to free difference from regulatory oppression, it should come as no surprise that queer scholarship has been greatly interested in the discussion of cross-dressing, transsexual, transgender, and hermaphrodite individuals; they are seen as the visible evidence that human sexuality, and socially constructed gender, cannot be reduced to fixed categories. Marjorie Garber takes issue with society's need to rigidly divide sexes into male and female: "why should we care if there are people whose biological equipment enables them to have sex 'naturally' with both men and women?"[44] The geneticist Anne Fausto-Sterling questions the medical drive to normalize deviant sexes, and writes that "hermaphrodites have unruly bodies. They do not fall naturally into a binary classification";[45] to bring this observation to its logical queer conclusion is to say that *all* bodies are basically unruly. Bodies systematically fail, in one way or another, to conform to notions of perfection, of health, of appropriate gender behavior, and ultimately of "normality." Eve Kosofsky Sedgwick points out that discourses of bodies and sexuality, even when produced within progay boundaries, can rest on "biologically based 'explanations' for deviant behavior that are absolutely invariably couched in terms of 'excess,' 'deficiency,' or 'imbalance.'"[46] In the case of Montgomery Clift, a central aspect of his post-1956 image is a marked dissonance from his former beauty, and from established notions of healthy masculinity, as his persona acquired a strongly disturbing aura. A queer analysis can highlight the ways in which Clift's disruptive quality, now inscribed in his body and appearance, radically challenged canons of male normality; a notable expression of this "abnormal" identity is the lack of overt sexual feelings.

The pathologizing drive of heteronormativity is virtually unchecked when directed at individuals who appear "asexual"; the lack of what is recognized as a "sex life" has proved to be one of the most durable taboos in Western society. Canonical notions of the "natural" adult body are inseparable from the presence of sexual activity, or at least from the wish for it; doctors, psychiatrists, and sex therapists routinely pathologize individuals who do not conform to what is deemed a healthy interest in sex. It is a largely unquestioned dogma that "sex is a natural function";[47] yet as queer contests identities and lifestyles traditionally considered abnormal, this process of denaturalization should also be applied to configurations that problematize the presence and nature of sexuality. It is remarkable that very little work has been produced on the social compulsion to have sex. A search for academic texts on celibacy will yield almost exclusively titles addressing religious practices, or the history of castration; a search for books on asexuality will mostly reveal material dealing with medicine and biology. A notable exception to this trend is made by a very few texts dealing, from a strictly female and feminist perspective, with the experience and implications of nonactive sexuality. Interestingly, these writers usually reject the word "asexual" because of its absolutistic and potentially judgmental connotations, as Leslie Raymer argues: "I don't like the word 'asexual.' I associate it with worms. It sounds prudish and tight-assed. 'Nonsexual' doesn't work, either, since I see myself and my lover as sexual beings. Nonpracticing, maybe, but sexual."[48] Likewise, Lisa Isherwood asks us to consider the inherent queerness of some celibate women, both religious and nonreligious, who have opted out of patriarchy through the choice of "erotic celibacy."[49] While the diverse implications of celibacy, nonpracticing sexuality, and asexuality need much further research in their relation to women's experience, it is also imperative to explore their links to cultural understandings of masculinity. As queer theory denaturalizes "normal" sexuality, gender, and relationships, it must address the extraordinarily deep association of orthodox male identity with rampant libido. Consequently, queering male sexuality leads to a reconsideration of the human relationships made available to men (and of course, by default, to women), and of their relation to, or dependence on, sexual activity. In Montgomery Clift's case, as his image became dramatically less eroticized after his accident, a queer assessment highlights his disruption of prescriptive patterns of sexual consumption; equally, Clift's eccentric relationships on and off screen subvert neat divisions between "sexual" and "nonsexual," positing what scholar Marny Hall calls a "borderland" zone "between or beyond the polarized categories of 'friend' and 'lover.'"[50] Kathleen A. Brehony advocates the need to acknowledge "the multilayered, complex, unique relationships among people,"[51] while Eve Kosofsky Sedgwick questions the common presumption "that everyone 'has a sexuality.'"[52]

Finally, queer theory has most recently been associated with the interrogation of time, and of the way normative social structures are temporally informed. Building on the notion of a dominant narrative of "normality," the identification of queer temporality exposes the fallacy of a "natural" human progression through time. The heterosexual norm, aiming to align human behavior to patterns of sexual and gender identity, is dependent on a specific temporal structure: heteronormativity is simultaneously framed and constituted by a time "that is linear, consequential and reproductive."[53] Elizabeth Freeman claims that society produces subjects through "chrononormativity,"[54] by ascribing meaning to human lives according to preestablished, time-productive trajectories. To queer time means to challenge the seemingly preordained trajectory of one's existence, recognizing instead the relative meanings of "past" and "present," and the temporal hybridity of subjective experience. Montgomery Clift's life is defined by an increasingly deviant temporality, which found powerful expression on screen in the last phase of his career. In assessing Clift's postaccident work, a queer reading deals best with the violent clash dramatized in the star's appearance: a literal embodiment of asynchrony, merging past with present, Clift was poised at a fraught (dis)junction that was simultaneously visual, semantic, and temporal.

Although spanning a relatively short period, the work of Montgomery Clift is characterized by his constant renegotiation of his screen presence, a feature that would befit an actor of significant longevity. The powerful significations of his heartthrob status coexisted with the deviant, unsettling evidence of physical and mental trauma; as the experience of pain was not hidden by Clift, but used as part of his performance and even flaunted in the face of public scrutiny, a queer critique goes against pathologizing interpretations, problematizing instead the notion of individual normality. By offering a queer assessment of the interaction of Clift's fluctuating identities, this book means to acknowledge that Clift's complex, at times troubling, screen presence is never the expression of something "wrong," "sick," or "abnormal"; indeed, this project is motivated by quite the opposite view. In his multiplicity of configurations, in his subversion of fixed categories, Montgomery Clift emerges as a positive, creatively defiant figure, open to possibilities of being that challenge the poverty of societal normativity. This book pays homage to Clift's expression of potential, choosing a queer theoretical approach insofar as it "describes a horizon of possibility whose precise extent and heterogeneous scope cannot in principle be delimited in advance."[55]

TWO

Irruption in Hollywood
The Beautiful Boy

Queerness as Sexual Ambiguity and Erotic Spectacle:
Red River and *The Heiress*

More than any other film starring Montgomery Clift, *Red River* has attracted retrospective critical attention. Casting the twenty-six-year-old Clift against an especially brutish John Wayne, this epic western depicts a classic yet deceptively simple tale of masculine struggle. *Red River* has been hailed as a key intervention in screen representations of male identity and Clift's role as Matthew "Matt" Garth as a template for his disturbance of gender patterns. Steven Cohan highlights the suggestive qualities of *Red River*'s dominant narrative, the opposition between the radically different masculinities Clift and Wayne represent: "the highly charged context between the soft boy and the hard man in *Red River* dramatizes such a shift in the mainstream culture's demands upon masculinity."[1] According to Amy Lawrence, in *Red River* "Clift's Matt stands toe-to-toe with John Wayne, insisting that Wayne and the western genre give way and revise their traditional definitions of manliness to accommodate Clift."[2] Barry Keith Grant points to the film's visual construction of a different masculinity, effected not only through the striking physical contrast between Clift and Wayne, but also by the close-ups of Clift's face in soft focus, a type of shot "usually reserved for enhancing the glamour of female stars."[3] Brett Farmer reads the film as a subversive homosexual parable, resonating "with the type of gay fantasmatic scenario . . . in which the 'tyranny' of patrocentrism is refused and an 'alternative' order of identification and desire is instated in its place."[4] Such claims testify to the enduring power of *Red River*, which aptly showcases Clift's blend of sexual ambiguity and gender disruption through a narrative resting on generational conflict and homosocial desire. Perhaps more than any other factor, Clift's irruption in the utterly traditional, "virile" western canon, against Wayne's hypermasculine presence, has ensured the film's status as a definitive example of Clift's subversive function. At the same time, *Red River* bears the unmistakable authorial mark of its director, Howard Hawks, whose oeuvre resonates with the interrogation of tropes of masculinity, often focusing on close relationships between men. From *A Girl in Every Port* (1928) to *The Big Sky* (1952), to *El Dorado* (1967), Hawks's films foreground the same intensely homosocial narrative, described by the director himself as "a love story between two men."[5]

It is significant that *Red River* is usually seen as the beginning of Clift's career, although it is not his first appearance on screen. While being indeed the first film he made, it was shot in 1946 yet only released in 1948, a few months after *The Search* had come out. A legal dispute between Howard Hawks and Howard Hughes, who claimed Hawks had stolen the plot from his own *The Outlaw* (1943), prevented *Red River* to reach the screen first. However, it is easy to see how the film may be used as the starting point for a study of Clift: apart from showing him at the youngest he ever was on screen, the film encapsulates his nascent persona and marks his full impact on audience and critics. While *The Search* had received superlative reviews, and gained Clift his first Academy Award nomination, *Red River* is the film that shot him to stardom; as Sidney Skolsky wrote, with *Red River* Clift "became a popular idol overnight."[6] There are obvious implications in Clift's stunning impact in *Red River*: it signals an unusually condensed screen presence, an exceptional amount of meanings traceable to his role and performance. Clift's portrayal of Matt encapsulates key traits of his star image, powerful and distinctive if just beginning to unravel; these traits will evolve and gain in complexity through Clift's career, or occasionally mutate.

Irruption in Hollywood

The shock of Clift's presence in *Red River* rests partly on his erotic self-display, on his open spectacle of sexually ambivalent masculinity. This erotic quality will become a huge part of Clift's persona, but it will be largely absent in his last films. Casting himself as a willing object of desire, in *Red River* Clift articulates a sexuality that defies categories and a contradictory, subversive relation to the masculine system in which he is placed; these subjective positions, variously expressed, will define him till the end of his life. Most analyses of *Red River* have focused on the homoerotic implications of Clift's performance: while this is a crucial aspect of the film's overall structure, and a defining factor in Clift's persona, it does not account for the range of meanings available, through Clift's presence, in *Red River*. A more useful approach to the film is to explore the ways in which it shows Montgomery Clift, in his first screen performance, to be a powerfully queer figure.

Red River begins its narrative in 1851, introducing one of the two main protagonists, Thomas Dunson (John Wayne), as a tough, hard-headed cowboy intent on moving south to start a cattle herd. Accompanied by his faithful servant Groot (Walter Brennan), Dunson however leaves behind his girl, Fen (Colleen Gray), telling her that he will send for her; he gives her a bracelet as a token of his commitment. Shortly after leaving, the two men see Indian smoke in the distance and fear that Fen may have been killed; indeed, when the Indians attack them later on, one of them is found wearing Fen's bracelet. Seemingly unfazed, Dunson kills the Indian and retrieves his bracelet as the attack is successfully overcome. Dunson's ruthlessly manly credentials are thus established, and confirmed in a later sequence: confronted by two emissaries of the landowner Diego, on whose land he is abusively feeding his cattle, Dunson shoots one of them dead, informing the other that the land now belongs to him. Between these two killing episodes Matthew Garth, a young boy (here played by Mickey Kuhn), crosses paths with Dunson. Matt appears on the scene as the traumatized survivor of an Indian massacre. He is wandering at random, taking the family cow with him, and is unable to speak coherently. Faced with this distressing sight, Dunson's solution is to slap the boy hard, but the boy's reaction surpasses expectations, as he quickly draws out a gun and threatens Dunson. Impressed, Dunson takes Matt with him to join forces and start a herd together. These events are the preamble to the film's main plot, which then moves forward fourteen years and shows Montgomery Clift as Matt, having just returned to Dunson after fighting in the Civil War. Through its brief prelude, however, *Red River* has set up its dominant narrative. Dunson, introduced as a cold-blooded murderer and a thief, is both compared to and paired off with Matt; their different but equal status has been made clear from the very start, as the film's initial credits announce the story of "a man with a bull and a boy with a cow." While Dunson is older and very tough, Matt is young and vulnerable; their respective "masculine" and "feminine" qualities are symbolized by their animals, a bull and a cow, which need to get together to create a herd. Yet if Matt has already signaled his different male identity, he has also forcefully held his own against Dunson, showing his willingness and ability to fight back; likewise, while Dunson's brutality increases as the film progresses, the film ultimately celebrates him despite all his faults. Since young Matt's first appearance, *Red River* therefore begins a confrontation between antagonistic yet overlapping masculine systems. On his return from the war, Matt finds Dunson in economic straits and planning to drive his herd a thousand miles north to Missouri, in what would be the first Chisholm Trail cattle drive through the Rio Grande. The drive promises to be danger-ridden, yet Dunson manages to enlist a group of men to follow him, with Matt and Groot. Just before they start their journey, they are joined by Cherry Valance (John Ireland), a young man who, like Matt, has a reputation as a skillful shootist; sparks of rivalry and strong attraction immediately fly between them. As conditions on the drive become increasingly hard, rumors of an easier, safer track to Abilene in Kansas fuels the men's discontent; Dunson refuses to change his plan, insisting in reaching Missouri. Dunson's dictatorial behavior soon reaches psychopathic levels: when one of the men accidentally starts a stampede, Dunson tries to kill him, but Matt prevents him from doing so. When two of the men later abandon the drive in protest, Dunson has them captured and announces he will hang them; again, Matt intervenes by shooting Dunson in the arm, this time taking charge of the men in an all-out mutiny. As Matt leads the group and the cattle on the new path to Abilene, Dunson vows to reach up with them and kill Matt. The specter of Dunson's presence haunts the men, but distraction arrives in the shape of a wagon carrying women and provisions; these are, however, under Indian attack, and Matt and his men come to their rescue. While engaged in fighting the Indians, Matt meets a girl named Tess (Joanne Dru), and after the Indians are repelled the two spend the night together; the next day, however, Matt must leave for Abilene. Tess is not alone for long, as hot on Matt's heels arrives Dunson; he discovers that Tess is wearing the bracelet he had once given to Fen, and then to Matt. After trying in vain to dissuade Dunson from pursuing Matt, Tess joins him in his search for her lover. The film approaches its climax as Matt makes a triumphal entry in Abilene; going back to his hotel at night, he finds Tess waiting for him. The next morning Dunson arrives in town; Cherry tries to shoot him to save Matt's life, but Dunson shoots him in return and proceeds in Matt's direction. Matt refuses to join the gunfight, allowing Dunson's bullets to get nearer and nearer to him; the exasperated Dunson drops his gun and punches Matt, and the two fall on the ground fighting, until Tess stops them. Shouting that their fight is ridiculous, as they obviously love each other, Matt's woman restores order; Dunson urges Matt to marry Tess and announces that Matt's initial will be now added to his own in branding their cattle.

Unsurprisingly, most scholars working on Clift have seen *Red River* as a narrative of male-to-male desire. Motivated by the relationship between Matt and Dunson, and resting on structures of masculine bonds, the film is a powerful representation of homosocial eroticism. Dunson's longing for Matt disrupts his patriarchal and harsh world; likewise, Matt's intensity and sexual enticement soon become the film's focus, undermining its overt validation of orthodox masculine claims. Clift's concentrated performance, defined by stillness, non-verbal expression, and a strong emphasis on his body, together with his extreme physical difference from Wayne, create Dunson's foil as a beautiful, erotically available boy. The age gulf between Clift (who looked even younger than twenty-six) and Wayne (who looked older than his thirty-nine years) crystallizes their characters' opposition as a generational crisis. However, if Clift's presence in *Red River* is inherently subversive of traditional virility, it is also in excess of the plain homosexual meaning it readily invokes. Not only is Clift at the center of conflicting structures of male desire, with Dunson and Cherry at their poles, he is also the active participant in a convincing heterosexual liaison. While Matt's romance with Tess implies a renegotiation of ho-

CHAPTER 2

moerotic relationships, his allegiance to Cherry and Dunson points to stronger identifications than generational grouping, and to ambiguous connections to his split homosocial system. Rather than just subverting the trajectory of male eroticism, Matt/Clift problematizes the very notion of male-to-male intimacy. If the shock of his presence rests partly on the tension between different sexual targets, it is equally based on his uneven, unspecified investment in any one of them.

Clift's ambiguous characterization of Matt is evident from his very first scene; a lot has been said of Clift's erotic self-display in *Red River*, and it is never more palpable than in his first appearance on screen. As a cut moves the action forward by fourteen years, the camera shows Dunson in the middle of the frame, crouching on the ground; he appears to be talking to no one in particular, yet to his left, slowly taking over the screen, the legs of two other men are visible. While Groot is soon recognizable as being farthest from Dunson, the figure in the middle is new to the film: it is Clift, who is standing still yet in a markedly relaxed attitude, with a foot resting on a stone and his arms loosely crossed on one of his legs. His shoulders are slouching, but his expression is attentive, listening to Dunson's speech without a comment; as the latter places a hand on Clift's leg to lift himself up, Clift helps him by taking the hand into his own. Dunson continues to talk, making eye contact with Groot, while Clift remains silent between them, looking in front of him as if absorbed in thought. All the while Clift is playing with a blade of grass, brushing it slowly over his mouth; his hips are slightly swung forward, and he still has not uttered a word. Finally, the camera tracks in on his face, as he places the blade of grass between his lips, takes it out again, and says a few words to Dunson. As the camera moves out slightly, Clift is exactly in the middle of the frame, slowly shifting his weight from one foot to the other while rolling a cigarette; though smaller than the two men beside him, he has by now focused the camera's attention entirely on himself. Through his deliberate use of his body, his drawing attention to his mouth, and his beautiful intense face, he has become the single interesting sight on the screen. Having prepared his cigarette, Clift gives it to Dunson, in a casually deferential gesture; he then takes Dunson's hands into his to help him light it. This whole scene captures Clift's show-stopping aura of erotic availability, which informs readings of Matt as a willing erotic object; Clift's enticing self-display embodies notions of male spectacle, inherently subversive of traditional gender patterns. This spectacle, however, is not so straightforward. Although Clift's erotic posturing in *Red River* is usually described as "passive," it is hardly that. On the contrary, his slow, deliberate movements exude self-control, which means control of his own display. Matt/Clift is offering a spectacle directed solely by himself, but to whom is it directed? Who, if anyone, is exactly its target, and what does it aim to elicit? Outside the diegetic space of the film, of course, the obvious end of Clift's eroticism is the audience. But the audience needs to channel its response through the film's available routes and to identify themselves with the object of Clift's performance; this is not easy to do, producing a first unsettling ambiguity around Clift. While the physical contact between Matt and Dunson has obvious implications of intimacy, the quality of their intimacy is suggestive but unclear; nor is Matt's erotic availability clearly displayed for Dunson. While his attitude toward him is attentive and relaxed, Matt offers no gesture or look hinting at an active sexual interest, nor, indeed, does Dunson show any for Matt. In this first arresting scene, Clift's erotic

Attracting the gaze: The adult Matt as he first appears on screen.

spectacle is primarily reflexive and self-contained: it signals a reveling in his own desirability, a hinting at unnamed possibilities. This ambiguous presence will be enhanced, rather than clarified, by the stark contrast of Matt's scenes with Cherry, where the sexual tension between them is astonishingly clear: by conveying notions of different intimacies with different men, Matt is complicating the articulation of his own desire. This split presentation of male-to-male longing is further unsettled by the relationship with Tess, in which Matt takes a heavily erotic role.

On one hand, *Red River* presents Matt/Clift as an erotic object, available to multiple gazes; on the other hand, he also emerges as a controlling sexual subject, independently exerting his erotic power. Clift's queer impact lies not simply in the difference between these layers of desire but in their overlapping, in his own fluctuation through bonding structures, in his being both objectified and in command. To better understand Clift's narrative and erotic meaning in the film, it is useful to refer to Eve Kosofsky Sedgwick's theory of homosocial desire. Sedgwick argues that while all patriarchal societies are built on homosocial networks, they are also inherently homophobic and misogynist. Their organization rests on a firm distinction between acceptable homosociality, which is presumed to exclude male-to-male sex, and unacceptable homosexuality, which is linked to the "feminine." Sedgwick suggests that a more accurate way of rationalizing patriarchal order is "to hypothesize the potential unbrokenness of a continuum between homosocial and homosexual—a continuum whose visibility, in our society, is radically disrupted."[7] Hunted, punished, and driven underground, homosexual desire is then "widely intelligible by being routed through triangular relations involving a woman."[8] The common narrative of two men fighting over a woman, contends Sedgwick, is the acting out of displaced male-to-male eroticism; she points out that "the bonds of 'rivalry' and 'love,' differently as they are experienced, are equally powerful and in many senses equivalent."[9] There are two key implications in Sedgwick's theory: one is that the links between homosociality, homosexuality, and patriarchy run deep. Homosocial belonging is by default complicit with the overt rejection of same-sex desire and must resort to erotic triangles to mask homosexuality and subject women. Second, to recognize the continuum of homosocial desire means to challenge normative sexual distinctions, allowing for an unstable spectrum of male-to-male relations. Crucially, Sedgwick questions the distinction between "sexual" and "nonsexual," preferring to identify "desire" as a powerful field of force between men, "the glue, even when its manifestation is hostility or hatred or something less emotionally charged, that shapes an important relationship."[10]

To apply Sedgwick's concepts to *Red River* is to recognize the coexistence of three conflictive, yet interrelated, erotic structures in the film, with Matt/Clift at their center. The first is the relationship between Matt and Dunson; tying Matt to the patriarchal system endorsed by Dunson, this homosocial bond is sustained by mutual desire, yet its continuum is conventionally disrupted by an erotic triangle, initiated by Dunson with Tess. When he meets her during his pursuit of Matt, Dunson rapidly assesses Tess as a suitable sexual partner, but only after having ascertained, through her possession of Matt's bracelet, that Matt loves her. Asking her to turn around and show him her body, Dunson then proposes that she should bear his own son. Just before this, as Tess was describing the pain she felt in being separated from Matt, Dunson had completed her sentence for her: it was "like if you had knives stuck into you." Although the film's overt narrative makes his words a reference to Fen, the woman that Dunson had tragically left behind, they are but a thin disguise for Dunson's unacceptable longing for Matt. Externalized as extreme hatred caused by Matt's betrayal, Dunson's passionate feelings for Matt—whatever their exact location on the "sexual" scale—are thus safely displaced on the pursuit of Matt's woman. Dunson's eventual suggestion to Matt, that he should marry Tess, comes only after she has effectively neutralized the men's mutual love; by publicly accepting their desire she has socially sanitized it, by virtue of her position as Matt's rightful (because female) mate. It is an unconvincing resolution, yet it is the only way to preserve a semblance of patriarchal order while preventing *Red River* from ending with a murder. At the same time, by reaffirming his loyalty to Dunson, Matt is accepting his place in the other's patriarchal system, as much as confirming his acquiescence to Dunson's desire for him, a desire, of course, that threatens that very same system. While it serves the film's normative ending, Matt's revival of his bond with Dunson is one more aspect of his ambivalent position, as the second erotic structure he occupies is the nonpatriarchal relation to Cherry.

CHAPTER 2

The scenes between Matt and Cherry occupy a relatively small portion of the film's total screen time, yet they are among its most memorable. From the moment they meet, the two young men engage in an intense exchange of stares while strutting around each other in a manner only describable as heavy flirting; their initial scene together is also the first instance in which Matt smiles repeatedly, staring sideways at Cherry with a playful expression. The open display of mutual attraction between them changes the film's mood, bringing in a strong erotic tension that is further emphasized by the dialogue. On seeing Matt, Cherry instantly decides to follow him by enlisting in Dunson's group, a move Matt piquantly rebuffs by saying they have already enough men. His words are spoken without conviction and only increase the atmosphere of tease. As Dunson leaves Cherry alone with Matt, he comments to Groot that the two young men will be "worth watching," as they have already started to "paw each other." The next scene sees Matt and Cherry competing in a shooting contest, but only after an extraordinarily blatant exchange: Cherry asks Matt if he can fondle his "good-looking gun," and offers him his own gun to touch. Matt complies, smiling invitingly as he hands him the gun, which Cherry duly caresses and declares to be "nice—awful nice." Once they have stroked each other's weapons, the two channel their energy into shooting cans, while Groot remarks from a distance: "they're having fun. Peculiar kind of fun." Through this all-too-clear erotic banter, Matt is inserted in a structure of intimacy without his doing or saying very much, just as in his first scene with Dunson, yet while this relative lack of action may partly support claims of Clift's "passivity," it belies the actively responsive quality he shows toward Cherry. More clearly sexual than his relation to Dunson, Matt's bond with Cherry is likewise enshrined in subversion. Through its open erotic nature, the liaison between the two younger men challenges homophobic patriarchal order, which Dunson symbolizes. It is significant that the Matt-Cherry relationship does not evolve into an erotic triangle, despite the fact that Cherry meets Tess and is attracted to her before Matt does. Sent ahead to check rumors of the wagon train carrying women, Cherry does not return to Matt and his men, preferring to wait for them in Tess's company. Later on, when Tess has been smitten by Matt and implores Cherry to help her get closer to him, Cherry complies. Both Matt and Cherry, therefore, have stepped outside patriarchy by externalizing their mutual desire, and by disrupting the bartering system that uses women as pawns in homosocial courtship. *Red River* dramatizes their insubordination through the mutiny against Dunson, which is led by Matt at the head of a group of gentler, potentially nonnormative men. These notably include Bunk (Ivan Parry), the sugar addict who unwittingly causes a stampede when stealing sugar at night, an activity deemed repulsively unfit for his gender (it is "like women liking whiskey," says Groot in disgust). Matt's allegiance to a nonpatriarchal, openly homoerotic system is thus sealed by his bond with Cherry; this is the film's aspect that has most vividly colored Clift's persona. His dissonant masculinity, expressed through his quiet speech, fluid movements, and almost frail beauty, is inseparable from his erotic ambivalence, and from his narrative role as alternative, sensitive leader. Matt's refusal to obey Dunson's cruel virile code fits Clift's image as a young rebel and strongly informs the film's structure of feeling, despite the ultimate permanence of the Matt-Dunson allegiance. Clift's emerging star persona is shaped through Matt and is suggestively confirmed by Clift's off-screen behavior: repulsed by the aggressive masculinity displayed by Wayne and Hawks, Clift wrote to a friend that "they laughed and drank and told dirty jokes and slapped each other in the back. They tried to draw me into their circle but I couldn't go along with them. The machismo thing repelled me because it seemed so forced and unnecessary."[11] The queerness of Matt/Clift is thus strongly based on his nonnormative homosocial bonds, yet it is also vastly increased by his unexplored desire for Dunson, and by his tangential but powerful attraction for Tess.

By eagerly responding to Tess's sexual advances, Matt forms a third erotic structure, which radically departs from the dominant, if dualistic organization of the film: homosocial desire, which had primarily defined Matt through his relations with Cherry and Dunson, is redundant in this heterosexual narrative. While male-to-male desire had been Matt's prevalent loyalty until Tess's arrival, with the latter the film's erotic focus shifts abruptly, yet paradoxically Matt is confirmed as belonging to a homosocial continuum. Just as homosociality and homosexuality are located along the same spectrum, so a queer reading of *Red River* must acknowledge that heterosexuality and homosexuality are also contiguous rather than separate: Matt/Clift endorses

CHAPTER 2

both in his own person, placed in a field including male-to-male desire (whatever expression this desire may take) as well as male-to-female attraction. To dismiss the sexual connotations of Matt's relationship with Tess is absurd. Within minutes of their meeting, Matt is crouching over Tess, ripping off her dress and sucking arrow poison out of her shoulder; soon afterward, she slaps him. The strong physicality of this first interaction is developed in their next scene together, set in the forest at night. Although distinctly unpredatory, Matt is highly responsive to Tess's erotic presence: he touches her neck and hair slowly and sensuously, then constantly shifts his position, expressing physical tension. His eyes rest on her with desire; when she kisses him, he takes her face in his hands and kisses her back. The clear implication of this romp in the dark is sex, just like in their later meeting in Abilene, when Tess surprises Matt in his hotel room. This time he advances toward her, grabs her with both arms and starts caressing her, while devouring her with his eyes; then he firmly places one hand on her mouth to stop her talking, and kisses her. It is not just a sexually charged scene, but also one in which Matt/Clift is remarkably active. Matt's behavior toward Tess, however, also points to an involvement beyond sex: his gift to her of Dunson's bracelet, a symbol of love, testifies to his emotional involvement. Cherry, while being an erotic and antipatriarchal companion, does not earn Matt's bracelet and shares no scenes with Matt once Tess has entered the narrative. However, Cherry remains Dunson's competitor, striving for a privileged place near Matt. The fact that Dunson, while pursuing Matt, shoots Cherry without a second thought shows his recognition of the younger man as a crucial rival. In fact, the bond between Matt and Dunson is unequivocally presented as one of love: though problematically contained by patriarchy, it is but a different facet of Matt's commitment to homoeroticism. In *Red River* Matt emerges as a split, extremely vital erotic subject, open to multiple modes of connection; his relationships overlap and parallel each other along a continuum of the social and the erotic, the homosexual and the heterosexual, revealing Montgomery Clift as a remarkably queer presence.

The Heiress is Clift's third film after *Red River* and *The Search*; while in some ways providing a departure from these previous works, it also signals continuity in the star's persona, confirming him as an ambiguous, yet undisputed object of erotic desire. One of the factors that attracted Clift to the role was the opportunity to play the villain, thus avoiding being typecast as the caring, sensitive champion. Based on Henry James's *Washington Square* and set in the 1840s, the film sees Clift as the suave fortune hunter Morris Townsend, ruthlessly wooing the rich but hapless Catherine Sloper (Olivia de Havilland). Unusually attired in period costume, and cast in the most unsympathetic role of his whole career, Clift plays Morris with skill and sophistication, presenting a convincing portrayal of calculation and greed. At the same time, Clift's performance also brings an unsettling complexity to his character, which combines with the narrative mystery around him to create an ambiguous protagonist, subversive of traditional notions of male sexuality.

The Heiress charts the relationships between Catherine and the two men who come to dominate her life: Morris, her suitor and object of her passion, and her father, Dr. Austin Sloper (Ralph Richardson). A naive young woman, pathologically insecure and socially inept, Catherine is the only child of her distant, emotionally chilly father. Dr. Sloper has never resigned himself to the loss of his wife, who died giving birth to Catherine, and constantly compares the beauty and charm of the former to the dullness and gaucheness of the latter. The film begins by showing Catherine, eager to please her father, agreeing to attend a ball with him and her chaperone, her silly and well-meaning aunt, Lavinia Penniman (Miriam Hopkins), who lives with them. The evening starts with Catherine's social mortification; she is unable to dance gracefully and is completely ignored by the young men present. Suddenly, however, she finds herself addressed by a dazzlingly handsome stranger, who invites her to dance. Encouraged by her aunt, who introduces the man as Morris Townsend, just returned from Europe, Catherine is swept on the dance floor and is instantly besotted with her partner. Morris is attentive and extremely charming, and this first meeting is soon followed by his assiduous, relentless courtship. Madly in love with her suitor, Catherine agrees to marry him against the wish of her father, who believes the penniless Morris is a gold digger, only interested in her daughter's inheritance. A fruitless interview with Morris's sister (Betty Linley), who is clearly under the spell of her brother's charm, only reinforces Dr. Sloper's opinion. Wishing to test both his daughter's

CHAPTER 2

determination and Morris's attachment, Dr. Sloper takes Catherine on a trip to Europe; her feelings for Morris, however, do not change during their travels. In the Slopers' absence, Morris insinuates himself into Aunt Penniman's confidence, becoming a regular visitor to the house and making liberal use of the doctor's wine and cigars. On Catherine's return from Europe, he immediately renews his pressing entreats to her and suggests an elopement. Morris's daring plan comes just after Catherine, unbeknownst to him, has had a painful exchange with her father: he has told her that Morris can only be pursuing her for her money, as she is devoid of any other attraction. Shocked and angered by the revelation of her father's opinion of her, but convinced of her lover's sincerity, Catherine eagerly agrees to elope with Morris, who arranges to come and collect her that night. She then informs him that her father, whom she never wishes to see again, will certainly disinherit her after they marry. The night comes, and Catherine anxiously waits for Morris, with her luggage ready, but he never appears. In grief and disbelief, Catherine is told by her aunt that she should have never informed her admirer of her loss of fortune; the final implications of these words crush her entirely. In the following days, Dr. Sloper falls gravely ill, but Catherine shows no feelings for him, even refusing to see him on his deathbed; meantime, she has discovered that Morris has gone west. A few years pass, and the still unmarried Catherine has become a self-possessed, bitter woman. Her monotonous existence is shattered one day as Aunt Penniman comes home with news of Morris: he is back in town, and wishes to see Catherine. Soon Morris appears, as handsome as ever; he implores Catherine to forgive him, saying that he only acted in her interest, not wishing to be the cause of her disinheritance. The two rapidly agree to marry and decide that Morris will return that same night, ready to take Catherine with him. At the appointed hour, Morris arrives and knocks at the Slopers' door, but he knocks in vain, as Catherine bolts the door and goes to bed, to the sound of Morris's desperate calling.

The Heiress is openly sympathetic to the plight of its heroine; its epilogue presents Catherine as being finally free from Morris, as she administers her cold-blooded revenge for the pain and humiliation he inflicted on her. At the same time, however, the film leaves no doubt of Morris's desirability as a prize sexual object. Through its narrative

Irruption in Hollywood

and visual texts, *The Heiress* constructs Morris/Clift as its sole erotic interest, a beacon of desire who has no competitors, either male or female. After two films in which he had appeared respectively as an army engineer and a cowboy, his beauty shining through "virile" clothes and activities, Clift here is deliberately packaged to give pleasure to the eye. Elaborately dressed in tight-fitting and frilly clothes, carefully groomed, with his hair and sideburns impeccably styled, he is ostensibly presented as a delectable sight. Diegetically, of course, the implication is that Morris has styled himself: a notion that heavily informs his performative, dandified character. The fact that his occupations appear limited to dancing, smoking cigars, and carrying his leather gloves, completes the association of Morris with aesthetic and sensual gratification. As the crafter of his own image, an image he uses for specific personal gains, Morris is also an active subject; this fundamental tension, between erotic object and controlling subject, crystallizes the contradiction his character signifies, the (dis)junction between appearance and essence.

The film's introduction of Morris highlights this contradictory quality. The frame initially contains only Catherine and her aunt sitting together, but it is soon partially invaded by the sight of a man's right arm; simultaneously, a suave male voice addresses the aunt and the niece. As the camera tracks out slightly, Morris is still hardly visible, but the portion of his back shown, and the direction his voice comes from, identify him as standing opposite the two seated women; the excited reaction his appearance provokes in them is clearly visible, leaving no doubt of the exceptionally pleasing effect he has achieved. Morris is thus dominating Catherine and the aunt through his literally superior position as well as dominating the screen through the build-up of anticipation created; his face has not even been seen yet. In this way, Morris is presented in a physically commanding stance, and as someone able to dramatically affect others through his presence; at the same time, the film is also highlighting his function as erotic spectacle, for the benefit of its female protagonists. This tension between Morris the subject and Morris the object is sustained throughout *The Heiress*, which again and again defines him as an erotic prize: "Isn't he the most beautiful man you have ever seen?" asks the enraptured Catherine to her father, while the clearly smitten Aunt Penniman describes him as,

CHAPTER 2

"A man who would be a feather in any girl's cap." Even the disparaging Dr. Sloper recognizes Morris's erotic value, as while attempting to persuade Catherine of her admirer's duplicity he tells her: "He could have had any woman." While Dr. Sloper's words are expressed through his view of Morris as an active cad, in the film's total structure of meaning they also signify "he could have been had by any woman." Morris, however, is at the same time a very effective subject, as his behavior motivates the film's plot; he not only instigates situations and events, but, just like Matt in *Red River*, is also in charge of his own erotic spectacle. Yet while Matt's self-display was integrated in the wider articulation of his character, and informed the expression of his multiple desires, Morris in *The Heiress* literally *is* his spectacle, albeit one ridden with ambiguity. Willing and fashioning himself as a vision, but with his thoughts, feelings, and history shrouded in mystery, Morris emerges as an act of performance, where the distance between performer and performative action is very uncertain. The opposition defining Morris as both object and subject is therefore also a contradiction between his appearance (his visible display as a pleaser) and his essence (his subjective intentions behind the display). This central ambiguity is obvious in his behavior as Catherine's lover. While exhibiting an outward urgency about their marriage, expressed through single-minded perseverance and verbal sentimentality, Morris shows no sign of sexual interest in the woman he is trying to seduce. Unlike in *Red River*, Clift's spectacle here does not disclose his own erotic charge, but only his power and determination to eroticize others. As Morris Townsend, Clift is erotically available but not accessible; his sexual aims, if any, are covered in secrecy. It is notable that Morris not only shows no physical passion for Catherine, but also that he does not even attempt to fake it; his performative range covers the routine characteristics of the ardent lover, apart from sexual ardor. Indeed, as soon as Catherine accepts his marriage proposal, he rapidly takes leave of her, without lingering in any passionate embrace. This erotic absence is, of course, in sharp contrast with established notions of the suitor, and as Morris presents a total lack of sexual interest in women in general, he is also deviating from models of "normal" masculinity. Nor is there any explicit indication that he may be attracted to men, and no rumors of past romances or scandals, with either sex, color his reputation. In fact, the only glimpse of erotic feeling Morris/Clift shows is visible in his contact with some inanimate objects, symbols of luxury and social status. While caressing the back of an antique chair at the Slopers', or moving his fingers over an art object, or touching other beautiful items of furniture and decoration, Morris/Clift conveys a sense of genuine craving: his hands move languorously, his eyes gleam with pleasure, even as he is engaged in a conversation about something else. He suggests a passionate coveting for things that, should they come into his possession, will match his own beauty and elegance, effectively becoming part of him; eroticism, for Morris, appears in fact to be self-reflexive. Whether showing off his physical appeal or responding to the sensuality of luxury, he is reveling in his own erotic persona. This self-celebration does not entail pleasure in his own sexual feelings, but rather an aesthetic appreciation of his value and power, as a highly sought-after erotic commodity. Simultaneously available and out of bounds, assiduous and detached, eloquent and enigmatic, Clift constructs a male lead whose sexual identity remains essentially closeted. Defined by discrepancy between traditional canons of the male lover and his ambiguous relation to them, Morris/Clift further unsettles social norms through the function of his erotic spectacle; effectively selling his body in exchange for security and status, he occupies a traditional female position. The feminization of Morris is emphatically dramatized by the manner of his engagement to Catherine. In a complete reversal of well-established social rules, he recoils from personally announcing his intentions to Catherine's father; rather than "manly" breaking the news to Dr. Sloper, and boldly pleading for his daughter's hand, he lets his fiancée do the preliminary work and only arrives on the scene afterward. Similarly, the end of the film sees Morris victimized, jilted by his lover and utterly powerless, in a typical female predicament. Once again, the "unmanly" connotations of Morris's situation are reinforced by Catherine's behavior: on their last meeting, when she must have already resolved to get rid of him, she presents him with a gift of jewels, sparkling diamonds she had bought for him in Paris. It is a very handsome present, befitting a man's dismissal of a high-maintenance mistress, and which, according to Catherine and her aunt, "really suits him."

Morris's deviant masculinity must be read in the context of his performative role; because he is constantly constructing himself as the irresistible Morris Townsend, he is literally offering a representation of male identity. This identity is highly subversive of normative patterns, something *The Heiress* further highlights through the contrast between Morris and Dr. Sloper, the only other male character in the film. Catherine's father offers an authoritative example of orthodox manhood, hard working, responsible, and deeply unfrivolous; this image is greatly strengthened by Richardson's performance, which is stately and confident, exuding virile solidity. Against this Victorian paragon of male virtues, Morris is immediately cast as his polar opposite, by being the visual and narrative embodiment of the Dandy. A fashionably radical figure in the mid-1800s, the Dandy was defined by an extreme love of beauty and fashion and stood for exciting decadence in a world of dull morality; importantly, and in flagrant defiance of Dr. Sloper's ethos, a Dandy would refuse to work or do anything useful, devoting himself solely to aesthetic pleasures. As Elisa Glick's research has shown, the Dandy's dictum was to do "absolutely nothing," true to the dogma that a Dandy "does not work; he exists."[12] Indeed, Morris has clearly no intention of finding employment; he once remarks to Aunt Penniman that Dr. Sloper can tirelessly work at his job, explaining his own different attitude by saying "some of us cannot."

The ambiguity Morris/Clift presents is thus based in gender subversion and sexual enigma; combined with Clift's arresting good looks, and with his established image as erotically desirable yet ambivalent, this ambiguity reinforces Morris's unsettling character. While *Red River* had contained some of the most erotically charged scenes of Clift's entire career, *The Heiress* sees him as equally beautiful and enticing, but sexually inaccessible and even unintelligible; he enhances his role's contradictions by giving a performance that is intense yet ultimately unreadable. Sexually indecipherable and biographically mysterious, yet powerfully present in his physical and social charm, Morris elicits speculations as to his nature and motives; he obviously carries secrets, which are never fully revealed, and the evil associated with his duplicity is only ever verbalized by Dr. Sloper. Morris's sister does not pronounce judgment on him, while Aunt Penniman is able to accept his mercenary scheme *and* to hold a most romantic image of him. The aunt's position is apparently illogical but close to that constructed for and by the audience. While Morris is apparently pursuing Catherine's wealth, he offers no insights into his alleged wickedness, nor can he be easily separated from Montgomery Clift as a sensitive, sympathetic young man, or from his status as covetable object of desire. Both in the diegetic space of the film and in the audience's participation in it, Morris/Clift constitutes an open secret, inextricably connected to issues of knowledge. In her account of queer identities and the closet in the nineteenth and twentieth centuries, Eve Kosofsky Sedgwick argues that historically, in Western culture, "knowledge meant sexual knowledge, and secrets meant sexual secrets"; the mystery around Morris is primarily signified as a sexual mystery, and the puzzle of his identity suggests a queer sexuality by being "distinctively constituted *as* secrecy."[13] Rather than being located at the junction between known and unknown, Morris/Clift *is* that (dis)junction: embodying the dialectics between deception and truth, between open and closeted, and between male and female, he is a quintessentially queer figure.

Clift was dissatisfied with his acting in *The Heiress* (as he was with many of his screen performances), yet it is difficult to imagine a better

Determined to please: Yet Morris remains inscrutable in The Heiress.

CHAPTER 2

rendition of a reprehensible, deeply alluring, and ultimately mysterious character. At one level of his performance, Clift plays the cad very convincingly. His speech is honeyed and suave, so evidently aimed at pleasing that it readily suggests calculation, and surely in no other film does he smile so frequently, yet so statically. His material greed is palpable, not simply when he is able to enjoy the Slopers' luxury, but also in the scene when Catherine tells him of her disinheritance: here his expression, which had been set to tenderness, noticeably falters. It is a subtly conveyed shift to coldness and displeasure, but one that Clift eloquently achieves through a sudden tension of his jaw, a deadly serious gaze, and the visible strain with which he continues their conversation. Yet while these are all pointers of duplicity and mercenary scheming, narratively confirmed by Morris's desertion of Catherine, they are complicated by other elements of Clift's performance. In his first scene, for example, Morris/Clift combines smooth talking and constant smiling with moments of disarming complicity. When Catherine is writing his name in her dance book, and is at great pains to hide that she has no other name written down, he very naturally shows her his own book, which is equally empty, and just as she had ineptly fumbled with the cord attached to the book, so he does too, giving her a quick glance of shared amusement. Moments later, when they are dancing together, he good-humoredly reassures her that her clumsy kicking of his legs is entirely his fault, as he is wearing the wrong type of boots. As the dance ends, and Catherine concludes her strenuous efforts to follow his steps, he observes her with almost childlike satisfaction and says: "very good!" These instances of unaffected behavior impede an absolute assessment of Morris; aided by his lack of open disdain for Catherine, and by script and camerawork that not once show his point of view, he remains ultimately deeply puzzling. Morris/Clift often conveys ambiguity through what he does, or does not, with his eyes; significantly, his parting look at Catherine after they have first met, a look she does not see, is totally inscrutable. As Catherine moves off the screen and the camera slowly tracks in on Clift, his face relaxes; his eyes are wide open and shining, almost dreamy. It is a look that may be interpreted in many ways, but its only obvious meaning is intense pleasure. Clift's ability to express emotions through his eyes is evident in all his work, yet if these emotions are connected to a female love interest, their exact nature is often unclear. Graham McCann has remarked that desire, in Clift's performance, "is often a very private, sometimes almost masturbatory, experience for him";[14] in *The Heiress*, Clift's look at Catherine goes even further, reverberating solely of its own pleasure. Because no hint of sexual feelings has preceded it (and none follows it), Morris's transfixed gaze signals a deeply personal, self-absorbed moment; its undefined desire can only be self-reflexive, even if it should be the desire of seeing himself rich. At the same time, when they are together, Clift not once looks at de Havilland as if he wanted to devour her with his eyes, a trademark of his heterosexual performances in his other films. Conversely, when making his marriage proposal to Catherine, Clift's eyes are hardly shown: most of the scene, including their kissing, is shot with him giving his back to the camera, or otherwise showing only a brief view of his profile, contributing to the uncertainty surrounding his motives. Yet as Lawrence Shaffer has argued, even when Morris's interaction with Catherine is documented through close-ups of his expression, all that one sees is "the determinedly charming face of Montgomery Clift . . . until the end it is impossible to determine the extent, if any, that Clift's face is a mask rather than a mirror."[15] The ongoing tension between mask and mirror, between surface and content, is an apt reference to the dandification of Morris's character. According to Elisa Glick, the Dandy is an essentially queer figure; while some of his traits, such as aestheticism and self-grooming, are easily referable to gay stereotypes, his queerness is best revealed by the complexity of his cultural positioning. The Dandy signifies the impossible reunification of contradictions; while reveling in the surface value of style and beauty, including his own, he also stands for a radical reevaluation of life's priorities, pointing to an alternative inner system that, however, remains elusive. The visible articulation of the Dandy's split subjectivity is the open secret of the closet; Glick concludes that the Dandy must perennially exist "in the dialectical relation between public and private, appearance and essence," in a fundamentally queer subjective location.[16] In *The Heiress*, Morris Townsend does precisely that. Morris's identity is closeted both narratively and through Clift's performance. He is known by his external image while remaining privately unknown, yet he is also always in the process of being known. Expressing a deviant masculinity and an openly concealed sexuality, Morris/Clift is the queer cusp between knowledge and secret.

Man-Boy Love and Queering Americanness: *The Search* and *The Big Lift*

The Search is set among the urban devastation of Allied-occupied Germany and focuses on a young Czech boy, separated from his mother during his imprisonment in Auschwitz. Free since the end of the war, but homeless, friendless, and in shock, the child runs away from the Allied authorities who are sheltering him and accidentally meets a US Army engineer on the street; the engineer takes him home and nurtures him, undeterred by the boy's evident mental confusion. The narrative charts the boy's recovery and intense relationship with his American rescuer until he is miraculously reunited with his mother at the very end of the film. *The Search* gained rave reviews on its release, winning several major international prizes, including an Academy Award for Best Screenplay; his two main protagonists, the US engineer and the boy, were also Oscar nominated. At the end of the film's premiere, a member of the audience asked the director, Fred Zinnemann: "Where did you find a soldier who could act so well?"[17] The answer was, of course, that Zinnemann had not found any "soldier" to play the part of engineer Ralph "Steve" Stevenson; the role had been given to Montgomery Clift, in what would be his first actual screen appearance. Thanks partly to his anonymity in *The Search*, partly to his astounding performance, Clift had produced a thoroughly convincing portrayal of the all-American soldier; in this sense, his presence both fits and informs the film's dominant narrative, where US power brings order and compassion to a Europe in chaos. At the same time, Clift's ambiguous masculinity combines with the intensity and idiosyncrasy of Steve's role, creating a powerful alternative text that complicates the plot. The result is a film underpinned by the suggestion that America and its Armed Forces are not monolithic or standardized but open to difference, to gender and sexual indeterminacy, and to relationships lying outside proscribed social models; in other words, the suggestion of a queer Americanness. Two years later, Clift would bring similar complications to another film set in postwar Germany, *The Big Lift*, this

Irruption in Hollywood

time playing the role of a sergeant in the US Air Force. *The Search* and *The Big Lift* are linked by obvious continuity in Clift's career: shot on location in Germany at a time of high Cold War tension, they also share marked "realistic" aesthetics, and a metanarrative centered on America as a redeeming force. In both films, an overt normative project is compromised by Clift's presence, creating a parallel text where notions of US "normality" are thrown into question.

The equation of Americanness with US military power is central to *The Search*. The film's narrative is framed by a binary structure where America, represented through its army and United Nations Relief and Rehabilitation Administration (UNRRA), is deployed to a defeated and ruined Germany; the condition of serving in the American Forces is added national poignancy by this oppositional setting. Americanness is thus automatically linked to notions of military organization, of control over oneself and others, and of traditional "masculine" attributes such as strength, emotional pragmatism, and heterosexual prowess. This happens despite the fact that the American military, meant as a defensive and offensive organization, remains mostly implied in *The Search*; instead, the film focuses on American rescue efforts, and specifically on the hugely difficult logistics of coordinating the movement of Displaced Persons (DPs) across Germany and liberated Europe. The affiliation with the US military, however, is a dominant feature of UNRRA, which is also strongly linked to notions of Americanness: although UNRRA was an Allied operational agreement, ratified by forty-four countries, it had been the brainchild of US President Franklin D. Roosevelt, and it remained directed by Americans throughout its existence. While the film shows a few token British officers involved in the rescue effort, the Czech boy's mother, Mrs. Malik (Jarmila Novotna) is the only non-American adult protagonist. The plot rests on the UNRRA director, Mrs. Murray (Aline MacMahon), and on US Army engineer Steve. These two Americans are never seen without their official uniform, thus being presented as inseparable from their country's national and military attributes; similarly, their roles as saviors directly inform the film's representation of Americanness. In this way the film constructs a master narrative of organized compassion, strongly inflected by notions of military and political order; indeed, the initial credits include the information that *The Search* was shot with the coop-

CHAPTER 2

eration of the US Army in Germany. Within this dominant structure of meaning, Mrs. Murray and Steve occupy pivotal roles. While Mrs. Murray introduces official Americanness, remaining a constant reminder of it throughout the film, it is Steve's appearance that triggers the plot's development, unsettling it at the same time. Causing an abrupt shift in the film's direction, for which, however, audience expectation has been elaborately built up, Steve/Clift also disrupts assumptions about Americanness and its "normality."

The film starts with a night shot of a derelict train station, soon entered by a robust woman in uniform, heading a similarly attired group. The woman, Mrs. Murray, is immediately identified as American by her accent, as she gives orders concerning the imminent arrival of a train carrying displaced children. Clearly sympathetic, yet brisk and in command, Mrs. Murray is next shown scrutinizing the train's cargo, with the aid of a torch; the camera follows her gaze over a mass of ragged, exhausted-looking children, still asleep. Her reaction to this pitiful sight is to tell one of her helpers, in a perfectly steady voice: "Ask them to get out." In just a few moments, the film has identified Mrs. Murray as the exponent of a much-needed compassionate initiative, but also as someone who is quite detached from her young charges; indeed, she can only reach them through an interpreter. As the children are woken up and ushered into a transport convoy, Mrs. Murray, in a voice-over, explains how the children fear anyone wearing a uniform, being the survivors of unthinkable horrors in concentration camps. The emotional effect of these words is heightened by the next scenes, which show the children being fed and prepared for bed; silent and ashen-faced, they present a ghastly spectacle of trauma and suffering. Through this initial sequence the film establishes a crucial depiction of Americanness. Mrs. Murray is remarkably lacking in traditional "feminine" traits, such as tenderness and the open expression of feelings; instead, the UNRRA director shows a clear bent toward the "masculine" and the "soldierly," reinforcing the association of Americanness with virility and military discipline. Rather than feminize or soften America's image, the presence of Mrs. Murray determines the film's overt discourse, where Americanness is synonymous with order and self-control. Not remotely a mother figure, she is the ideal exponent of a mighty national power, carrying out vital relief work but remaining emotionally uninvolved. There is nothing subversive, however, in the "virility" of the UNRRA chief; with her character left unexplored, and her role limited to showcase US organizational achievements in post-war Europe, Mrs. Murray is upholding the status quo. This image of America as well meaning, yet "manly" unconnected to the feelings of those needing rescue, is forcefully expanded in the next sequence. Here Mrs. Murray interviews the displaced children one by one, filing their details and making arrangements; unable to communicate with them in their native languages, she again needs an interpreter to mediate the conversations. But she is also incapable of showing empathy through nonverbal means. When a little girl narrates how, in a concentration camp, she was forced to collect the possessions left by the people being gassed and found her mother's things among them, Mrs. Murray briefly falters. Yet without making direct contact with the girl, she turns to the translator and tells him, "Well, say something to her." This incapacity to reach out to the suffering children bears enormously on the film's narrative, as it will be entirely reversed by the arrival of Steve/Clift: he will mark a special channel of transmission between children and grown-ups, where communication includes language yet also bypasses it. Mrs. Murray's total lack of emotional currency, mirrored by her linguistic incapacitation, will be countered by the excess of Steve's availability to the boy he rescues.

Through these first sequences the film defines Americanness as a force of pragmatic, institutionalized compassion, striving to bring "normality" to Europe; in doing so, it also presents the war children as inhabiting an opposite dimension from the Americans, as their distressed appearance, erratic behavior, and recent history mark them as distinctly "abnormal." This oppositional structure is crystallized by the appearance of Karel Malik (Ivan Jandl), the Czech boy who will be the film's young protagonist. The most visibly "abnormal" of all the children, Karel is so utterly traumatized that he refuses to speak; his eyes are wide open with terror, and he seems to have no memories, not even to know what his name is. A flashback explains Karel's grim history: the son of a Czech intellectual, he was taken to Auschwitz with his mother, but the two were eventually separated. The boy's last sight of his mother was through the wire fence that divided them. As the film cuts back to the present, and to Karel being questioned in vain by the

CHAPTER 2

interpreter, Mrs. Murray gives orders for the boy to be sent to a special refugee camp, which deals with particularly difficult cases. During transportation to this camp, Karel and other children manage to escape from the UNRRA authorities; their fear of uniforms makes them believe they are going to be killed. Scattering in all directions through the streets in ruins, the children are difficult to reach for the officers in charge of them, and Karel and another boy manage to avoid recapture. They find themselves by a river, and Karel's companion fatally dives in, to be drowned by the strong current; Karel himself runs away from the scene, but his knitted cap falls in the water and floats adrift.

The Search thus establishes Karel's persona as deeply traumatized, impossible to communicate with, and terrified of people in uniforms; next, the film presents the audience with the harrowing story of Karel's mother, Mrs. Malik. She is revealed to have survived Auschwitz, to know that her husband and daughter have been killed, and to be wandering around Germany in search of her son. Mrs. Malik has a very sensitive, expressive face, marked by suffering and exhaustion; the film shows her going from one refugee camp to another, until she is erroneously told that her child is indeed sheltered in a camp, and that she will see him immediately. The almost unbearable gush of joy is soon shattered, as Karel's mother discovers that this child, calling himself Karel Malik, is not her son, but a Jewish boy who adopted her child's name when it was not answered in a roll call. The powerful emotions stirred by this sequence are concentrated on Mrs. Malik, an icon of motherhood, defined by the sweetness and longing visible on her face; she makes a striking comparison with Mrs. Murray, becoming the film's symbol of motherly femininity.

At this point *The Search* has been running for thirty-three minutes, but it has only been a prelude to what happens next. As the camera cuts to a desolate landscape of urban ruins, Karel comes into view, barefooted and ragged; on the nearby road a jeep is parked, and a long shot shows an American soldier in it, eating a sandwich. Unlike every uniformed figure seen until now, this man appears relaxed, almost slouching in his car. The camera closes in alternately on the soldier and Karel, who exchange glances; then, in a sudden movement, it closes in on the soldier, showing a full view of Montgomery Clift's face. At this moment the film introduces desire in its text. As Steve/

Clift looks up, making prolonged eye contact with the boy, he reveals a stunningly beautiful face; his eyes are huge and radiant, beaming with liveliness and kindness. It is not simply that Steve is the first remotely good-looking character in the film (and will be the last); his beauty has an almost shining quality, all the more striking among the grimness and deterioration that has dominated the screen so far. Twenty-seven years old, Clift looks younger than he is, fresh and totally charming; in a single close-up, he focuses on himself the multiple gazes of the camera, of Karel, and of the audience. This shot crystallizes Steve as the film's focal point, and as its object of desire; coming at a stage in the plot where hopelessness and desolation have been steadily mounting, Steve is the natural target for the audience's and Karel's longing. The beautiful man in the jeep seems to promise, and will indeed bring, much-needed relief to the film's narrative; however, this relief contains unsettling elements, which will complicate the apparent linearity of *The Search*.

As intimated by his first appearance, Steve is the bearer of hope and love in Karel's life; the film charts the development of an almost ob-

Desire enters the film text: Steve's first appearance in The Search.

CHAPTER 2

sessive relationship between the two, as the boy's fear of military uniforms is replaced by a passionate attachment to Steve. Karel grows so attached to his rescuer that he literally cannot bear to lose sight of him; living together in the same house, the boy takes on the role of Steve's companion, and by the end of the film the two even share the same bedroom. On his part, the US Army engineer becomes completely absorbed by Karel, centering his life on the boy's needs; his feelings for the child are so strong he cannot leave him behind and decides to take him home with him to the United States. All this points to a mutual excess of feelings, to a craving for each other's presence that goes beyond traditional social patterns—adult males are not meant to be so close to little boys unless they are their own offspring, and especially if the adult in question is a young, strikingly handsome US soldier. Moreover, orthodox notions of handsome US soldiers are linked to ideas of aggressive masculinity, muscular physicality, and rampant heterosexuality, all traits that Steve/Clift does not possess. However, the disruptive structure dominated by Clift in the film has its beginning somewhere else: in the channeling of audience desire through the boy's passion for him. The spectators' longing for Clift has a narrative and erotic base, which is actively strengthened by his performance: throughout his presence on screen, entirely devoted to his scenes with the boy, Clift is intensely available, foregrounding his emotional openness but also his body. There cannot be many actors who match Clift's motility in *The Search*. Steve/Clift never remains still, getting up from his seat, slumping in an armchair with his legs outstretched, then sitting up again and tilting his body toward the camera; next, he is suddenly near the boy, affectionately squeezing his arms, placing his face near his while he talks. All his movements and postures demand attention, and attention he gets, both from the boy and the camera. An abundance of two shots frame both protagonists in close-ups, showing Karel's enraptured gaze on Steve, and Steve's luminous face turned on him. The audience is thus positioned in an unsettling arrangement because its response to Steve's erotic appeal is mediated through Karel, the only available route. The film's articulation of desire is therefore constructed along profoundly queer lines. By producing a male-to-male narrative of longing, *The Search* goes against traditional parameters of gender and sexuality; as this narrative is also one of man-boy love, accepted rules of generational relationships are also disturbed.

It is important at this point to qualify the possible implications of this dual narrative of desire. According to Eve Kosofsky Sedgwick, there is a need for queer theory to posit alternative models of the child in relation to sexuality; she speaks of the reductive possibilities offered by existing views of children as "totally volitional, unproblematically 'active,'" or instead as "totally passive and incapable of relevant or effectual desire."[18] She proposes instead that a child may be seen "as being sometimes in a position to influence—obviously to radically varying degrees—*by whom s/he may be seduced*" (Sedgwick's emphasis).[19] While Sedgwick is careful to acknowledge that "seduction" takes place in "a continuum that extends to, but is not fully defined by, the experience of a child who is in fact assaulted or raped,"[20] *The Search* firmly locates boy-man desire outside scenarios of physical sex, or indeed of any kind of coercion. While Karel may be seen as being seduced by Steve, this seduction does not imply any sexual action, intention, or even feeling on Steve's part; instead, it designates the boy's active/passive choice to be attracted and enamored by Steve. Likewise, Karel's attachment to Steve is not sexually developed, yet it does contain a sensual element, a need for Steve's corporeal presence and closeness; in this sense, the boy's attraction for the man has the same quality of a child's attraction for, and pleasure in, his mother's body. Adult sexuality is thus removed from the foreground, as Clift's self-display, if erotically inviting, remains untargeted and ultimately self-reflexive. While Clift's portrayal of Steve makes him desirable and available, it does not develop his sexual persona; his intense, self-conscious use of his body points rather to a suspension, to a delay in the activation of sexual feelings. Delay still contains an erotic potentiality, leaving Steve/Clift poised along a border zone that, however, he never trespasses; man-boy love in *The Search* is effectively contained by sexual delay, assuring the film's safeguard of notions of children's safety. As Kathryn Bond Stockton remarks: "Delay is seen as a friend to the child. Delay is said to be a feature of its growth: children grow by delaying their approach to the realms of sexuality, labor, and harm."[21] However, while Steve gives off no sexual signals toward Karel, he displays a platonic love for the boy that allows Karel the "choice to be seduced." The film's structure of desire is therefore

CHAPTER 2

operating at two levels: the audience is erotically captivated by Clift, and is guided to channel this erotic attraction through the boy's infatuation for him. At the same time, the boy's sensual yet nonsexual desire is facilitated and nurtured by Clift, through his layered performance that defines him as both object of desire and mother surrogate.

The feelings Steve expresses for Karel are clearly in excess of the accepted "norm"; the two are not biologically connected, and there is no apparent reason why a young US Army engineer should take a displaced child home with him. As Steve's housemate, US Army officer Jerry (Wendell Corey), points out, the easily found reason for this behavior is that Steve is a "sucker," having fallen for the boy's touching appearance. In this instance Jerry is a reminder of American "normality," of the emotional detachment employed by the US Forces in dealing with DPs. Jerry's analysis of the relationship between Steve and Karel rests on his alignment with national standards and on the acknowledgment that his fellow American is somehow different from the others; when Jerry arrives home and finds the boy with Steve, he asks "Who picked who up?" But if Steve's decisions regarding the boy are patently outside the "norm," they are made profoundly more so by the way Clift performs his scenes with Karel. Although never sentimental, Steve's treatment of the boy is defined by intensity and closeness; he shows deep absorption in aspects of the child's routine usually seen as "feminine" tasks, such as teaching him, carefully supervising his clothes and appearance, and making sure he eats properly. Above all, there is a degree of tenderness in Steve's behavior that emerges at key moments, adding a feeling of strong intimacy to their relationship and marking Steve not as a father figure for Karel, but as an odd combination of mother and partner. This is never more obvious than in a crucial sequence in the last part of the film when Karel momentarily disappears; his eventual reunion with Steve is one of the most emotionally charged scenes in *The Search*. Karel runs away because, in a sudden memory flash, he remembers his mother as he had last seen her, in Auschwitz behind a barbed wire fence; frantic with anxiety, he asks Steve to go with him to look for her. Before Steve can summon up the courage to tell him what he believes, that his mother is dead, the boy runs away, confused and distressed. In a previous sequence, the audience had seen Karel's mother, Mrs. Malik, being told that her son was

Irruption in Hollywood

dead; the boy's knitted cap, found floating in the river, had convinced UNRRA of his drowning. After collapsing with shock and spending a period of recovery assisting children in a UNRRA camp, Mrs. Malik had decided to go on the road again, unable to give up her search for her child, whose death she refuses to believe. When, on Karel's disappearance later on, Steve runs after him, he displays the same devoted stubbornness as the boy's mother; after driving around the city in vain, he still won't listen to Jerry's entreaty to give up the search, just as Mrs. Malik had previously refused to listen to Mrs. Murray, and to accept her boy's death. Steve and Mrs. Malik are thus clearly linked by the film's narrative, as the only two people in Karel's life who are irrationally determined to find him. When Steve finds Karel again, however, the scene of their meeting evokes diverse emotions, crystallizing Clift's ambiguous performance as surrogate mother and male companion.

It is Jerry, driving the jeep with Steve, who spots Karel in the distance; Steve then gets out of the car, saying that he must speak to the boy alone. He walks toward Karel, but stops a few steps before reaching him; with his face turned toward him, and his back to the camera, he just says "Hello." Clift's face is not shown at this moment, but his voice compresses so much emotion in a single word, that it invites an almost dizzying expectation from the audience. Karel looks at him, disoriented and poised to flee again, but Steve/Clift adds: "Hey, don't run." The boy rushes to embrace him. Steve returns the embrace, keeping the child pressed against him, gently stroking his hair and telling him not to cry; they remain like this for a few moments, with their arms around each other. It is a distinctly "mother and child" posture, immortalized as such in countless paintings and sculptures; at the same time, Clift's intense and tender attitude makes the scene not so dissimilar from a lovers' reconciliation. It is a romantic rather than sexual quality, hinting at a special intimacy between man and boy; while adding an extra layer of tension to their relationship, it also marks the unsettling positioning of audience desire. The overall result is a combination of multiple, equally queer strands; Montgomery Clift was aware of at least one of them, as he insisted on reshooting this scene. Although Clift did not explain to Zinnemann why he was unhappy with his performance, the reason was that while speaking to Karel, he had instinctively called him "dear"; the reshoot, which went into the final cut, does not contain that word. Clift revealed this in a letter to a friend: "he wrote to Rick in New York that if that scene were printed, the audience was sure to think him homosexual for having said 'dear' to a boy."[22] It is painful to think of Clift's anguish about the social perceptions of one, common word; it is also indicative of the power of cultural constructions of homosexuality, and of man-boy relations. While the film stays clear of any sexual implications, the relationship between Steve and Karel is clearly defined by love, a love that exceeds prescribed social limits both narratively and performatively. Indeed, "man-boy love" seems the most apt description for the bond between the protagonists. As Kathryn Bond Stockton points out, it is possible to use "the phrase 'man-boy love,' which to many ears denotes pedophilia, to connote a range of ways in which men and boys might say they love each other, including wanting to live together."[23]

The queer relationship between the US soldier and the boy thus veers toward platonic longing and homosocial complicity. Steve and Karel share jokes and understandings of their own and clearly see themselves as a pair. When Jerry announces the arrival of his family

Together again: The reunion of Steve and Karel is deeply emotional.

from the United States, Steve immediately replies that he and the boy can sleep in the attic; later on, when Jerry's wife and children are sitting down to dinner, Steve puts the final touches on Karel's outfit, which includes new shoes he bought for him, and tells him, "We'll go downstairs and knock them dead." At the same time, Steve's role as a mother surrogate is forcefully signaled throughout the film; it is remarkable that Steve and Mrs. Malik never share a frame together, not even at the end, when the reunion between mother and son takes place in front of Steve, who is, however, confined off screen. The two love objects in Karel's life cannot be seen at the same time, as they are not compatible, being articulations of the same motherly function. Likewise, the final return of the boy to Mrs. Malik is inevitable, not just because a child is expected to have only one mother, but because Steve is not simply a mother substitute but also a male companion and object of desire; the reestablishment of the mother-son couple is the obvious route back to "normality." Steve and Karel have met and loved each other within a context of "abnormality"; Karel, the least normal of all the displaced children, has been reached by the only adult who is also markedly atypical. Steve/Clift not only acts against accepted models of the US soldier, he also looks different: he is defined by a striking lack of "masculine" attributes, including a complete absence of heterosexual interests. Although Clift was physically fit and healthy when he shot *The Search*, his appearance is extremely slim and delicate, almost feather-light; his face is exquisitely beautiful, rather than manly attractive, and his incessant movements are always graceful. The overall impression is that of a gorgeous-looking creature, whose gum-chewing and general banter do not manage to fully virilize. This ambiguous image is reinforced by the lack of heterosexual narratives; there is not a hint of Steve's past or present interest in any woman, and Clift himself, in his first-ever screen appearance, is necessarily devoid of romantic or erotic baggage. The only relationships Steve is engaged in are with Karel, and with his housemate; although Jerry is married with a family, he is initially presented alone, sharing a self-contained environment with his army colleague. When one day the two men have a discussion in front of the boy, Jerry regrets it immediately, saying: "We want to bring him up right, don't we?" This domestic set-up has been read as intrinsically homoerotic,[24] and indeed, to some extent, Steve and Jerry

CHAPTER 2

do resemble a couple with a child. However, the possible queer subtext of Steve's life with Jerry is left undeveloped, as the film then reinforces Jerry's utterly "normal" nature as an emotionally detached US serviceman and a family man. Jerry notices the oddity of Steve's nonapproach to women with amusement, in a scene when Steve and Karel are showing off the boy's progress in learning English. Jerry places a series of drawings and photographs in front of Karel, who accurately names in English, as Steve taught him, the images they reproduce. When Jerry shows him a picture of a seminaked pin-up girl, the boy promptly responds: "Tomato"; Jerry's reaction is to suggest to Steve that he "sticks to building bridges." What Steve has in fact achieved, by displacing the word "tomato" onto the pin-up, is the elision of female sex appeal from language. Verbal language fulfills a pivotal role in the relationship between Steve and the boy: not only does Steve manage to get Karel to speak again, he also provides a new semantic system for him. In another significant scene, Karel asks Steve what is the meaning of the word "mother"; Steve is at a loss, incapable of explaining the concept in words, and finally points to a photo of two dogs, one smaller than the other. Again through a process of displacement and elision, Steve has linked "mother" to a generic animal picture, deleting the mental image of the female parent and presenting the boy with his own system of queer signification: the two dogs together could certainly symbolize Steve and Karel.

Man-boy love in *The Search* thus relates subversively, yet obliquely, to the film's overt discourse, which promotes Americanness as the "natural" and "normal" way to be. Clift's portrayal of Steve does not create an anti- or non-American character; it rather provides an unorthodox, yet believable, protagonist, suggesting that Americanness might be different; indeed, that it might be queer.

The Big Lift is set during the Berlin Blockade (June 24, 1948–May 12, 1949), when the Soviet authorities, in an effort to gain control over the Allied-divided city, blocked all road and rail access to its American, British, and French sectors. In response, the US and UK military organized an airlift of colossal dimensions, which successfully managed to keep Berlin provided with coal and food; the Soviet decision to end the blockade was seen as a political humiliation for the USSR and an unmitigated triumph for the Western Allies. Against this Cold War background, *The Big Lift* focuses on two US Air Force sergeants involved in the airlift, Danny MacCullough (Montgomery Clift) and Henry "Hank" Kowalski (Paul Douglas). While Hank is middle-aged and deeply embittered against the Germans after his experience as a prisoner of war, Danny is young and trusting, and eager to explore Berlin. The contrast between Hank and Danny forms a central strand of the narrative, as does their changing relationship to the German women they date. Determined to "instruct" his girlfriend, Gerda (Bruni Löbel), in the meaning of American democracy, Hank gradually sheds his own prejudices, developing a sympathetic approach to Gerda and her fellow Germans. Danny, on whom the film concentrates, starts seeing Frederica (Cornell Borchers), and rapidly comes to rely on her; on their first date, because of an accident to his US uniform, he is forced to wear German civilian clothes and must therefore hide from all military authorities, including his own. To be found not to be wearing his uniform would mean the loss of his sergeant stripes, plus incalculable complications with the Soviet powers and US military police. Suddenly vulnerable, Danny is practically and emotionally led by Gerda through the perils of blockaded Berlin; after this ordeal he falls in love with her and proposes marriage, ignoring Hank's advice to distrust the cool, somewhat shifty Frederica. As their wedding is about to take place, Danny finds out that Frederica has been deceiving him all along, planning to marry him only in order to reach her German husband, an ex-SS living in the United States. Stunned and hurt, Danny leaves Germany to go back home, just as news arrives announcing the end of the blockade, and the American Forces' victory over it.

An explicit propaganda effort, *The Big Lift* is stylistically defined by a strive for "realism": not only it is shot on location, but all the US military personnel on screen, with the exception of Clift and Douglas, are real-life US servicemen playing themselves. With most of its cast consisting of genuine American soldiers (a fact immediately communicated to the audience in the initial credits), the film visibly connects masculinity to the strength and power of the American Forces. Even more obviously than in *The Search*, militarized virility is presented as intrinsically American, as the blockade setting entails a visual and narrative emphasis on US nationality. Likewise, the only soldiers seen in any detail are from the United States; the other Western Allies are virtually absent from the screen, and so are the Soviets, leaving the Americans to stand for martial virility without comparisons. Yet Americanness is also opposed to the implied threat from the USSR as well as to the moral and urban ruin of postwar Germany; in this way it is heavily linked to notions of "normality," and indeed the airlift's practical goal is to restore normal living conditions. Most didactically, through Hank's and Gerda's discussions about democracy, Americanness is directly contrasted to the abnormality of Nazi and communist dictatorship. The film's end reasserts the dichotomy of Americanness versus alienness, revealing Frederica's duplicity and providing a normative closure, as Danny returns alone to the United States. This restoration of the American protagonist to the American "norm" mirrors the end of *The Search*, when Steve goes back home leaving Karel in his mother's care and is presumably separated from the boy forever. The final shot of Danny in *The Big Lift*, which shows him boarding an America-bound plane, is followed by Hank's comment on the defeated Soviet blockade, and by the proud observation that US planes can take off in all weather conditions. In this sense, *The Big Lift* is an impeccable propaganda feature, asserting and celebrating American virtues; similarly, at one level of meaning in the film, Danny/Clift is comfortably inserted in the system—masculine, military, and national—to which he nominally belongs. In a parallel subtext, however, the film's dominant structure is disrupted by Clift's de-virilized, de-sexualized, and partly de-Americanized presence. Specifically, the film's central representation of Americanness, made inseparable from orthodox masculinity, rests on the compulsive repetition of the same normative pattern; Clift interrupts and fractures the film's reenactment of Americanness, exposing it as constructed and unstable. Functioning as a glitch in the American national and gendered repetition, Danny/Clift becomes the locus of powerlessness and queer destabilization.

True to its dominant propagandistic mode, *The Big Lift* does not waste time in establishing its key issues: the film starts with footage of the Soviet authorities imposing their blockade on Berlin, and of the Western Allies united in defiance, while an American voice-over details the actions of "the Reds." An abrupt cut then widens the frame, revealing a cinema screen showing beautiful girls in swimsuits, enthusiastically cheered by an audience of US servicemen. As the projection is

Irruption in Hollywood

interrupted by the announcement of a personnel meeting, the camera focuses on Danny and Hank, both Air Force engineers. Danny's first line in the film is to express disappointment about the meeting, as it will force him to miss his date for the evening. Followed by the banter of the others, who offer to stand in for him with his date, Danny and Hank reach their assembly point, where they are told of their imminent departure; they rightly suspect their destination will be blockaded Berlin, where they will have to "feed the Krauts." From the film's beginning, therefore, and through the next sequences showing the men's flight to Germany and their work for the airlift, Danny is presented as being at one with the American army he serves. His behavior highlights a randy interest in women and a wisecracking sociality with his mates; his appearance is that of a gum-chewing, slightly cocky young man, just like the rest. It is true that Clift's physical beauty, and his established star status, necessarily make him stand out; but this effect is partly tempered by the way he is shot, mostly in long or medium-long shots, with only brief close-ups. In a scene where the arrival of the US Navy provokes the frantic teasing of the Air Force men, Danny/Clift is seen from some distance, but in a prominent position, standing on a vehicle and leading the others in a song. The protagonist is thus shown as a fitting member of the American military, although his difference from Hank, who is more senior and prejudiced, is regularly emphasized. The two men, however, share a keen interest in "schatzies," local German women, and Danny's initial adherence to heteronormativity is pointedly shown in his encounter with Frederica. The two meet because the US authorities have staged a radio and photo event to celebrate the airlift and the Berliners' gratitude; Danny is randomly chosen to receive the gifts of the city's population. Once Frederica has thanked him on behalf of the women of Berlin, she and Danny are urged to kiss for the photographers; after this, Danny, with what looks like well-practiced timing, asks her for her phone number. As he walks back to the plane, Frederica's number in his hand, Danny jumps for joy, throwing his bag in the air with an attitude suggesting victory; indeed, the word "score" would be an apt caption for his image. While all this has been going on, however, there have been hints that Danny's fit in the American male system, despite appearances, may not be total or perfect. When the press shouted "kiss" to the couple, Danny planted a shy, small kiss on Frederica's lips, which drew complaints from the reporters. Frederica then embraced him and kissed him passionately, this time amid the cheers of the crowd. It was but a moment of sexual timidity, or uncertainty, on Danny's part, yet consistent with the ambiguous persona Clift had by now established. His physical appearance also marks Danny/Clift as somehow different; while slightly older-looking and less ethereal than in *The Search*, he is still elfin in comparison to the other soldiers, and a positive waif next to the burly Hank/Douglas. As the film progresses, an increase of close-ups highlights the delicate beauty of his face, in marked contrast to the average, rugged looks of the other male characters. The combination of all these factors makes for disruptive potential, fully developed through Danny's relationship with Frederica, and the experiences he undergoes in Berlin; in order to appreciate his subversive impact, however, it is necessary to examine the film's aggressive reenactment of virilized, militarized Americanness.

The Big Lift combines plot development with an inordinate amount of Air Force footage; rather than limit military elements to a contextual background, the film constantly emphasizes US martial prowess through narrative asides, visual references, and motifs. American planes, endlessly repeating their journeys to and from Berlin, are almost always present, either in lengthy scenes outside and inside the aircrafts, or through the loud engine rumbling heard over the dialogue. With their male pilots and personnel controlling them, the planes are a straightforward symbol of gendered Americanness, incessantly engaged in self-performance. Airplane scenes are combined with images of radar and other flight and ground equipment, often in close-up or extreme close-up; the impressive power of US war technology, in the hands of the soldiers who control it, becomes a virtual extension of the film's average American male. While the plot charts events in Danny's and Hank's lives, the screen never lacks for long the presence of the US military machine, and of the collective of men who both serve and command it. The key scene of the radio and photo-story event, when Danny and Frederica first meet, is preceded by an extravagant display of US artillery on parade. Even toward the end of the film, when the audience may be reasonably preoccupied with Danny's love story, this is abruptly cast aside by a shift to US bravery and skills. In a narratively

Irruption in Hollywood

unrelated sequence, Danny finds himself on board a plane trying to reach Berlin, and soon falling prey to thick fog. One of the plane's engines then catches fire, making for a perilous descent back to the air base; the tense return operation is shown in close detail, focusing on the pilots' steady nerves, matched by Hank's calm presence at ground control. As the plane on fire touches down, and all the men get out safely, the film has shown once again a superb US maneuver; just as the airlift itself, the successful rescue of the plane is due to American masculine courage, good judgment, and superior ability. Significantly, Danny has taken no part in this achievement, being only an engineer on board and thus a passenger; extraneous to this particular triumph, he is in fact soon to be defeated in his own experience with Frederica. The film nevertheless strives to frame its narrative by its dominant view of Americanness, articulated through a process of constant reenaction and the reiteration of a collective display of traditional masculinity. This emphasis on military prowess is accompanied by a verbal evocation of America: the US soldiers, bored and lonely, regularly mention their own towns and states back home, while Hank's discussions with Gerda include quotations from the US Constitution. This pervasive construction of Americanness, relentlessly bombarding the audience, is disrupted once Danny leaves the US air base for Berlin and begins his involvement with Frederica.

As discussed in chapter 1, Judith Butler points out that gender is constantly being enacted, always in the process of producing itself, and is therefore both constructed and performative; the need for gender identities to incessantly self-repeat shows their provisional and threatened status. Because heterosexuality relies on established and compulsory gender patterns, it follows that gender is always heterosexually determined; hence, Butler argues, a deviant sexual orientation can denaturalize gender patterns, revealing their performative construction.[25] Butler's theory can be usefully applied to *The Big Lift*: gender and national identity merge in the film, whose primary structure of meaning relies on the obsessive repetition of a powerful, militarized, and traditionally male Americanness. Militarized masculinity, of course, carries implications of rampant heterosexuality; indeed, more than other versions of masculine identity, it is heterosexually overdetermined. As Danny enters Berlin to eagerly meet his schatzie, he is wearing his full

CHAPTER 2

US military uniform, for the first time in the film; however, his compliance with the performance of US virility is about to be interrupted and subverted.

Danny finds Frederica busy at work in a bombed-out site almost entirely reduced to rubble. Frederica's job involves collecting and carrying bricks and stones: a heavy, physically demanding task that Danny observes incredulously. Frederica, however, appears comfortable and confident in her occupation; her body, though not unfeminine, looks stronger than Danny's, and her assured demeanor matches her solid appearance. As they walk through the city together, Danny stops to offer some cigarettes to two men who are painting a column; one of them accidentally spills paint on Danny, making his US uniform instantly unusable. Frederica takes Danny home, gives him the clothes of one of her neighbors, and takes charge of the cleaning of the uniform; because of power shortages and scarce facilities, Danny won't be able to get it back until the next day. At this point Danny begins to lose, first of all, the visual marks of American masculinity: stripped of his uniform, he first wears a bathrobe in Frederica's home, then a full set of German civilian clothes, complete with cap. All these garments belong to Stieber (Otto Hasse), who is not only Frederica's neighbor but also a German spying for the Russians; he himself volunteers this information to the astonished Danny. The film moves forward, showing Danny and Frederica traveling by public transport, then meeting Hank and Gerda for dinner; in these scenes Danny wears Stieber's clothes, attempting to pass unnoticed by the ubiquitous US military, indeed by any authority, as his loss of uniform is made worse by his accidental lack of identification papers. Sitting powerlessly in a train carriage where Soviet policemen are carrying out a search, Danny is increasingly bewildered and dependent on his female companion. His position of social and political superiority, the innate privilege of US troops in Germany, has volatized; looking like a down-and-out local, he is wearing clothes belonging to a Russian spy and must avoid at all cost his own people, the US Forces. The film's constant display of Americanness, of which Danny is meant to be part, has been disrupted, even broken, and with it Danny's confident masculine status. He must now follow Frederica's guidance on where to go, when to speak, and who to avoid or trust; indeed, Danny's position has been reversed, as he has effectively swapped places with the German population. Vulnerable and quite helpless, Danny has also been placed in a traditionally female position. The power switch between him and Frederica is visibly signaled by the film's focus on their appearance. As Danny bemoans his own scruffy German outfit, she replies that she doesn't have to look like that, as she gets all her clothes sent from "friends" in the United States.

The events that follow complete Danny's de-Americanization. Having finally reached, with Frederica's help, the restaurant where Hank and Gerda are waiting, Danny soon notices American military police entering the place to check people's identity cards. Unable to leave the restaurant, he jumps on the stage, pretending to be part of the group of local performers singing "Chattanooga Choo Choo." After a few seconds, however, Danny realizes that the familiar American song is now being sung in German; as he clearly cannot follow the lyrics, he is left to fool around and hope not to be noticed. Shortly afterward, the film offers the most poignant moment in Danny's destabilizing progress as he and Frederica find themselves followed by US military police;

De-Americanized: Danny passes for a local riding the subway in Berlin's Soviet sector, with Frederica at his right.

CHAPTER 2

in order to avoid them, the two end up in the Soviet sector and are suddenly surrounded by questioning Soviet authorities. Anxious and lost, unable to talk without revealing his American identity, Danny is rescued by Frederica's nerves of steel: she tells the Soviet officers, now joined by American and British ones, that Danny is her German husband, shot in the throat during the war and thus not able to speak. This scene sees Danny literally silenced, with his Americanness wiped out; as Ralph Stern writes, "identity and voice are ceded altogether."[26] Initially presented as an all-American sergeant, Danny has now ruptured the film's smooth repetition of American masculinity. Simultaneously causing and signifying interruption, the feminized, de-militarized, de-Americanized Danny has exposed the illusory, performative nature of Americanness; in other words, he has assumed a queer position in relation to his masculine identity. At the same time, through the loss of his male American status, Danny has also forgone the realm of the film's "normality," moving to the anomalous position of looking like a local, yet without knowing what a local would know. Cast into the experience of "abnormality," while unequipped with any insider or outsider epistemology of the "abnormal," Danny is doubly alienated; the easy slip into identity—any identity—is denied to him.

Yet while Clift's role, appearance, and star persona, all concur in the creation of a disruptive subtext, it is Clift's performance as Frederica's lover that completes the subversion of American masculinity. In stark contrast to traditional patterns of male behavior, and to his own initial acquiescence to standard models of US soldiers, Danny's erotic relation to Frederica is ultimately ambiguous, casting a blow to associations of militarized masculinity with (hetero)sexual prowess. Danny's first pursuing of his schatzie follows predictable lines: he quickly obtains her phone number, then rushes to Berlin to see her. As the couple spend time together traveling through the city, and dining at the restaurant, Danny actively seeks physical contact: he places his arm around Frederica as they jump on a bus, later repeating the action while they are having a drink, with the excuse of making a toast. While they are drinking, he takes her by surprise and kisses her. Danny's display of sexual initiative, however, takes place in public, and is limited to mild flirting; as the evening progresses, his behavior becomes less playful and more emotionally charged, but also less sexualized. Danny and Frederica are shown dancing together to a romantic-sounding German song; later on, Frederica sings while playing the piano, attentively observed by the increasingly enraptured Danny. In this particular scene, Clift begins to markedly distance himself from the performance of the randy soldier: he lays his face on top of the piano, encircling himself with his arms almost in an act of self-protection, casting an intense yet shy gaze on Frederica. It is a posture expressing a mixture of longing and detachment that, to some extent, characterizes all of Clift's heterosexual performances. In the context of *The Big Lift* it is a dissonant image, heralding more significant deviations in Danny's behavior as a US soldier. In a later scene, Hank and Gerda wish goodnight to Danny and Frederica. Danny is to spend the night at his girlfriend's place, waiting to retrieve his cleaned uniform in the morning. As Hank is about to leave, he quietly imparts instructions to Danny on how to "get to first base." The next scene, however, shows Danny sleeping alone in a single bed, while Frederica is awake and doing some ironing, with a somber expression on her face. As he wakes up, Danny groggily starts talking about electricity rationing. There is absolutely no suggestion that "first base" may have been reached, or even attempted; the conversation, nevertheless, becomes increasingly more intimate, with Danny expressing emotion and compassion for the hardship Frederica endures. Now the camera gets closer to the couple, framing them together, and subdued lighting aids the feeling of blossoming romance; there are no erotic sparks, however. At no point does Danny/Clift indicate, with a gesture or a look, that his interest in the woman next to him is of a decidedly sexual nature. Frederica, whose tone of voice is cooler and steadier than Danny's, says: "Danny, I think you love me just a little," to which he replies, "more than just a little." They kiss, and the scene is cut. While it is certainly possible to read a prelude to sex in all this, the strength of Danny's erotic interest in Frederica remains unclear; conversely, there is no doubt of his passive role, and of his girlfriend's control of the situation. Indeed, Danny is already being manipulated by Frederica, who extracts, but does not reciprocate, a declaration of love from him. The scene is significant in the film's treatment of its central relationship: not only is it the only moment remotely linked to the possibility of sex, but it is also the last intimate exchange between Danny and Frederica, who are afterward shown either surrounded by other people, or separately.

CHAPTER 2

Their remaining scenes together contain no hint of erotic tension. The night at Frederica's thus assumes a representative status in *The Big Lift*, suggesting Danny's intensity of feelings, but leaving a question mark on his sexual intentions and activity.

In terms of the film's dominant performance of American masculinity, Clift's sexual behavior provides a fracture, a clear interruption in the structure of militarized virility. From the film's beginning, when US soldiers greeted the pin-ups on screen by cheering loudly, gesticulating, and literally jumping up from their seats, male Americanness has been translated into assertive, uncomplicated sexual enthusiasm for the opposite sex. Danny/Clift was included in this initial performance; however, by the time Hank reconfirms the pattern by advising him on seduction techniques, the younger American has deviated from the course traced out for him. His behavior when alone with Frederica suggests that his endorsement of male Americanness was, in fact, just a performance; in relation to the American "norm," the film's protagonist is effectively de-sexualized. Danny is revealed as a subject beyond normative repetition, and male Americanness is shown to be a construction, neither "natural" nor "normal." Importantly, however, Danny's de-Americanization does not imply the total negation or deletion of his national origin. Just like Steve in *The Search* had posited a different way to be American, so Danny in *The Big Lift* does not abandon the structure in which he is inserted. While fracturing and exposing the performance of gender and nationality, Danny still returns to the United States, as a member of its air force; as in *The Search*, a normative closure in *The Big Lift* reaffirms, on one hand, the "rightness" of America as its protagonist's ultimate destination. At the same time, Steve and Danny go home incorporating a profound difference in their being American; by remaining linked to their original system, they denaturalize it, challenge it, and subvert it. In both *The Search* and *The Big Lift*, Montgomery Clift has helped to effect the queering of Americanness.

THREE

The Peak of Stardom
Desire, Multiplicity, Deviancy

Social Disruption and the Closet:
A Place in the Sun and *I Confess*

The years 1951–53 see Montgomery Clift at the peak of his fame. Worshipped by fans, hailed as one of Hollywood's hottest properties, and Oscar nominated twice, Clift starred in three high-profile films; while these roles further consolidated his image, they did so by crystallizing his essential multiplicity. A reluctant murderer in *A Place in the Sun*, a priest oppressed by secrets in *I Confess*, a tough yet vulnerable army misfit in *From Here to Eternity*, Clift imbued each role with sexual ambiguity. Matched to the films' narratives of social deviancy and transgressive desire, Clift's presence evoked an astonishing range of queer identifications.

A Place in the Sun remains, together with *Red River*, the most critically discussed of all of Clift's films. Through a powerful plot combining a love triangle with crime and guilt, *A Place in the Sun* places Clift at its center simultaneously as perpetrator, victim, and object of desire; coupled with a very young Elizabeth Taylor, in a composite image of almost impossible glamour and beauty, Clift's persona in the film achieved an enduring iconic status. Writing retrospectively, scholars

CHAPTER 3

have seen Clift's character, George Eastman, as a typical expression of his star image; this assessment is based on notions of youthful rebellion and erotic power, and on the identification of a subtext of closeted homosexual desire. *A Place in the Sun* is based on Theodore Dreiser's novel *An American Tragedy* and focuses on the socially ambitious George and his dramatic involvement with two women: the homely, working-class Alice Tripp (Shelley Winters) and the beautiful, wealthy Angela Vickers (Elizabeth Taylor). The film begins with George hitching a ride, aiming for the town where his rich relatives, the Eastmans, own a successful swimsuit factory. Belonging to a poor and estranged branch of the family, the son of a devout woman working in a religious mission, George nonetheless exploits his connections to get a job in the factory; there he begins an affair with Alice, despite his uncle's express ban on relationships with the employees. At the same time, through his rare forays into the Eastmans' social circle, he meets Angela, and the two fall rapidly and passionately in love; yet George seems unable to abandon Alice, and keeps both relationships going in a complex web of deception. Soon a crisis ensues, as Alice tells George she is pregnant and presses for him to marry her. George agrees, yet desperately bides for time, managing to leave town to follow Angela to her vacation by the lakes. Trying to gain acceptance from the socially superior Vickerses, and reveling in Angela's adoration, George starts conceiving to murder Alice as his only possible way out; just at this point Alice unexpectedly arrives on his trail, phoning him from the train station near where he is staying. Pathetic and scared, she threatens to expose their relationship and her pregnancy to George's hosts and family, unless he marries her immediately. Panicked, George leaves the Vickerses with an excuse, and while still thinking about murder, he takes Alice to the registry office—but they find it shut. Now George grasps his last chance of getting rid of Alice. Knowing that she cannot swim, he takes her for a lonely night ride in a boat, on a deserted lake, intending to drown her. Once in the boat, however, George agonizes over his plan and finally realizes he is unable to go through with it. Yet the boat accidentally capsizes, and the film then cuts to George reaching the shore alone and running back to the Vickerses. The police soon trace him there and charge him with Alice's murder. The defense takes the view that George desired to kill Alice, but did not do so, and is therefore innocent, but the jury

The Peak of Stardom

finds him guilty. Stunned and confused, waiting for his execution in jail, George admits to the prison's chaplain that he could have saved Alice when she fell in the water, but did nothing instead. Angela then appears at his cell; in a heart-wrenching farewell, she promises to go on loving him forever. George, fazed and bewildered, is then escorted to the electric chair.

Superbly directed by George Stevens, with a tense plot and an imposing music score, *A Place in the Sun* nevertheless depends on Clift's performance for its haunting impact. Clift's acting is painfully intense, and his total immersion into character turns the film into George's emotional tour de force; Clift famously prepared for his last sequence by spending a night in the death row of San Quentin state prison. Likewise, in the climactic boat scene, George's moral torment is evident through his anxiously darting eyes, copious sweating, and physical restlessness. As well as earning him a second Academy Award nomination, Clift's portrayal of George generates sympathy for his predicament, placing the audience in an ambivalent position; George's uncertainty as a murderer gives the film its lasting power to shock. Yet while informed by moral confusion, the ambiguity defining George/Clift is equally found in the intricate sexual structure he weaves around himself. Combining social and sexual transgression, Clift constructs a deviant protagonist, resonating with notions of excess, illicit desire, and the closet.

Film scholars have identified George's relationship with Alice as having a clear homosexual subtext. Hidden and forbidden, tinted with guilt, and carried out in liminal spaces such as darkened rooms or cinema halls, the George-Alice affair is, according to Steven Cohan, much more meaningful "when one reads Alice *as if* she were a male lover."[1] Kylo-Patrick R. Hart sees Alice's metaphorical maleness as key to the film's narrative, and a source of "gay male spectatorial engagement."[2] However, to see a queer narrative only in the George-Alice liaison is to ignore the extent of Clift's sexual ambiguity in the film; Clift's queerness is not expressed through a single closeted relationship, but rather in the coexistence of multiple, contradictory desires. As George, Clift inhabits not one but several closets, emerging as a split subject in a fragmented narrative of craving and belonging.

As discussed in the previous chapter, in *The Heiress* Morris/Clift was constituted by secrecy, defined by the contradiction between known

CHAPTER 3

and unknown; Clift's character in the film essentially *was* the closet. In *A Place in the Sun*, instead, George/Clift is primarily identified by conflictive knowledges: Alice knows him in a certain way, Angela in a different way, through narratives that are mutually exclusive and mutually hidden. A cardinal issue in the film's structure is that neither relationship is uniquely closeted; they both are. Indeed, according to Eve Kosofsky Sedgwick, the idea that the closet should be single-meaning is a historical fallacy; she exposes an established cultural code "by which the-articulated-denial-of-articulability always had the possibility of meaning two things, of meaning either (heterosexual) 'nothing' or 'homosexual meaning'"; this code informs "a discourse in which there was *a* homosexual meaning, in which all homosexual meaning meant a single thing."[3] The closet is pervasively present in *A Place in the Sun*, yet it has different meanings, problematizing the codified invocation of a monolithic gay subtext. This is anticipated by the film's initial sequence, which establishes George as relating to two incompatible worlds: the poor, shabby environment he was brought up in, and the Eastmans' flashy upper-class milieu. In other words, he does not fully belong to either and is thus set up for a dualistic narrative. The film begins by showing George hitchhiking on a highway, carrying very little luggage, and wearing a leather jacket which, with its still-visible seams where an emblem was removed, looks second hand; he is obviously too poor to afford public transportation. While standing on the side of the road, George notices a poster advertising the Eastman swimsuit brand; he smiles at it, with pleasurable recognition. Seconds after, he looks in fascination at a girl speeding past him in a luxury convertible, though she does not see him; it is Angela. After finally getting a lift to town, George arrives at the Eastman headquarters, where the gatekeeper treats him contemptuously; however, the latter immediately changes his attitude when George shows him a handwritten card from his uncle, the Eastman boss. As he makes his way to his uncle's office, George looks patently out of place in the atmosphere of business and wealth surrounding him; his extremely awkward, self-conscious demeanor emphasizes his discomfort. Yet the secretaries, who know he is an Eastman, treat him with solicitude, immediately putting him on the phone with his uncle, who is still at home. Thus the film introduces George/Clift through signs of social ambivalence, which

The Peak of Stardom

are confirmed in the scenes that follow. Just before his arrival at the Eastmans' home for a first visit, George is discussed and strongly objected to by his family, on the grounds of his being a social embarrassment; later, when he has arrived and is trying to make conversation, Angela breezes in greeting everyone, yet once again she does not see him. Next, George is shown going to work with his cousin, who warns him of the company rule against "any of us" socializing with the girls working in the factory; such a ban, he insists, "is a must." Not knowing who he is at first, the factory girls greet his arrival with wolf whistles; subsequently, however, Alice will express reservations about being seen with him, remarking, "if you're an Eastman, you're not in the same boat as anyone." Too working class for the Eastmans, too Eastman for his working-class colleagues, George is brought to dissimulate each of his sides in turn. Later in the film, when George has been arrested, the district attorney, Marlowe (Raymond Burr), asks the Vickerses: "None of you knew this boy was leading a double life?" These words are not simply, as it has been argued,[4] a suggestive reference to the closet represented by Alice. While George's affair with Alice had been kept a secret from the Vickerses and Eastmans, so had his love for Angela been hidden from Alice. George's "double life" is literally, symmetrically so: its two sides knowingly coexist only through his privileged viewpoint, until he is "outed" from both his closets. However, while George as a subject is primarily defined by a dualistic structure, with Alice and Angela at its poles, this configuration is complicated and fragmented by his other secret identities. It is notable that George hides not only his two girls from each other, but also his mother and background from both. When he and Alice first walk together one evening, they come across a religious group singing hymns on the street. George's face is immediately cast in shame and fear of recognition. Without saying a word to Alice, he averts his gaze and moves quickly away from the scene. Similarly, when his uncle insists he phones his mother in Angela's presence, George complies only very reluctantly, attempting to shield his conversation from Angela, and Angela's existence from his mother. Later on, he will only speak about his upbringing when forced to do so by Angela's father, who interrogates him after complaining of knowing nothing about him. Lastly, George's own living space, his modest rented room in town, is never entered by Alice, Angela, or anyone else; his scenes there show him always alone, hinting at yet another hidden identity, that of the young bachelor. The ambiguity defining George/Clift is thus partly the effect of conflictive knowledges about him; at the same time, the separate discourses constituting him are produced and reflected through his split subjectivity. Motivated by mutually exclusive needs and loyalties, George/Clift is characterized by the polymorphic ambivalence he both exhibits and inhabits; consequently, he is equally defined by the excess of his desires, which makes him outreach the rules of established social patterns. This multiplicity is given its chief expression through George's connection to Alice and Angela, and through his ultimately undetermined, unresolved relation to heterosexual desire.

In its explicit narrative, *A Place in the Sun* works hard at containing George's disruption; the protagonist is presented essentially as a poor young man who, in pursuing the American Dream, has gone tragically astray. George's transgression is primarily identified with his relationship with Alice, which leads to the possibility of the ultimate social breach, murder, and to the death of both. Certainly, guilt and subversion are openly associated with the George-Alice strand of the plot, sustaining its interpretation as a closeted gay subtext; however, George's relationship with Angela is also underlined by unsettling elements, which make it equally suggestive of a queer meaning. In its dominant narrative, the coupling of George/Clift and Angela/Taylor is not only validated but also celebrated by the film: the two actors' exceptional beauty, the similarity of their perfect features and glossy dark hair, and their obvious chemistry on and off screen, offered director George Stevens and producers at Paramount a ready-made, double-star act. Indeed, the sensational effect of their joint appearance had been already exploited by Paramount, as early as in 1949: Clift had been literally ordered to attend the premiere of *The Heiress* with Elizabeth Taylor, whom he had never met, but who was already cast as Angela Vickers. Their presence together at the premiere had been extravagantly documented through live TV coverage, press articles, and photos; rumors of a love story and impending wedding followed, unhindered by Taylor's nine-month-long marriage to Conrad Hilton Jr. in 1951. By the time *A Place in the Sun* was released, in August 1951, Taylor was newly single and bound to Clift by an intimate friendship that would only end with his death. The Clift-Taylor connection was therefore part of Clift's star baggage since 1949 and guaranteed to generate publicity; it also facilitated the film's depiction of an exceptional love story. George and Angela are linked by eternal love (it will survive the grave) and framed by an abundance of extreme close-ups of their faces together. Conversely, the tainted quality of George's affair with Alice is visualized through Winters's sharp difference from Taylor: while Taylor is confident and luminously beautiful, Winters is insecure and depress-

A match made in heaven . . . with some initial help from Paramount. Montgomery Clift and Elizabeth Taylor at the premiere of The Heiress, *1949. The Kobal Collection.*

CHAPTER 3

ingly mousy. Even so, George's desire for Angela is effectively an act of social subversion, whose abnormality can be read in the "excessive" symbiosis between the couple, and in their apparent lack of sexual activity.

It is true, of course, that George blatantly infringes workplace conventions, and the Eastmans' rule, by starting to date Alice. Of his two girlfriends, Angela is presented as his most "natural" choice, despite the social gulf between them: this "naturalness," however, only makes sense in view of the tenuous thread of the family connection, or from the perspective of aggressive social climbing. It is actually much more obvious for George to frequent and marry Alice, who comes from the same working-class environment as he, and who shares a similar history: they have both left their homes to come to town in order to get jobs at the factory. Moreover, George has got Alice pregnant, and the logic of the time would see nothing more desirable than their marriage. The ordinariness, hence normality, of the relationship between George and Alice transpires from the context around them; if their sexual affair is framed by dark cinemas, bedrooms where they are forbidden to be together, and parked cars at night, it is also true that this situation is presented as common to countless young heterosexual people. When George and Alice first chat in the cinema, as the lights come on after the film, they are surrounded by couples passionately kissing; George poignantly glances at them. Later on, when they are in the car and the police arrive to move them on, they are parked not far from other cars containing other couples, all seeking a space for sexual intimacy. In stark contrast to George's relationship with Angela, the George-Alice affair is framed by a contextual sexual narrative that is deeply normative. It is 1951 and the sex lives of young, unmarried, heterosexual Americans are strictly controlled. At the same time, young males are expected to display a robust sexual appetite for the opposite sex, which is precisely what defines George in his initial attachment to Alice. George's sexual attraction for her, however, is narratively castigated by the film, even as it vitally affects plot causality through Alice's pregnancy. The prime motivation of *A Place in the Sun* is George's all-consuming, quasi-mystical love for Angela, and in this light his prior erotic interest in Alice appears completely out of place. George/Clift is expected to find fulfillment in his union with Angela/Taylor, who is his

The Peak of Stardom

soul mate and, in terms of beauty and charisma, also his equal; the tryst with the shabby Alice/Winters is a fatal lapse on his part. In fact, the supposed "naturalness" of George's love for Angela is based on spiritual affinity and a shared aesthetic of beauty rather than on sexual passion; the fact that George's sex drive is evident only with the uglicized Alice, whom he doesn't love, profoundly disrupts the film's intentional coupling of its two main stars. Yet there is no mistaking Clift's erotic charge in his early scenes with Winters, which count among the most openly sexual of his career. On their first outing together, he kisses her passionately, saying afterward, "I wanted to do this for so long"; his voice is low and excited. As he walks her home, he keeps stopping to kiss her, finally grabbing her outside the door and holding her in a tight embrace; when she moves away, he grasps her face in his hands to kiss her again. In the later scene in the car, he cannot keep his hands off her: he starts caressing her neck, then kisses her forcefully, moving his whole body on top of hers. When they finally find themselves outside her window, Clift exudes sexual desire: he presses himself against Winters, kissing her neck and mouth, then sighs with frustration until he manages to get into her room. As she follows him there, he takes her in his arms and holds her tight, dancing along to the music on the radio; the room is almost totally dark, and only their silhouettes are visible. Clift says softly: "this is nice," then takes her to the edge of the frame, and they become indistinguishable; their speech is muffled, yet her voice is clearly repeating "oh, George . . ." Successful seduction was never signaled more clearly.

Through his behavior with Alice, therefore, George/Clift injects deep ambiguity into his persona. While his relationship with Alice is normative, even banal in relation to the social frame of *A Place in the Sun*, it becomes highly transgressive in the film's structure of feeling, which rests on the love story between George and Angela; this is presented as extraordinarily emotional, almost a matter of life and death, yet effectively devoid of any sexual content. Most importantly, George/Clift acquires queer connotations through his liaison with Alice, but not simply because he structures the affair along patterns of secrecy and guilt. Alice does indeed represent *a* closet in George's life, but what the closet hides is not Alice in herself, but the fact that George has had sex with her. It is the closeting of sex, which Alice's pregnancy

CHAPTER 3

is in danger of revealing, that contributes to George's double life; coexisting with his romantic, nonsexual passion for Angela, it casts George/Clift in a light of multiplicity and contradiction, constructing him as an erotically ambiguous subject. George's sexual secret is more than just a burden, it is the product of two parallel systems he inhabits; his closets confine him, but what they hide is the unbound scope of his subjectivity, replete with conflicting desires and unmanageable excess.

The relationship between George and Angela is secrecy-ridden and defined by a powerful symbiotic attraction: it is the meeting of same with same, united in a dimension only they can understand. It is notable that whenever they are together, they remain always on the periphery of the social scene they find themselves in; this is openly shown in the sequences at the Vickerses' summer house, when George is constantly arranging for him and Angela to be alone, despite the presence of a vast crowd of guests. Even when having dinner with everyone else, they sit together at the very edge of the table; they appear to interact solely with each other. But the furtive nature of their relationship is visible from the start, in the scene at the Eastmans' ball, when they first talk of their mutual love. From the moment they arrive, they seek distance from the other guests, and as they start dancing together they are mostly shot in a succession of extreme close-ups; they may be in a room full of people, but they are patently detached from the context. The fast editing, juxtaposing their beautiful faces, has also the effect of almost merging George and Angela into a single entity. As they hold each other tightly, their heads are very close, highlighting their physical similarity: even their hairstyles are similar, with a big quiff swept back on the forehead. When George tells her that he loves her, Angela visibly panics, saying with great alarm: "Are they watching us?" Whoever "they" may be, they obviously must not witness their nascent love, and she quickly takes him outside, closing the door behind them. Only then she confesses that she is in love with him too. In view of their huge passion, and in relation to cinematic conventions of love scenes, it is remarkable that George and Angela wait quite some time before exchanging a single kiss; instead, outside the ballroom, they repeat how much they love each other and make detailed plans for spending time together in the summer. These plans include Angela cooking breakfast for George, but do not extend to erotic fantasies; no hint of sexual urgency is detectable. There is a sense that erotic action is secondary to their love, that their belonging together is beyond physicality; indeed, George tells her "I guess maybe I loved you even before I saw you." George and Angela manifestly cannot bear to be apart, linked by an unnamed yet powerful feeling of identification; to be sure, an enduring legacy of *A Place in the Sun* is its images of Clift and Taylor together, their faces so close they touch, twin icons of radiant beauty. On set, when rehearsing their scenes, Clift famously played Angela's role several times, feeling he could show Taylor how to approach her part.[5] While the great love uniting George and Angela implies desire, it is chiefly a desire for mirrorlike self-completion; their relationship is not openly sexualized by the film, which instead emphasizes sameness and complicity.

The merging of identification and desire, according to Eve Kosofsky Sedgwick, is the established cultural structure for "*homo*-style homosexuality" and one of the main assumptions underpinning modern epistemologies of the closet.[6] While stressing that this is a well-established way in which the closet is known, Sedgwick is keen to show the

Angela and George reveal their mutual love.

inaccuracy of one of its premises by arguing that "sameness" is not dependent on sharing the same biological sex. Indeed, the expansion of notions of sameness to nonhomosexual relationships is a concept at the heart of queer theory. Leo Bersani's theorization of "homo-ness," for instance, is based on what he deems an initially homosexual mode of relating to others, which he calls "*near*-sameness," which he also sees as shared by nongay people.[7] A queer reading is then clearly applicable to the relationship between George and Angela; this is not only closeted but also based on a "*homo*-style" sameness that merges desire with identification. Importantly, it is a relationship that disrupts traditional erotic patterns by positing eternal love without its sexual consummation.

George is thus defined by two primary closets, which constitute him as an ambiguous and subversive subject. Firstly, his closeted lives are incompatible, splitting him between carnal desire and mystical affinity; secondly, the sum of these contradictory cravings produces an excess of scope—that is, of meaning—that marks George as all-reaching and uncontainable, as someone daring to want too much. Crucially, while George's two conflicting relationships contain strong queer suggestions, they also unsettle normative sexual behavior in their explicit articulation. By presenting George as randy with Alice yet celibate with Angela, they position him obliquely in relation to heterosexual masculinity. In the emotional, existential, nonsexual drama that defines George's involvement with Angela, and which *A Place in the Sun* emphatically validates, the protagonist's conformity to orthodox virility is ultimately uncertain. It is entirely typical of Montgomery Clift to produce, through the same character, two opposing patterns of male desire; his sexual ambiguity is all the more striking in the film's triangular structure, where once again he is cast as erotic magnet. With no male competitors, and desperately wanted by both female protagonists, George/Clift is the film's clear object of desire, the focus of a sexualized gaze that not even Angela/Taylor can attract by herself. As he often was in his previous films, Clift is patently on erotic display in *A Place in the Sun*, something evident from the beginning: dressed in a plain, tight-fitting t-shirt, he turns heads and provokes whistles at work, while his presence at the Eastmans' party, in full evening dress and with cigarette in his mouth, finally stops Angela dead in her tracks. Characterized by an immense eagerness to please, as much as by the awareness of his own power of attraction, George/Clift translates his erotic sway into a "cruising sexual swagger" that is also "androgynous,"[8] signaling his unqualified availability. However, unlike in *Red River* for instance, this time Clift's erotic spectacle has no male targets in the film's diegesis; his sexual ambiguity is articulated through contradictory, heavily subtexted heterosexual narratives, whose suggestions of closeted desire open up, but never resolve, a range of queer possibilities. As in Sedgwick's discussion of the closet, a queer reading of Clift's persona in *A Place in the Sun* highlights "the possible plurality of meanings behind the unspeakables."[9]

George Eastman is punished by the film, sent to the electric chair for a murder he has desired but not committed, yet being actually guilty of letting Alice drown. The criminal act of assisting Alice's death defines George's transgression in ethical terms; in its tracks, however, it carries a bundle of contraventions the film cannot contain or condone. Guilty of concealments and deceptions, of social duplicity and disruptive sexuality, George is above all culpable of irreconcilable cravings, of ambitions of privileged knowledge and exclusive control. What is ultimately penalized is George's aspiration to know and have all, to subvert the implicit rules of life inside and outside the closet. A useful way of conceptualizing George's transgression is again to consider Sedgwick's work, specifically its notion of the epistemology of the closet as a two-way structure. Sedgwick argues that "an ability to articulate the world as a whole . . . may well be oriented around the tensely attributive specular axis between two closets: in the first place the closet viewed, *the spectacle of the closet*; and in the second its hidden framer and consumer, the closet inhabited, *the viewpoint of the closet*" (Sedgwick's emphasis).[10] In *A Place in the Sun*, George attempts to reunite in his experience both the spectacle and the viewpoint of the closet by being simultaneously inside and outside his secret lives. However, wholeness, or "the ability to articulate the world as a whole," eludes him, as by breaking the convention of the single-meaning closet he effectively courts his doom. It is true that, to a limited extent, Alice and Angela share George's positioning, aware as they obviously are of the secretive nature of their own relationships with him; George, however, is alone in experiencing simultaneously the viewpoints, as well as the spectacles, of all his closets.

CHAPTER 3

This peculiar combination of ubiquity and division is strongly emphasized by Clift's performance, whose power of ambivalence constructs George as someone both intensely present and mysteriously detached. As Judith M. Kass has observed, *A Place in the Sun* is an ideal vehicle for Clift's complex screen persona, "the quality he possessed of appearing removed from others around him—as though he is both a participant in the action and an outsider looking on. . . . He is both private and exploding out of himself."[11] Unlike his closeted partners, George has no existence beyond his multiple deceptions, which make up his life not as an unbroken entity but as a cumulative act of fragmentation. As Clift himself commented, George is "the kind of guy who has some charm, but basically he conceals and dissembles about everything."[12] By aiming for a privileged position, as the sole inhabitant and surveyor of a multifaceted network of secrecy, George defies the tacit rules of the closet: his excess is effectively the subversion of subversive orthodoxy. Against the compulsion to remain in one's socially allocated slot, even when this is the fraught structure of the homosexual closet, George/Clift strikes for multiplicity and contradiction; the transgression of *A Place in the Sun* rests on the queer disobedience of his protagonist.

Montgomery Clift plays a Catholic priest in Alfred Hitchcock's *I Confess*, a man caught in a complex narrative of secrecy and deception; to a noirish plot steeped in false appearances and unreliable knowledge, Clift brings a striking performance based on nonverbal meaning, engulfing his character in the overbearing presence of the closet. The film was bound to produce a power tussle, as Hitchcock's legendary dictatorial tendencies and maniacal reliance on a prearranged storyboard clashed with Clift's obsessive intervention in his roles. On occasion, Clift had no choice but to obey his director. In a key scene near the end of the film, for example, when he is coming out of a courthouse, Clift was told to look up toward the opposite side of the road, to facilitate a cut to the next scene. "I don't think I would look up," remonstrated Clift, to which Hitchcock's swift reply was, "Well, you'd better look up, or else";[13] in the final cut, Clift's gaze duly moves upward in this scene. At the same time, the final cut also shows how Clift's alterations of his lines, often radical truncations of the original dialogue as documented in his script notes, were mostly retained by Hitchcock.

The film sees Clift as Father Michael Logan, a parish priest in

The Peak of Stardom

Quebec City, whose rectory employs the German refugee Otto (Otto Hasse) and his wife Alma (Dolly Haas) as caretakers. In the secret of the church confessional, Otto tells Logan that he has murdered the lawyer Villette, when Villette caught Otto stealing in his home. Stunned and distressed, and obliged by religious rule not to reveal Otto's confession, Logan the next day makes his way to Villette's house, where he had previously arranged to meet his former girlfriend, Ruth (Anne Baxter), who was being blackmailed by Villette. His unexplained arrival on the scene, and his visible familiarity with Ruth, arouse the immediate suspicion of police inspector Larrue (Karl Malden), who is in charge of the case. Larrue's suspicions are soon confirmed by the account of two witnesses, who saw a priest leaving Villette's house late on the previous night. Indeed, as shown in the film's first scene, Otto had committed his crime wearing a priest's garb as disguise; he had later placed the cassock, stained with Villette's blood, in Logan's room in order to incriminate him. The clutches of the law rapidly close on Logan, as Larrue interrogates Ruth and discovers the reason for Villette's blackmailing. On Logan's return from World War II, before he became a priest, he had met up with Ruth again, unaware that she had married during his absence. Caught in a violent storm in the countryside, the two had been forced to spend the night in Villette's summerhouse and had been surprised there by him in the morning; their compromising situation had allowed the lawyer to blackmail Ruth, while also giving him the power to disgrace Logan. Larrue hears these details after having questioned Logan in vain, as the priest refuses to talk about his ex-girlfriend or the murder in a double effort to preserve Ruth's reputation and obey his religious vows. However, now Ruth herself tells Larrue the story of her shared past with Logan, in the presence of the latter and of her husband, Pierre (Roger Dann), through a series of flashbacks. Ruth and Logan had been in love, but he had then volunteered to fight in World War II, eventually breaking every contact between them; she had therefore married Pierre, hoping to start a new life. When Logan had returned from the war, however, she had realized she still loved him, but he had changed while being away, a change that would lead him to become a priest. Coming back to the present, Ruth confesses that the night of Villette's murder Logan was with her, as she had asked for his help in dealing with the blackmail; yet instead of providing him with an alibi, her words aggravate his position by furnishing him with a reason to kill the lawyer. Once the autopsy establishes that Villette was killed after Ruth and Logan had parted, the priest is arrested and put to trial. Throughout all this, Logan stubbornly refuses to tell what he knows about Otto, not even to save himself from hanging. The jury believes Logan to be guilty, yet reluctantly acquit him because of insufficient evidence; outside the court, however, an angry mob is ready to lynch him. As the priest tries to make his way outside, under police protection, Otto's wife breaks down from her feelings of guilt and is about to scream the truth. Otto silences her by shooting her dead. Understanding at last who is the real murderer, Larrue chases Otto, who is clearly dangerous and ready to do anything. Logan, trying to persuade Otto to give himself up and spare more bloodshed, advances toward him; Otto raises his gun and aims, but Larrue shoots him. Logan is safe, and Ruth goes back home with her husband.

I Confess is a text crisscrossed by threads of erroneous beliefs, deceptive identities, and transgressive desires; holding all of these together is Logan's refusal to talk, a poignant silence that, far from denoting nothingness, is highly productive of meaning. By emphatically not saying what he knows, or even what he feels, Logan points to the very mystery he is leaving unsaid: his silence is constitutive of something that, even when ostensibly uncovered or named, remains elusive until the end. At first the priest's muteness seems to concern two issues only: Otto's confession of Villette's murder, and Logan's past and present relationship with Ruth. However, Logan is also totally silent about his reasons to break up with Ruth and join the priesthood, and his reticence in this regard greatly informs the ambiguity that surrounds him. Aided by a sparse spoken part, which Clift himself reduced to a minimum, and by an abundance of close-ups tracing his facial expressions, Logan/Clift performs his silence as a willed act; in so doing he places himself in a closed yet open location, in the blatantly hidden position of the closet. According to Eve Kosofsky Sedgwick, the condition of being in the closet can be conceptualized as a silent speech: "'Closetedness' itself is a performance initiated as such by the speech act of a silence—not a particular silence, but a silence that accrues particularity by fits and starts, in relation to the discourse that surrounds it and differentially constitutes it."[14] Clift's performance as Logan is indeed one of perfor-

The Peak of Stardom

mative silence; his closet is not simply indicated, but effectively created by the poignant gaps in his speech, in relation to the various narrative discourses around it. Logan's communication, or rather lack of it, is defined by the omission of required explanations; to Larrue he not only conceals Otto's guilt but also refuses to give any details about his own whereabouts on the night of the murder, so as not to mention Ruth. With Ruth herself, his dialogue is characterized by a lack of explanation for his choice of the priesthood, and by an absence of clear replies to her belief in the persistence of their mutual love. In both situations, Logan speaks through a form of preterition, which Sedgwick identifies as a prime form through which the closet is articulated and known.[15] Defined by the Encarta Dictionary as "the act of passing over something or leaving something out," the repeated act of preterition locates Logan in the closet on several major accounts: as a man wrongly accused of murder; as Ruth's ambivalent ex-lover; as the suspect of a sexual liaison with Ruth that leaves them both open to blackmail; and as an enigmatic, wholly unexplained priest. If Logan's persecution, on one hand, readily suggests Hitchcock's theme of the transference of guilt to an innocent protagonist (evident throughout his oeuvre from *Sabotage* to *Strangers on a Train*, from *Shadow of a Doubt* to *Vertigo*), in *I Confess* the emphasis is on secrecy and disobedience rather than contagious evil. Trapped in the multiple facets of his closet, Logan/Clift is entangled in a net of sexual ambiguity and social transgression, investing his role with powerful queer connotations.

The figure of a Catholic priest may readily suggest conformism and an adherence to the status quo; in *I Confess*, however, Father Logan stands out as a misfit, deviating from both religious and secular societies. If Logan's predicament is chiefly motivated by his obedience to Catholic doctrine, it still has the immediate result of placing him in net transgression of a basic community rule: the idea that an innocent man collaborates with public justice in tracing a criminal. Through his refusal to talk, Logan makes his own innocence hidden from all, ironically closeting the one secret that would reintegrate him in a law-abiding, Christian society. Logan's unshakeable noncooperation is plainly evident from the start, when Larrue first questions him, and it is reinforced by changes Clift made to the script: his original reply to the inspector was meant to be "I can only help you as far as I'm capable,"

CHAPTER 3

but Clift replaced it with a curt "I'm not able to help."[16] Logan's closet, of course, is forced upon him by external dogma: not only by the inviolability of confession, but also by the ban on priests' association with women, and on married women's with other men. The observance of these rules, however, turns Logan into a murder suspect, while the occultation of his relationship with Ruth, once discovered, only adds further ambiguity to his position. On both accounts, Logan loses his status as a worthy member of Catholic society and is hunted by the police and implicitly cast out by his fellow priests. Not even the jury's acquittal will restore his credentials. The oblique, ambivalent relation of Logan to his religion is clearly marked by the film; as the priest walks the streets in anguish, before resolving to face the police who want to arrest him, the camera shoots him from above, showing him overwhelmed by menacing dark crosses on the churches' roofs. At the same time, ominous loud music underlines Logan's oppression. Likewise, during the trial, which sees him on his own against a uniformly hostile court, a large crucifix is constantly visible in a prominent position on the wall. Even more forcefully, the key moment of Otto's revelation is entirely shot from inside the church confessional, a physical closet, framing Clift in a highly claustrophobic view. While Otto is barely discernible outside the narrow grate he speaks through, the camera captures Clift in an extreme close-up, showing only part of his face, most notably his eyes, and his left hand raised near his temple. Clift's hand contracts and de-contracts in nervous tension, while his eyes dart around anxiously, with no object to rest on; he is confined, trapped by Otto's words and their consequences. Logan's closet is visibly taking shape around him, and from now on the priest will be in an increasingly isolated position, ambiguously relating to his environment.

However, while Logan's behavior in regard to Otto's crime deviates from normative social patterns and places him at odds with the very same religion that dictates it, the protagonist's chief transgressions are clearly marked as sexual. The closet through which Logan is positioned to society at large, that of an innocent man and potential blackmail victim, is but the counterpart of his far more mysterious, closeted sexual identity. Logan's main ambiguity is linked to his relationship with Ruth and to his decision to become a priest. Suggestions of illicitness are attached to Logan's closeness to Ruth from the film's beginning, as the two are first shown together through the point of view of Inspector Larrue: the camera rests on Larrue's suddenly alert, extremely suspicious gaze, then cuts to Logan outside Villette's house. Through Larrue's eyes, the priest is shown touching Ruth on the arm and leading her away from the scene. At this stage in the narrative, Larrue lacks the slightest motive to link either Logan or Ruth to the murder, so his obvious alarm casts an aura of doubt on the couple that necessarily hints at something else. As the film progresses and Ruth tells the story of their relationship, Logan's feelings and motives are not only unexplained but also increasingly opaque; the silence he opposes to her revelations constructs his more impenetrable closet, aided by Clift's ambiguous performance and by the film's careful use of flashbacks and editing. The enigma Logan presents to Ruth is also one for the audience, who largely see him through Ruth's subjectivity, and whose own attraction for Clift is channeled through the woman who so obviously desires him.

The notion that Logan's priesthood is a deviation from the "norm" is implicit in *I Confess*, which organizes a main narrative strand around a clear polar structure: the choice of being a Catholic priest is directly poised against the choice of heterosexual love, as Logan is presented as having chosen the priesthood *instead* of Ruth. Logan's religious vocation, therefore, automatically acquires a queer meaning; its defiance of heteronormativity is confirmed through Ruth's resentment of it, implicitly highlighting the homosocial, homoerotic associations investing an all-male community. It is remarkable that Logan's only instance of possible self-explanation, the long talk he has with Ruth on his return from the war, is not given to the audience to hear; it is shown through a flashback with Ruth's voice-over, and its meaning is further clouded by Ruth's dismissal of it, as she clearly does not grasp Logan's point (whatever this may be) or even take it seriously. The ex-boyfriend's dramatic shift, from romance and passion to remoteness and chastity, remains enigmatically described as "a change." Nor does the dialogue between Ruth and Logan, at any point, provide clarification; in a key scene when they meet on a ferry at Ruth's request, after she expresses her reluctance to accept Logan as a priest, he tells her: "I chose to be what I am—I believe in what I am." What he actually "is," and how and why he is "it," however, is not explained; not once in the film does Lo-

CHAPTER 3

gan refer to God, or to Catholicism, or to any religious feeling or vocation. The only person to know what the priesthood means to Logan is Logan himself, and this never spoken, yet pointedly hidden knowledge constitutes his priesthood as a closet. Sedgwick argues that the knowledge/ignorance opposition has special reverberations for epistemologies of the closet. She points to the cultural process "by which 'knowledge' and 'sex' become conceptually inseparable from one another—so that knowledge means in the first place sexual knowledge; ignorance, sexual ignorance."[17] In *I Confess*, Logan's choice to become a priest acquires a sexual rather than spiritual meaning, which is reinforced by Ruth's consideration of it in wholly secular terms. Guiding the audience as the only character with a prior knowledge of Logan, she cannot understand his "change," even less believe in its overt consequences—namely, his apparent chastity and the end of his love for her. While Logan's unheard talk to Ruth after the war has the narrative place of a "coming out" scene, it ultimately discloses nothing; this simultaneous openness and closure, however, is in itself redolent of the closet. As Judith Butler argues, "being 'out' always depends to some extent on being 'in'; it gains its meaning only within that polarity.... *Outness* can only produce a new opacity; and *the closet* produces the promise of a disclosure that can, by definition, never come."[18] Indeed, Logan's coming out to Ruth produces only a new enigma, which is equally true for the audience. If, on one hand, the Catholic priesthood heavily hints at a choice of homosociality or homosexuality above the heterosexual norm, it is also true that the film does not furnish Logan with any male erotic interest, nor does it make him the object of another man's desire. The mystery surrounding Logan's loyalty to the priesthood is symbolically articulated through the narrative role of the cassock. While Clift wears the Catholic priest's uniform through most of the film, so that his portrayal of Logan becomes primarily associated with it, Otto also uses the cassock as a disguise and a false piece of evidence. Worn by the murderer, then cast off and exploited as crucial proof against the innocent Logan, this religious garment clearly guarantees nothing in itself; nevertheless, it is specifically Logan's own cassock, as he testifies in court. Logan's condition of being a priest, therefore, cannot be fully explained through any external sign, yet it ultimately defines the pro-

The Peak of Stardom

tagonist above all other descriptions; what it defines is a silent knowledge, a substantial yet closeted state of being.

Logan's essential ambiguity greatly rests on Clift's performance in his scenes with Anne Baxter, and on the film's alternation of flashbacks with Logan's present as a priest. The couple's prewar love story is never given any dialogue, so its meaning rests partly on Ruth's desire-charged narration, and even more on the visual rendition of their relationship. These scenes show Logan as a passionate lover, mostly framed in the act of kissing Ruth. Their last moments together, before he leaves for the war, are especially poignant: the two are dancing slowly, and Clift holds Baxter's body tightly, touching her face with his and keeping his eyes closed. The camera lingers briefly on his entranced expression, then it shows him raising his head, suddenly recalled by the leaving soldiers. He looks at Baxter with deep anguish and grabs her forcefully, kissing her in a frantic manner suggesting despair; he then leaves abruptly, only to immediately return for one more kiss, and a parting look full of pain. It is a brief scene, but Clift makes it resonate with love and pathos. By contrast, the next flashbacks show Logan/Clift as deeply ambivalent toward Ruth on his return from the war, shifting from tenderness to detachment; this ambivalence carries through to the present, when the priest's verbal reticence with Ruth is matched by manners varying from availability to aloofness. Between the film's two diegetic spaces, therefore, the passionate prewar time and the fragmented, forbidding present, there lie these more recent flashbacks, of which the most significant is the scene of the night at Villette's house. The clandestine hours during the storm are mystery-ridden yet display more than a clear hint of a sexual connection, while crucially linking past and present through narrative causality. In so doing, the night at Villette's effectively ties Logan the lover to Logan the priest. The scene sees the couple running to find shelter under the pouring rain; they enter the deserted summerhouse, and here Logan's behavior, which had been quite distant, changes abruptly. He looks at Ruth intensely, as if he had suddenly realized something; he sits near her and begins to touch her wet hair first, then her face. It is an intimate, very sensual gesture, which creates a palpable physical tension between them; whatever follows, however, is not to be seen, as the film cuts to an external shot of the summerhouse, isolated under the downpour, and then to Ruth's face in the present, completing her story. Slowly, almost deliberately, with a vacant look in her eyes, she says, "there was no way I could get in touch with my husband," adding after a pause, "it stopped raining in the morning." The whole sequence is exuding sexual meaning, and Ruth's elliptical narration, entirely bypassing the hours of the night, points to a secret happening. Indeed, as Amy Lawrence convincingly argues, Ruth's words are instrumental in suggesting sex, in a script where any direct reference to it had been removed to please the censors: "Hitchcock . . . finds a way to restore enough ambiguity so that audiences could imagine the possibility of sex while the filmmakers could deny it."[19] Ruth's speech is followed by a reaction shot of Logan, listening to it in the police station: he first looks downward, obviously ill at ease, then raises an alert gaze toward Ruth. He appears agitated and aware at the same time, but the exact significance of his expression remains unclear. Indeed, the whole of Ruth's narration has been interspersed with close-ups of Logan in the present, his face always expressing profound discomfort; he has not uttered a single word, never interrupting her story of shared romance and unremitting desire. The result of these converging narrative planes is that the priest is strongly eroticized as the two Logans merge into one, just as they are merged in Ruth's mind; combined with Clift's nuanced yet inscrutable performance in the whole film, this erotic aura informs the sexual ambiguity of the protagonist. At the same time, of course, in social terms Logan's eroticization is both subversive and disgraceful; it thus fulfills exactly the condition of being in the closet. In this regard, it is interesting to consider Clift's notes about his trial scene, when his relationship with Ruth is revealed to the jury and the audience. Ruth's testimony consists mainly in an account of their love story and is constantly interrupted by the accusations of Prosecutor Robertson (Brian Aherne), who openly claims she and Logan carried on a sexual affair after he returned from the war. On his script, next to this sequence, Clift writes: "result of testimony" and "feeling shame."[20] Feelings of shame seem unlikely to refer to Logan's keeping of the sanctity of the confession, but would be appropriate to the "outing" of his sexual secrets. The priest's closeted sexual identity is, to a large extent, resting on the ongoing presence of Ruth in his life.

A key exchange between Logan and Ruth takes place on the ferry,

The Peak of Stardom

after he has become a suspect for the police; they meet in public, although they are aware of being under surveillance. Despite this unfavorable situation, their conversation is intimate, focusing on his current predicament and, especially, on their relationship. Logan urges Ruth not to compromise herself, not to tell the police of their meeting the night of the murder; she replies that she doesn't care about her reputation or her husband, adding: "I love you, Michael. I have always been in love with you." At this point, according to the script, Logan should have said "no!," but Clift eliminated this line;[21] instead, he merely looks at her, silent and troubled. Later on, after repeating that her feelings have not changed, Ruth asks him: "are you afraid of me? Why? Why?" Logan/Clift does not reply; he looks at her with a serious gaze, yet the briefest hint of a smile plays at the corner of his eyes and mouth. It is a disconcerting, unreadable expression. She goes on: "you're in love with me, you've always been in love with me, you haven't changed"; he now hurriedly says, "Ruth, I have changed, you have changed too." While being a rare intervention on Logan's part, this phrase does not directly address her allegation, the notion that he is in love with her; in fact, he has allowed the words to be said, just as he allowed her to express her love for him. Although Logan clearly seeks some distance from Ruth's obsessive longing, by alluding to the "change" that has come upon them, his words and manner are not forceful enough to dispel ambiguity. Once again, the rapidly changing expressions on Clift's face point to an inner agitation, yet they remain indecipherable. This scene establishes Logan as the object of Ruth's erotic desire, yet it does not clarify to what extent he is complicit in that desire, which is transgressive of the rules regulating the conduct of both married women and priests. Crucially, it is also a desire that is counter to Logan's hypothetical embrace of homosexuality. The overall attitude emanating from the priest is one of stubborn passivity, which allows at least for a silent participation, for his acceptance of being the target of Ruth's sexual passion. At the same time, Logan's blank-filled style of communication maintains his sexual identity as a secret, pointing to a clear deviation from Ruth's uncomplicated heterosexuality; indeed, the closeted relation of Logan to his ex-lover is highlighted by Ruth's incessant pursuit of him, a virtual hunt that oppresses and ultimately threatens him, unwittingly exposing him to a murder charge. Logan's queerness rests on

CHAPTER 3

his multifaceted life in the closet as much as on his oblique connection to sexual categories. Be it the chastity of the priesthood, the desire of heterosexual lovers, or the homoeroticism of male-only environments (which, before Logan's ordainment, notably included the army), they are all ambiguously relevant to the protagonist. Each of these potential sexual niches is permeated by Logan's eroticized status in the film.

To cast Montgomery Clift as a Catholic priest, of course, could not but multiply the ambiguous erotic charge that unsettles Logan's character. Clift's star image in 1952–53 was inseparable from notions of huge sex appeal, yet in *I Confess* he is not only dressed in a severe black cassock, but also ostensibly separated from any erotic possibility. As Father Logan, he would be expected not to even *think* about sex. This initial conflict between star and role is vastly complicated by the relationship between Logan and Ruth, as much as by the film's camera work. Although Clift is at times seen through a long shot, the lens mostly avoids a full view of the cassock, focusing instead on his face in a multitude of close-ups. Indeed, the film makes the most of Clift's looks from the very beginning, in the scene that precedes Otto's con-

Eroticized: Father Logan is singled out as the object of desire in I Confess.

100

fession. Clift is first seen very briefly through a window of the rectory, wearing his priest's garb, as he notices Otto entering the church opposite; he is then shot full-length as he himself goes into the church. After asking "Who's there?," Clift advances toward the camera, then stops, anxiously looking upward; his face is now clearly shown in close-up, at the center of the frame, with his eyes wide open and his lips slightly parted. It is a shot that pointedly shows Clift as extraordinarily attractive. Taking a candle to find his way in the darkness of the chapel, Clift again moves nearer the camera, getting closer to Otto at the same time; Otto is sitting down, almost hiding, and Clift leans forward to talk to him, towering above him and holding the candle next to himself. In the heavy obscurity of the church, key lighting now powerfully illuminates Clift, while the candle shines directly yet softly on his face. For a moment his beauty is made to look surreal, bathed in light, his features appearing singularly polished and unlined. This series of shots firmly establishes Logan/Clift as the film's locus of beauty, as its object of desire.

This is not to say that Anne Baxter is presented as anything less than a very attractive, glamorous leading lady; indeed, the film emphasizes her elegance and sexiness, as in the dinner party scene when her guest the prosecutor reveals Logan's imminent arrest. At this pivotal moment Baxter wears a striking, off-the-shoulder black gown, which perfectly showcases her figure and luminous blonde hair. As Ruth, however, Baxter is placed unequivocally in the role of the chaser; although her husband desires her, her narrative coupling is not with him but with Logan, and it is always she who actively pursues him. Likewise, Baxter is given a suitable amount of close-ups, yet these are usually part of a sequence where she is either reminiscing about Logan or telling him that she loves him; her function is to confirm the priest as the film's prime sexual attraction. Lastly, Baxter's persona certainly did not rest on erotic appeal as dramatically as Clift's did at the time, nor did she carry a comparable baggage of sheer stardom. In Clift's case, instead, a potent, established aura of erotic desirability combines with Logan's role as object of desire. As in every other film he had made until then, in *I Confess* Clift is not only beautiful, he is also the only man on screen to be even remotely so. Alone among his fellow priests, Ruth's husband and friends, and Karl Malden, Logan/Clift stands out as an erotic

CHAPTER 3

exception; his looks signal his sexualized function, and thus also his deviancy from normative ideas of Catholic priests. Clift's star image, of course, was not simply erotically charged, but carried a strong quality of sexual ambiguity; his popular perception as "an enigma" matches and reinforces the mystery surrounding Logan. As this mystery is never explained, the priest remains in his closet, and it is given to Ruth to provide the final, the only utterable conclusion about Logan: "He could never love me enough." There is no indication of what "enough" or "not enough" may consist of, and why. Elusive of every category, yet ambiguously present through his powerful silence, Logan/Clift does not reveal himself; his closeted life hides the secrecy of multiple possibilities, the queer potential that forever disrupts the norm.

The Queerness of the American Soldier: *From Here to Eternity*

Montgomery Clift had long been planning a collaboration with Italian director Vittorio De Sica, yet the result was a bitter disappointment for both of them. *Stazione Termini*, also released as *Indiscretion of an American Wife*, is an overmanipulated feature, heavily marked by the two men who fought over its control: De Sica himself and producer David O. Selznick, both of whom released their own, slightly different version of the film. Entirely set in Rome's main railway station, and charting the end of the brief affair between Giovanni Doria (Montgomery Clift) and American housewife Mary Forbes (Jennifer Jones), *Stazione Termini* is heavily encumbered by the respective priorities of Selznick and De Sica. An extravagant amount of close-ups of Jennifer Jones (imposed by husband Selznick) is matched by an equally disproportionate number of extranarrative characters, ranging from noisy priests on an outing to a woman about to give birth (De Sica's insistence on contextual "realism"). With the dialogue meant to be written by Truman Capote, who, however, abandoned the job after just a couple of pages, the film is an ill-assembled story of extramarital lust, followed by the heroine's guilt and decision to return to the United States. As Giovanni, Montgomery Clift is cast in a role that is by far the most conventional and heteronormative of his career. He is jealous, dictatorial, and passionate by turns, running through the predictable gamut of Italian stereotypes (just like the film as a whole appears to run through stereotypes of neorealism,

The Peak of Stardom

from squalid exteriors to assorted down-and-out characters). In one key scene that is De Sica's most superfluous addition to his rendition of male Italianness, Clift even slaps Jones in the face, out of resentment for her departure. To his everlasting credit, however, Clift plays Giovanni to near perfection, crafting a wholly convincing portrayal of patriarchal frustration and lover's anguish; while his performance is never less than brilliant, it does not rescue the film's visual and narrative chaos, and could not impede its critical and box-office failure. Most importantly, *Stazione Termini* stands out among Clift's work for its total lack of queer or subversive content. Not every scholar has shared this view. Amy Lawrence has focused on the scene when Giovanni and Mary are surprised by railway staff, while kissing in an empty train carriage, and are consequently taken to a police station under threat of arrest. Lawrence claims the idea of a heterosexual couple being arrested for kissing is preposterous, and that the subtext of this incident must be a closeted queer one.[22] While this is a suggestive interpretation, it does not account for the realities of Italian society in the 1950s, realities that would continue to be firmly in place well into the 1970s. The list of Italians charged with "indecent behavior in public" on slight displays of physical intimacy is a long one. In fact, the police episode is the most straightforwardly realistic of the whole film, depicting an almost routine rite of passage for Italian heterosexual couples. Accordingly, this book will not deal further with *Stazione Termini*, while noting how the film interrupts the queer continuity of Clift's career. Another 1953 film, the third screen appearance for Clift that year, is instead crucial in terms of his star trajectory; it is the immensely successful *From Here to Eternity*, which crowns the peak stage of Clift's stardom.

Montgomery Clift was never a soldier in real life, being rejected by the draft in World War II because of a rare chronic illness, amebic dysentery; it is remarkable, however, that his screen persona is significantly linked to military roles, as he is cast as part of the American army in almost a third of the films he made. Of all these armed forces characters, none has proved as memorable, as vividly associated with Clift's image, as that of Private Robert E. Lee Prewitt, the protagonist of *From Here to Eternity*; the role gained him a third Oscar nomination. In this film Clift manipulates notions of military virility to an extent unparalleled in his career. In *The Search* and *The Big Lift* Clift had played a US

CHAPTER 3

army engineer, but while the military connection was crucial to both films, Clift's narrative engagement was primarily with relationships outside the army. Similarly, although *Raintree County* will see Clift enlisted with the Northerners in the American Civil War, and *The Young Lions* as a Jew serving in the US army in World War II, these roles will be only marginally identified with the condition of being a soldier. In *From Here to Eternity*, instead, the inner and outer lives of Clift's Prewitt are entirely conflated with his position in the American military; consequently, Clift's portrayal of Prewitt bears massively on issues of institutionalized masculinity. The result is a highly disruptive portrayal of the American soldier, which resonates all the more for its strict connection to Prewitt's idiosyncratic, passionate vision of the US army. In a sense, Clift's role in *Eternity* exemplifies to an extreme degree the traits that had come to define his star persona: Prewitt is an ambivalent misfit, whose deviancy is expressed through the toughest, most stubbornly defiant personality Clift ever brought to the screen. At the same time, Prewitt is also intensely vulnerable and morbidly sensitive; inserted in a powerfully homoerotic narrative, his identity as a soldier is a combination of subversion and military loyalty, of fierceness and tenderness. Clift's physical appearance in the film is, in subtle ways, different from what it had been. It does not break continuity in his star image, but the film's use of it informs Prewitt's impression of brittle strength, conveying an almost aggressive, yet sexually ambiguous, masculinity. Clift's physique was naturally very slight, and he was uninterested in bodybuilding; to play Prewitt, however, he had trained intensively for months to develop his muscles. On screen he therefore appears in top physical shape, stronger than he ever did before or after, matching the script's description of Prewitt as "deceptively slim."[23] This muscular effect is accentuated by having had his hairy chest and back shaved and deliberately displayed in scenes where he is stripped to the waist. As the film is mostly shot in and around army barracks, Clift's body is shown off not just to the audience but also to his fellow soldiers; forced to dig trenches by vicious officers who hate him, the shirtless Prewitt/Clift takes his punishment in open view of his squad, as if he were an item on display. The masculine context of these scenes, the only instance of partial nudity in Clift's career, is emphasized by Clift's looks and heavy physical labor. With his dog tags conspicuously hanging on his well-toned pectorals, his arms visibly pumped up, and drenched in sweat for the effort of digging, Clift is as virile as he could ever be, for the benefit of his all-male audience. Conversely, in his scenes outside the barracks with his girlfriend, Alma (Donna Reed), he is always covered up, wearing a loose Hawaiian shirt that doesn't highlight his shape. Dressed as a civilian in the company of women, Clift is not made to openly connote eroticism.

If the star's body aids the construction of an ambiguous sexual meaning around Prewitt's character, his face informs the creation of a struggling protagonist, straining under the load of conflictive and socially unsanctioned desires. Thirty-two years old while shooting *Eternity*, Montgomery Clift is still extremely beautiful, yet in close-up his face shows traces of his worsening physical and mental state. By then a full-blown alcoholic suffering from blackouts, and severely addicted to a range of prescription drugs, Clift has a slightly rough, worn-out look, with an unusually heavy gaze; his face readily suggests an internal fight, which becomes Prewitt's struggle against both fragmentation and conformity. Of course, Clift had often conveyed supreme tension in his past performances, most notably in *A Place in the Sun* and *I Confess*. In these films, however, the violence of George's and Logan's pain had been visually softened by Clift's appearance, which was defined by the pure, serene quality of his beauty. By contrast, Prewitt's suffering is visibly raw and unmitigated, adding poignancy and strength to the protagonist's struggle. *From Here to Eternity* stages Prewitt's fight for his own vision of self: inextricably caught in his self-definition as a soldier, Prewitt/Clift battles to affirm an essentially queer identity.

From Here to Eternity is based on James Jones's best-selling novel, set in the US army base of Schofield Barracks in Oahu, Hawaii; the time is 1941, shortly before the Japanese bombing of Pearl Harbor. The plot focuses on Prewitt and two other soldiers, Private Angelo Maggio (Frank Sinatra) and Sergeant Milton Warden (Burt Lancaster), and begins with Prewitt's arrival at the barracks. A talented bugle player, Prewitt had requested a transfer from his previous post after another soldier had been undeservedly made top bugler in his place; the transfer had cost him his rank of corporal. Prewitt is also a champion boxer and is immediately pressured to compete in the next boxing championship to bring prestige to his new company and gain a promotion for Captain

CHAPTER 3

Dana Holmes (Philip Hober). Prewitt refuses to comply, having given up boxing after accidentally blinding a friend during a fight; his uncooperation makes him the target of vicious bullying, as several officers and soldiers gang up to give him "the treatment," a brutal regime of physical and mental humiliations. Warden, however, takes a strong liking to Prewitt and tries to help him; Maggio, hotheaded and devoted, stands by Prewitt and gets himself in trouble. Prewitt's steadfast refusal to box never falters, as he stoically meets each wave of abuse; his only relief comes through bursts of bugle playing and trips to town with Maggio, where he meets Alma, a beautiful and sympathetic nightclub hostess. Attracted to and comforted by Alma, Prewitt proposes marriage, but she refuses him saying that a soldier is not good enough for her. Meantime, Warden has started an affair with Holmes's unhappy wife, Karen (Deborah Kerr), who asks him to train as an officer in order to be transferred somewhere new, where they can be together. Warden, however, who loathes the idea of being an officer like Holmes, cannot bring himself to do it. Throughout all this, Prewitt and Warden have been playing a cat-and-mouse game around each other, trying to hide their strong mutual attraction; slowly, however, their relationship intensifies, while it becomes clear that they also share a hatred of abusive authority. They are both deeply shocked when Maggio, accused of insubordination, is sent to the notorious "stockade," a sadistic place of confinement ruled by the psychotic Sergeant "Fatso" Judson (Ernest Borgnine). Indeed, news soon leaks out of the stockade that Fatso is systematically hitting Maggio with an iron rod; one night, as Prewitt and Warden are sitting together outdoors, a badly beaten Maggio arrives on the scene, having managed to escape; he dies in Prewitt's arms. Distraught, with tears streaming down his face, Prewitt places himself by the loudspeaker near the barracks and plays a mournful, emotional piece on the bugle; his next move is to go to town and find Fatso. After a brief fight, Prewitt stabs Fatso to death; then, badly wounded in the chest, he goes AWOL and hides at Alma's house. A few tense days go by. Warden, preoccupied with Prewitt's disappearance, covers up his desertion; he also ends his affair with Karen, unable to commit to her and become an officer. Finally, on December 7, Japanese planes attack Pearl Harbor. As Warden takes charge and organizes his men for counterattacks, news on the radio reaches Prewitt, who is still at Alma's, ill

The Peak of Stardom

and weak from his wound, and mostly drunk. Immediately sobered up by the news of the Japanese attack, Prewitt frantically gets ready to leave Alma and rejoin his company, despite risking severe punishment for having gone AWOL; Alma begs him to stay, promising him that they will get married if he does. Prewitt, unshakably determined to go and entirely focused on his army's needs, does not heed her and leaves abruptly; as he runs through the island trying to reach his base, he is spotted by an army patrol, who seeing his civilian clothes order him to stop. Prewitt doesn't stop, and is shot dead. Warden, greatly distressed, arrives to identify his body. The film ends with Alma and Karen leaving Hawaii on the same ship, grieving for the men they could not keep with them.

James Jones's novel was considerably expurgated in its film adaptation, as producers were keen to obtain the collaboration of the US army, and specifically the use of the original Schofield Barracks in Hawaii. Among the many changes brought in to please the military, the approved Daniel Taradash script omits the novel's explicit descriptions of the viciousness of the stockade, as well as some clear allusions to homosexual liaisons; both Jones and the director, Fred Zinnemann, were unhappy with the final script, feeling it had been excessively toned down.[24] Nevertheless, the film remains a formidable indictment of the corruption and senseless brutality found in the American army; it equally maintains an overwhelming homosocial emphasis, to the ultimate detriment of heterosexual relationships, and a strong homoerotic current. While the plot follows Warden and Maggio closely, Prewitt dominates the film: his defiance of authority, his conflictive love for the army, and his powerful, often ambiguous emotions motivate the narrative. Through a deviant military identity, Prewitt expresses a deviant masculinity, without negating either his maleness or his belief in the army; instead, his character denaturalizes orthodox notions of the soldier and the man, positing a queer alternative that has its roots in the army itself.

According to Judith Butler, the notion of the military is not unconnected to that of homosexuality; on the contrary, it actually *depends* on it through a negatively derived construction of its own identity.[25] Pointing to the explicit prohibition of homosexuality in the US army's Don't Ask, Don't Tell policy (DADT),[26] and to its implicit prohibition in every representation called forth by the notion of "American army," Butler concludes that traditional concepts of military maleness rest on the negation of homosexuality for their self-affirmation. Butler argues that, paradoxically, the army effectively produces and reproduces homosexuality by insisting on its prohibition, not only as a practice, but even as an utterable entity ("don't ask, don't tell"): "the homosexual subject is brought into being through a discourse that at once names that 'homosexuality' and produces and defines this identity as 'an infraction against the social.'" Considering Sigmund Freud's contention that the repression of male-to-male desire is the prerequisite for the attainment of socially legitimate manhood, Butler claims the army produces what she calls "the masculinist citizen" as a self-denying homosexual. To renounce a desire, however, is not to eliminate it, but rather to preserve it; referring to Freud's *Civilization and Its Discontents*,[27] Butler notes that "within renunciation, desire is kept intact" and that "the libido is not absolutely negated through repression, but rather becomes the instrument of its own subjection." Butler derives that the employment of the libido against desire is the source of the pleasure found in the application of the prohibition: "prohibition becomes the displaced site of satisfaction for the 'instinct' or desire that is prohibited . . . because this displaced satisfaction is experienced through the application of the law, that application is reinvigorated and intensified with the emergence of every prohibited desire."[28]

Butler's discussion of DADT provides vital clues about the construction of military masculinity, highlighting how the army calls forth specific identities through discourse, by interpellation of the military subject. In other words, the army interpellates the masculinist citizen by demanding the renunciation of his potential homosexual identity; at the same time, the army interpellates the homosexual as the antithesis of the soldier, as someone who has failed to be produced as masculinist and to negate his homosexuality. The army's creation of the homosexual rests not only on his nonmasculinism but also on his perceived danger for the military community, as he is seen as "an infraction against the social." Lastly, the army's persecution of homosexuals can be explained as the gratification of homosexual desire, which the masculinist citizens have successfully repressed. In the face of this formidable discoursive and practical strategy on the part of the military,

Butler advocates a queer response of nonalignment, a disavowal of the army-created "homosexual." In line with the queer rejection of fixed categorization, she champions "the distance between something called 'homosexuality' and that which cannot be fully interpellated through such a call."

Butler's argument can be ideally applied to *From Here to Eternity*: the core of Prewitt's drama rests on a military discourse of interpellation and renunciation, on a coercive system of identification that Prewitt defies and subverts. As a soldier in the American army, Prewitt is first of all interpellated as a masculinist citizen, and this primary interpellation is clearly articulated in the film as the demand for a series of renunciations. Indeed, the very beginning of *Eternity* introduces its protagonist in relation to what he is asked to give up; at the same time, it also shows Prewitt's alternative view of his military self, and his ambiguous erotic status. Reporting to Captain Holmes, who interrogates him together with Warden, Prewitt/Clift is framed standing up between his two superiors: he is neatly wearing his uniform, his arms are rigidly folded behind his back, and his gaze is concentrated and fierce. As in the script, Clift appears "immaculate, decisive—the picture of a soldier,"[29] a deceptively masculinist look that while affirming his belonging to the army belies the different kind of soldier he is. Indeed, he is immediately questioned about his reason to quit his former corporal position, and he is criticized and derided for his feelings about his bugle playing; next, Holmes announces that he expects him to box for the regiment. As expressions of pain and defiance rapidly pass over Clift's face, he briefly states his refusal to box after the tragedy involving his friend, emphasizing his stance by repeating the same few words: "I quit fighting." As one of the first sentences of a newly arrived soldier to his captain, it is a remarkable statement, to which Holmes retorts, not illogically: "you may as well say 'stop war' because a man got killed!" When Holmes then tries to bribe him with the promise of a job as company bugler, Prewitt's reply is instant and curt: "not if it means fighting." This brief scene establishes Prewitt's character and his complex position inside the army. Through Holmes's comments and orders, the US military has asked Prewitt to renounce his strong feelings about his musical talent and about the friend he has accidentally blinded; in other words, the army has ordered Prewitt to renounce his identity as a very sensi-

CHAPTER 3

tive man and passionate musician, to deny his "instincts or desires." As a prize boxer who refuses to box, Prewitt is explicitly regarded by Holmes as a soldier refusing to soldier, and this will remain the army's official view of him. Prewitt will be regarded as a subversive element, a rebel who will not acquiesce to be interpellated as a "proper" soldier, thus forgoing his admittance to the legitimate world of manhood. Indeed, by deciding to quit boxing Prewitt is letting the army down, choosing to follow his intense emotions instead of reveling in his physical prowess; he is thus betraying the notions of virility he is asked to conform to, and so rejecting the imposition of a masculinist identity. In 1941, when the film is set, and in 1952–53, when the film was made, the existence of homosexuality was, more than ever, a precondition for the US army to define itself against; hence, Prewitt's interpellation as a masculinist soldier implicitly contains a sexual reference, a request for homosexual self-denial. Holmes's attempt to prohibit Prewitt from accessing key parts of himself, such as his love of music and his horror of hurting a friend, are symbolic of the prohibition of a homosexual

Refusing to obey: Prewitt is defiant against Holmes's pressure.

The Peak of Stardom

identity. Likewise, Prewitt's refusal to be molded into an orthodox soldier suggests the nondenial of male-to-male desire.

The sexual implications of Prewitt's character already emerge from the film's early sequences and are complicated by their coexistence with Prewitt's external conformity to ideas of martial virility. In the scene preceding the exchange between Holmes and Prewitt, the latter meets Warden for the first time; Prewitt is playing pool on his own, waiting for Holmes to arrive, and Warden enters the poolroom to tell him to move on. A series of two shots frames them both in medium close-up, as their eyes meet and they acknowledge each other; then, as Warden says "I've heard about you," the camera moves closer on Clift's face in a reaction shot. Clift keeps his gaze fixed on Warden, while his features, which had been tight and self-contained, relax and break into a smile; for a moment, his eyes exhibit the shining quality that so often typifies them, but which appears only sparingly in *Eternity*. At the same time, there is a fleeting but clear glint in his gaze, as he replies smiling: "I've heard about you too." It is the briefest of scenes, but Clift uses it to convey interest and attraction toward Warden, and a palpable thrill in his presence. Later on, during Prewitt's grilling in Holmes's office, it is Warden's turn to feel the allure of the new connection; although he initially performs his sergeant part, mocking Prewitt's "hurt feelings" about the bugling, he soon starts to consider the newcomer with obvious fascination. Looking up at Prewitt from his desk, Warden slowly stops what he is doing, staring at him with an entranced expression, a habit he will maintain throughout the film.

As the narrative progresses, Prewitt is firmly integrated in homosocial alliances of love and desire through his relationships with Maggio and Warden. Simultaneously, the army's official and vicious elements single him out as someone deserving "the treatment." Identifying him as a subversive in need of punishment, "the treatment" effectively constitutes the army's next interpellation of Prewitt: while it does not expressly term him a homosexual, it openly interpellates him as a bad soldier, who has refused to comply with his masculinist duties. The army's effort to represent Prewitt as a failed military man is clearly shown in the film, through the specific forms of abuse he receives. Prewitt's persecutors take delight in divesting him of his soldierly skills: officers make him trip on purpose during exercises, accuse him of marching

CHAPTER 3

out of step, and deliberately steer him into puddles during maneuvers, always punishing him for these supposed mistakes. During a routine demonstration in weapon assemblage, the experienced Prewitt is the first to finish building his rifle, yet the commanding officer disgraces him by insisting that he has done it wrong. Just as significantly, Prewitt is perpetually assigned to menial tasks of a feminizing nature, such as washing up dishes and scrubbing floors; in an especially poignant scene, he is on his knees cleaning the gym floor, looked down upon by the regiment boxers he has refused to join. The army's interpellation of Prewitt as a failed soldier is highlighted by the clothes he must wear on these duties: generic fatigue outfits, resembling a denim suit, devoid of any obvious military association. By separating him from the attributes of masculinist soldiers, the army clearly defines Prewitt as "an infraction against the social," an aberration against martial homogeneity; this discriminatory attitude is powerfully shown throughout *Eternity*, despite its last-minute rehabilitation of the army through Holmes's dismissal. An unlikely resolution to the endemic brutality of Schofield Barracks, Holmes's eventual disgrace was added to the script at the request of the US military in a blatant change to Jones's text, and through a scene that made Zinnemann "sick" whenever he watched it.[30] In fact, the viciousness displayed and sanctioned against Prewitt, and the excited glee of its tormentors, are convincingly explained through Butler's discussion of DADT: Prewitt is mercilessly punished because to do so satisfies the army's repressed desires, as the displaced fulfillment of forbidden instincts lies in the administration of the punishment itself. Likewise, the extreme ferociousness of Prewitt's "treatment" is readable in the context of an "antisocial" diagnosis on the army's behalf, of the implicit identification of Prewitt as a homosexual, and thus as a "dangerous and contagious" threat. This dual interpellation, as a deficient soldier and a menace to the military community, is one from which Prewitt sensationally distances himself. If, on one hand, Prewitt refutes the army's masculinist call by privileging his own feelings, he also constantly reasserts his identity as a committed soldier through his personal vision of the army, his boundless love for it, and a behavior that is often distinctly "virile."

Prewitt's self-fashioning as a military man thus rests on a dualistic basis, which subverts categorizations. As a soldier, Prewitt not only asserts his right to be sensitive and emotionally vulnerable, he also claims the entitlement to defy the army's authority; having refused to box, he later avenges Maggio's death by killing Fatso, and then he goes AWOL. While all these actions are eventually the making of his doomed fate, the film unquestioningly validates them, and they do not remotely erode Prewitt's belief in his identity as a soldier. Indeed, when Alma tells him he is risking his life by crossing the island after going AWOL, effectively a deserter amid army patrols who will not recognize him, Prewitt does not believe her; in his copy of the script, Clift adds the words "They'll know I'm a soldier" to his dialogue with Reed.[31] Prewitt's unshakeable certainty of his military identity is stressed by his adherence to notions of physical strength and resilience, powerfully expressed by Clift in his performance. In stark contrast to his attitude in previous films, when he was often characterized by slouching, hunched shoulders, and a tentative tone of voice, in *Eternity* Clift exhibits an extremely upright, tough posture: his back is perfectly straight, his step decisive, and his speech brusque. If he exudes tension and hurt since the first scenes, he mostly achieves it through a darkening gaze and a taut jaw, or a subtle flinching of his face, which is instantly suppressed; while his drained, roughed-up features suggest intense pain, his behavior denotes a habit of tough self-control. On the whole, Clift's stance in the film indicates skilled preparation in the face of attack—the epitome of soldierly masculinity. In fact, Prewitt's military courage is inscribed in his very resistance against the army's "treatment" and is again stressed in Clift's personal script notes: in another addition that does not feature in the film's final cut, Clift writes "they can't break me—I'm too good a soldier" into his lines.[32]

Prewitt's commitment to a military identity translates and feeds into his vision of the army, which is grounded in male kinship and male-to-male love. Far from being "an infraction against the social," Prewitt claims as his society a homosocial, homoerotic community of soldiers; if ideally this is an American army based on equality and homofriendliness, in practice it is the army of Prewitt, Maggio, Warden, and their allies. A system within a larger system, Prewitt's military brotherhood still relates to the impersonal, often monstrous machine that contains it, through the link of a powerfully felt symbolic value. Over the film's subversive collective of nonmasculinist men, who refuse official inter-

CHAPTER 3

pellations, towers their idealized notion of the army as whole: a male-bonding structure, a nurturing haven for soldiers' mutual affection and desire. This is why Prewitt, addressing the conflict between his loyalty as a soldier and the horror of his "treatment," tells Alma that he can love the army even if the latter "doesn't love him back"; his passionate belief in the armed forces rests on his ideal of what these ought to be as much as on his specific allegiance to individual male relationships. While advocating the nondenial of "instincts and desires," thus crucially disrupting official interpellations of the US soldier, Prewitt's own army is also, symbolically and practically, the American army; indeed, when the Japanese attack Pearl Harbor, Prewitt heatedly remarks that they have attacked "the best army in the world." Through Prewitt's subjectivity, the subversive and the privately felt overlap with the officially represented, effectively queering the film's portrayal of the US army. Rather than negate soldierness or maleness, *From Here to Eternity* de-naturalizes these concepts, disrupting social and military expectations of the American soldier; its overt plot validates Prewitt's queer vision of the army, and its strong homoerotic subtext emphasizes it.

Through the intersecting personal narratives of Prewitt, Warden, and Maggio, the film foregrounds intense attachments between men, ultimately privileging homosociality above heterosexual relationships. Although Prewitt is initially very attracted to Alma, his attraction appears rooted in the need for comfort; as it is often the case in his performance with female love interests, Clift is physically affectionate toward Reed, but the extent of his sexual involvement remains uncertain. Indeed, in their scenes together there is a palpable sense of maternal coziness, an impression that Alma's role is to provide reassurance and sweetness to the troubled Prewitt. When they are alone together, in a discrete lovers' parlor at Alma's nightclub, Prewitt's express desire is that his girl would "snuggle up to him": erotic intimations are entirely missing. Maggio's arrival soon interrupts the couple's intimacy, yet Prewitt is far from annoyed and greets his friend with a radiant smile; it is notable that in the whole film, Prewitt will smile in that way only to Maggio. Likewise, more than once Prewitt will give up his chance to be with Alma in order to rescue Maggio from trouble. Maggio himself, though loudly declaring that he likes girls, is never linked to any woman; while he introduces Prewitt to the delights of the nightclub, his behavior on the dance floor, surrounded by female beauties, is clown-like and virtually asexual. The exception to Prewitt's and Maggio's detachment from heterosexual eroticism is, of course, Warden, whose relationship with Karen is emphatically based on sex (and whose lovemaking on the beach, tame as it may appear today, is nonetheless immortalized as one of cinema's sexiest moments). Although Warden's heterosexual passion is highlighted in the film, it is ultimately discarded in favor of a life of active service in the army; just like Prewitt, who chooses to leave Alma and join his company at war, Warden decides to abandon his woman to stay by his men. Significantly, Warden's ending of his affair with Karen is linked to his rejection of a career as an officer; again like Prewitt, Warden refuses the masculinist interpellation, in this case shaped as the call for being an ambitious soldier who wants to command others. "I always hated officers," reiterates Warden with passion, not prepared to betray his feelings or deny his identity; implicitly, therefore, his refusal of masculinist self-denial posits the nondenial of homosexuality. It is notable that while Prewitt and Warden renounce monogamous commitments to their women, this is not through the desire for heterosexual promiscuity, which would be in fact normative soldier behavior; on the contrary, they give up Alma and Karen in order to literally run back to an all-male existence. The wisdom of preferring the army to the company of women is enshrined in the lyrics of "Re-Enlistment Blues," the film's chief musical theme. Jazzily played by Prewitt on his bugle mouthpiece while Warden and others join in a chorus, the song centers on a soldier betrayed and robbed by a woman, thrown out of a bar while being called "queer," and finally realizing that reenlisting in the army is his best option. Diegetically functioning as the melancholic score of drunk and bored soldiers, "Re-Enlistment Blues" effectively spells out the film's preferred scenario: the opposition, even the incompatibility of army love and heterosexual love.

This implicitly avowed split marks the choice of homosociality, and homosocial desire, above that of heteronormativity; textually and subtextually supported throughout *Eternity*, this choice is endorsed most significantly in Prewitt's final leaving of Alma. Having been visibly depressed since going AWOL, living at Alma's in a state of drunkenness, Prewitt is instantly returned to sobriety and action by the thought of rejoining the army. Excited and collected at the same time, snapping

CHAPTER 3

back into strength and willpower, Prewitt also shaves and smartens up his appearance to meet again his fellow soldiers; during these preparations, he is totally oblivious to Alma's tears and pleas, even as she proposes marriage in the attempt to stop him. Almost hypnotically, Prewitt is clearly feeling the lure of a love greater than any other, as the army's need and his own need of the army simultaneously recall him. The last exchange between Prewitt and Alma finalizes his priorities; hardly aware of her presence anymore, without a glance of regret or affection, Prewitt tells her "I'm sorry" with chilling detachment, and rushes out of her house. On his way out, he switches all the lights off, "because of the blackout outside," a gesture that becomes a visual symbol of his termination of their relationship.

If narrative developments foster the construction of a homofriendly discourse, a clear homoerotic subtext underpins the film's overwhelmingly homosocial bias. Since the first scene when their eyes meet above the pool table, Prewitt and Warden are increasingly linked by mutual attraction, which is revealed only cautiously at first. When Warden ingeniously saves Prewitt from court-martialing, a soldier comments on his protective action by telling Warden "maybe you like him," and receives a defiant reply: "maybe I like him." In a scene where Prewitt, worn out by the brutality of "the treatment," gives vent to his feelings through a passionate burst of bugle playing, Warden cannot take his eyes off him, looking completely entranced. Later on, Prewitt is struck by fascination with Warden. After witnessing Warden rescuing Maggio from a knife fight with Fatso in a bar, Prewitt appears shaken and smitten at the same time. Rising quickly from his chair to follow Warden, who has stormed outside, Prewitt murmurs, "he's a good man," staring wide-eyed in his direction. Prewitt's immediate arousal, his running after Warden, and Warden's obvious satisfaction as he sees him joining him outside, are strongly redolent of traditional "pulling" situations; only usually, of course, Warden would have attracted a woman and not a man. The erotic quality of the relationship between Prewitt and Warden is at its most evident in a key scene outside the barracks. Both moderately drunk, they sit next to each other; Prewitt casually lays his hand on Warden to steady himself. As they talk, Warden begins to caress Prewitt on his arm and back; he does this for a while, then he strokes his head and ruffles his hair very tenderly. Prewitt, passively accepting

The Peak of Stardom

Warden's touch, looks available and perfectly comfortable; their dialogue stresses their close bond, as Warden says "we stay together" to Prewitt, who forcefully repeats, "Prewitt stays here till the bitter end." Given that rank separates the two men, and that until now they have not socialized as friends, it is an extraordinarily intimate scene, a very blatant display of attraction. Their good looks and fit appearance emphasize the homoeroticism of the Prewitt-Warden couple; Montgomery Clift and Burt Lancaster are the most attractive men on screen, and the film showcases their bodies and nobody else's. However, while they both appear half-naked at times, Lancaster is deliberately eroticized in his love scene on the beach with Kerr, while Prewitt's body is displayed only to the male gaze: it is there to be looked at by other men, but is not actively engaged in erotic activity with either sex. Indeed, narratively and visually, Clift in *From Here to Eternity* is once again an object of desire: Warden and Alma both want him, though he is ambiguously related to both.

To these two dominant relationships, Prewitt's feelings for Maggio add further uncertainty, enhancing the protagonist's undefined

Homoerotic: Prewitt and Warden are powerfully attracted to each other.

CHAPTER 3

sexual identity. On a basic level, the friendship between the two is articulated through wisecracking camaraderie and mutual support, and thus presented as a traditional "buddy" association; however, the very notion of male bonding is replete with ambiguities, and these are amply highlighted in the exchanges between Prewitt and Maggio. While not displaying the erotic tension defining his connection to Warden, the alliance with Maggio brings out some of Prewitt's most obvious expressions of love. The tenderness underlying their relationship finds its climax in the scene of Maggio's death, and in the emotional piece of music through which Prewitt mourns his loss. As soon as the runaway Maggio appears in front of him, crawling and visibly ill, Prewitt takes him in his arms; it is a very intimate embrace, with their faces so close they are almost touching. Maggio encircles Prewitt's neck with an arm and collapses to the ground, while his friend keeps his grip on him, crouching down by his body. Skinny and wasted, Sinatra here looks fragile next to Clift, whose strong yet delicate hold of him expresses protection and nurturing; his hand entirely covers Sinatra's thin shoulder, and gently squeezes it, while his gaze is glued to the dying man's face. As Maggio unfolds his tale of abuse in the stockade, he feverishly grabs Prewitt's shirt, then his arm; the other never shifts his position, whispering "buddy, buddy . . ."; when Maggio closes his eyes, and Warden says "he's dead," Prewitt still does not move, as if frozen by emotion. The film then cuts to Maggio's empty bed in the barracks, while the sound of a mournful music fills the air; after showing the soldiers stirred by the melody, the camera moves on to Prewitt at the bugle. A long shot locates him by the loudspeaker, in the vastness of the empty courtyard, and then a close-up reveals that he is playing and crying copiously at the same time; it is an emotional, intensely lonely image. Alternating the sight of his distressed face with shots of the respectful attitude of his audience, the film prolongs and emphasizes the sight of Prewitt's unstoppable tears; no other event has made him cry, and this reaction marks the enormity of his grief. Combined with the powerful effect of the bugle melody in the silence of the night, the overflow of Prewitt's emotion conveys a sense of romantic despair. Narratively and visually, it is the seal of his love for Maggio. While this sequence leaves erotic questions unresolved, it casts a weight of passionate feelings on the relationship between the two friends, which exceeds the boundaries

The Peak of Stardom

of orthodox male behavior. At the same time, Maggio's death stresses how Prewitt's homosocial attachments are situated in an antiauthority space: a rebellious figure, Maggio has been murdered by the vicious, official military power represented by Fatso and Holmes, a power Warden has tried to oppose and contain throughout the film. Prewitt's alliance with Maggio and Warden, steeped in homosocial desire and the refusal to obey, is thus the expression of the protagonist's rejection of the army's masculinist call. However, this does not signify the army's success in the interpellation of Prewitt as a homosexual; on the contrary, Prewitt's identity can emphatically not be conflated with military notions of homosexuality. Steadfastly reaffirming his self-definition as a proud soldier, and his belief in an ideal army based on male love and nurture, Prewitt is refusing the terms of the antithesis between soldierness and homosexuality; indeed, he is refusing the antithesis itself. In so doing Prewitt interposes an unbridgeable distance between his sexual identity and the army's interpellation, realizing the queer resistance Judith Butler advocates. Pondering on the fact that Prewitt is not usually able to explain himself through words, and tends instead to express feelings and thoughts through his behavior, Montgomery Clift said: "Prew is a limited guy with an unlimited spirit."[33] The unlimited quality of Prewitt's character makes it impervious to categories; refusing to be bound by external interpellations, in *From Here to Eternity* Clift shapes its protagonist through rebellion and multiplicity, confirming once more his own subversive and queer persona.

FOUR

The 1956 Car Accident and a New Queerness

Trauma and Fragmentation: The Accident and *Raintree County*

Montgomery Clift turned down every film role he was offered between 1953 and 1956; while shunning Hollywood, he chose instead to return to Broadway in 1954, producing and starring in a controversial version of Chekhov's *The Seagull*. The film that finally brought him back to the big screen was *Raintree County*, a sweeping Civil War drama in which he played the protagonist, John Shawnessy. The reasons why Clift accepted the role remain uncertain: he had strong misgivings about the script, and famously hated the film, which he described as "a monumental bore" and "a soap opera with elephantiasis." Clift's biographers tentatively cite financial need as one of his motives in making *Raintree County*, as well as his desire to work again with Elizabeth Taylor, who costarred in the film as John's unhappy wife, Susanna.[1] Whatever the reasons, Clift started shooting *Raintree County* in April 1956; nearly half of it had been completed when, the night of May 12, Clift left a dinner party at Elizabeth Taylor's, drove down the Beverly Hills canyons and, allegedly half asleep, crashed his car into a telephone post.

CHAPTER 4

Endless speculations surround Clift's alcohol and drug intake that night, even though some of those present—Taylor's husband Michael Wilding, Rock Hudson, and Clift's close friend and fellow actor Kevin McCarthy—always insisted that he had hardly drunk and was completely lucid. The most supported account of the events, and the one repeated by Clift himself,[2] is that he was simply exhausted, already weeks into an intensive shooting schedule that saw him act in almost every scene; he was also suffering from lack of sleep.[3] What is certain is that Kevin McCarthy was the first to arrive on the spot of the accident, as he had been driving ahead of Clift and had suddenly noticed his disappearance from his rearview mirror; he found Clift's Chevrolet "crumpled up like an accordion against a telephone pole."[4] Unable to get inside the car, whose doors had jammed shut, McCarthy ran back to Taylor's house for help; when they finally managed to get to Clift, still trapped inside, they found him breathing but only semiconscious, bleeding very heavily and visibly choking on something. A steely nerved Elizabeth Taylor stuck her hand inside his throat, to find that he was suffocating on two of his own teeth, knocked down there by the blow; she removed them, thus probably saving his life. It took the ambulance half an hour to arrive on the scene, yet it was only a matter of minutes before a storm of paparazzi descended on it, alerted through the gruesome system of celebrity reporters who loitered around police stations waiting for emergency calls.[5] Clift, however, was hidden from view by Hudson, McCarthy, and Wilding, who formed a barrier around him to stop the journalists from taking photos; as a result, no public record of Clift's battered face and body ever existed. Yet if no images of Clift himself were available, the mangled appearance of his car was; as Amy Lawrence perceptively comments, "the accident itself was traumatically visible through news photos of the car, the wreckage standing in for Clift's ravaged body."[6] This dramatic visual evidence had gone around the world by the following morning, thanks to UPI and Wide World news agencies, in a spectacularly publicized scoop.[7]

The physical damage Clift had suffered was indeed huge, and his blood loss alone had nearly killed him; yet incredibly, no part of his body was severely affected aside from his face, which had borne the full impact of the crash. His left cheek was heavily lacerated, and both jaws were broken in four parts; his nose was broken in two, and the sinus

The 1956 Car Accident and a New Queerness

was fractured. One of his upper cheekbones was cracked; his mouth was virtually ripped apart, with a hole through his upper lip. Teeth were missing. Remarkably, the reconstruction of this wrecked face would involve no plastic surgery; Clift's left cheek was instead wired, the broken bones were reassembled, and his mouth was, somewhat messily, sown back into place. The accident's toll caused Montgomery Clift untold physical and mental pain, as well as triggering long-term changes adversely affecting his psychological state, his addiction to prescription drugs and alcohol, even his capacity to have sex; the most immediate and visible consequences, however, were centered on his appearance. While Clift's back and neck had also suffered a blow, and he would never recover from whiplash, the wreckage the crash caused was inscribed in his face; only his eyes and ears remained the same. The loss of a nerve in his left cheek meant that nearly half of that side of his face was paralyzed; his features appeared thickened, his nose had changed shape, and his upper lip looked like "a repaired harelip."[8] In addition, the broken sinus had caused a permanent change to his voice, which from now on would be lower, nasal, and at times croaky. Severe as these physical alterations were, and personally devastating to Clift, they were still very far from turning him into a monstrous figure; the total effect was one of uncanny, disturbing difference from his former looks. Clift's face was not scarred, nor was he deformed in any way; he had not spectacularly plunged into ugliness. The discrepancy between his pre- and postaccident faces, however, was so extremely powerful to inform perceptions of Clift as "disfigured," a notion that persists to this day, as any Internet search for his name will reveal. The representation of Clift as a somewhat deformed man did not rest so much on what he had become, but rather on the tragic loss of what he had been. To anyone who was familiar with his beauty, be it his fans or his friends, he appeared changed to the point of nonrecognition. People who knew him "reacted with shock or embarrassment when they saw his new face. Often he simply wasn't recognized."[9] The words of Jack Larson, one of Clift's closest friends, exemplify common reactions to the star's new appearance: "He looked completely different. His mouth was twisted. A nerve had been severed in his left cheek so that the left side of his face was practically immobile—frozen. His nose, that perfect nose! was bent—crooked—out of shape. He looked stuffed, that's the only way I

CHAPTER 4

can put it."¹⁰ Clift's lawyer, Jack Clareman, also focuses on the gap between Clift's two faces: "He'd been so spectacularly handsome. People used to gasp when they met him. Now they gasped for a different reason."¹¹

In the light of such viscerally dramatic accounts, it is tempting to argue that Montgomery Clift remained a good-looking man until his death; however, in order to assess the development of his postaccident image, it is vital to consider it in relation to his former appearance. The issue at stake, massively affecting his career and star persona, was not how more or less handsome Clift now was; it was rather the inescapable, painful comparison between his looks before and after the crash. Unlike most men, and other stars whose image had not rested on such perfect features, Clift was pitted against an ideal he could never match up to: his own appearance until May 12, 1956. His beauty had been so total and flawless to be completely unusual, and, in terms of contemporary masculine standards, almost unnatural; this faintly "abnormal" quality had informed his overall deviant image, but in a dazzling, erotically appealing way. As Clift's biographer, Robert LaGuardia, eloquently describes: "Before, it had been a mutant, supernatural face, devastating because each part had seemed charged with a separate life force."¹² LaGuardia is much less convincing, however, when arguing that Clift's new face was "normally imperfect":¹³ a face that was almost half-paralyzed, and thus asymmetric and partly static, could not fit established canons of bodily normality. Partial yet obvious, the objective changes in Clift's appearance merged with the memory of his previous looks, producing a twisted, eerie version of his well-known self. A fan magazine put it succinctly: "Montgomery Clift looks strange."¹⁴ This "strangeness" could only have a negative impact on Clift's established status as object of desire; as one of his biographers writes, he found himself overnight to be "a damaged commodity in an era of handsome rebels."¹⁵

The perception of Clift as a ruined beauty affected his star image in a complex way. In a powerfully visual sense, continuity was broken, yet the break itself became part of his image, forever linking the past to the present, confirming the importance of physical appearance in Clift's total signification as a star. This utter emphasis on Clift's looks was evident in the way that MGM, the studio producing *Raintree County*, han-

The 1956 Car Accident and a New Queerness

dled the accident crisis: their press release on May 14, 1956, carried a headline that did not highlight Clift's medical condition, nor hailed his survival, but simply stated, "Monty Clift Won't Be Scarred by Crash." The publicity effort to foster a belief that nothing had changed was, however, very short-lived, as on May 23 Clift's doctor told reporters that his patient would require "further treatment."[16] From this point onward, news of Clift's horrific injuries would slowly leak to the press, reaching a feverish peak when he went back on set, nine weeks after the accident.

In order to conceptualize Clift's trajectory as a star, it is useful to refer to Richard Dyer's notion of stardom as a "structured polysemy." Dyer argues that the range of meanings attached to a star are multiple yet structurally organized; while in some cases the elements making up a star's image may reinforce one another, in other instances these elements may be in a relation of opposition or contradiction, "in which case the star's image is characterised by attempts to negotiate, reconcile or mask the difference between the elements, or else simply hold them in tension."[17] Until the 1956 accident, the contradictions inherent in Clift's image had been primarily centered on his sexual identity, specifically on his lack of conformity to a neat sexual and gender orientation. Traditional notions of the heterosexual heartthrob had jostled with strong homoerotic suggestions; likewise, Clift's status as a sex symbol had coexisted with erotically passive or asexual performances in some of his films. These contradictions had never been resolved, yet had been organized in a total image of powerful, queer ambiguity; in this sense, the conflicting sides of Clift's persona had effectively reinforced one another, contributing to his overall "enigmatic" perception. The single element that had contained and defined Clift's contradictions was his almost surreal beauty; this beauty had given visible coherence to the ambivalent, multiple meanings of Clift as a star. After the car crash, Clift's essential ambiguity will be reshaped by a new contradiction, the one between his former and new appearances; these two facets will not be reconciled but will remain forever held in tension, as the notion of "Montgomery Clift" will call forth images of his preaccident career, of the accident itself, and of his current looks and state of health. In other words, the trauma of May 12, 1956, with his immediate and long-term consequences, will become an integral part

CHAPTER 4

of the polysemous structure of Clift's stardom. As Dyer points out, "structured polysemy does not imply stasis; images develop or change over time."[18] As mentioned in the previous chapter, Clift's appearance had in fact subtly altered well before his accident, as simple aging had combined with the routine abuse his body was subjected to. Massive amounts of alcohol and prescription drugs, chain smoking, and an erratic diet had started to leave their mark, yet any change had gone unnoticed in the four-year gap between *From Here to Eternity* and *Raintree County*. The physical and mental havoc the 1956 crash caused, while a turning point in itself, also acted as a catalyst for existing or developing changes in Clift's looks and fitness; in addition, the representation of his "enigmatic" aura started to lean conspicuously in the direction of psychological anomaly. A history of emotional fragility, depressive tendencies, and assorted addictions was suddenly incorporated in the leveling trauma of Clift's broken face. Alongside the discursive rupture that certainly occurred in his image, there was a simultaneous thread of continuity in the foregrounding of notions of deviancy; the next phase of Clift's career will be defined by their intensification, and his queer identity will be increasingly expressed through narratives of social "abnormality" on and off screen.

The dynamic polysemy structuring Clift's image thus gained new dimensions, where physical and mental "difference" acquired a more alien meaning; rather than simply disruptive or subversive, Clift was more and more perceived as deviating from the "norm." The most basic expression of this shift was visual. Not only was Clift now distanced from his former beauty, which, "unnaturally" perfect as it had been, had constituted his own normality, he was also moving away from the established standards of successful leading men, based on strict notions of bodily fitness and attractiveness. For most of Clift's public and fans, the car accident heralded a visual trajectory of deterioration, as Clift became gradually afflicted by a plethora of illnesses. Although his health often fluctuated, the next ten years would see him significantly aged and frail, in a seemingly unstoppable process culminating in his gaunt, exhausted look in *Freud*. In *The Defector*, released after his death, Clift appeared as a still-handsome man looking desperately, almost unbearably ill. Yet while his physical decline took place in stages, Clift's worsening mental state was sensationalized almost immediately after

The 1956 Car Accident and a New Queerness

the accident. In the aftermath of the crash, when Clift was struggling to cope with his condition and the pressure of being back on set, popular attitudes toward him started to shift. What had been baffled fascination turned into a less sympathetic view; the star's disturbing physical change was merged with perceptions of an antisocial, psychologically unsound individual. During the location shooting of *Raintree County* in Danville, Kentucky, MGM allowed packs of reporters free access to cast and crew: their most repeated question was, "What's wrong with Monty?" Although Clift tried to hide from them, columnists avidly lapped up every glimpse of him, and pronounced the star "hellbent on self-destruction."[19] Hugely stressed and drugged-up at the same time, wrapped up in his pain and his acting, Clift provided an ideal target for press speculation, as a screenwriter on set remembers: "I've never seen anyone under such pressure, except in combat during the war. . . . He gave the impression of being charged up all the time without ever exploding."[20] The *Boyle Country Courier-Journal* reported on August 19: "Clift's recent automobile accident has done things to him. He hardly looks himself in repose." Clift was in fact so horribly tense he literally dripped with sweat and was forced to change his shirt up to eight times a day.[21] In the last weeks of shooting, gossip reporters, including Hedda Hopper, informed their public that Clift was "pathologically disturbed,"[22] while those working with him were hardly more tolerant, as an MGM story editor recalls: "Monty's ordeal was so naked it disgusted and frightened a lot of people."[23] Even Clift's fans were becoming less indulgent. When a group of local enthusiasts near the *Raintree County* set threw a party in his honor, they fully expected him to attend. As the shattered, pain-ridden Clift never appeared, and Elizabeth Taylor kept away with him, incensed fans were quoted in the press accusing the pair of "complete lack of consideration for their public"; the incident made international news, notably in the British *Daily Mail* with the headline "Elizabeth Taylor and Clift Booed by Angry Fans."[24]

If Clift's motives in accepting his role in *Raintree County* remain unclear, there is less speculation about his decision to return to it, just nine weeks after the accident. Despite pleas from his agent and from long-time girlfriend Libby Holman, who believed he was in no condition to go back to work, Clift must have felt the huge pressure of a project costing MGM $6 million, the highest film budget in Holly-

CHAPTER 4

wood history at that point. Perhaps even more, Clift may have badly needed the psychological boost of returning to some sort of normality; indeed, Elizabeth Taylor allegedly feared he might have killed himself if unable to go back on set.[25] As a consequence of returning to acting while in the grip of pain and posttraumatic stress, Clift's presence in *Raintree County* is inevitably shaped by his physical and mental condition. Combined with the film's random mix of pre- and postaccident material, and a rambling script acutely lacking in character delineation, Montgomery Clift's own drama fundamentally affects the production. As the protagonist, Clift especially suffers from the script's poverty of insight and nuances: his identity as John is incomplete, emerging as the disjointed aggregate of occasional flashes of self-articulation. At the same time, John is a figure caught in a parallel and highly fragmented narrative, the discursive burden of "before and after" now attached to Clift as a star. The result is a film that, through Clift's image, is visually disturbed and disturbing, lacking finality and alternately expressing disorder and blankness. In Clift's career, *Raintree County* stands out as a text about personal chaos, presenting him as a split subject in the midst of conflicting representations. If plot and script deficiencies play a large part in the film's messy effect, it is Clift's uncanny appearance that disorients the most; at a primary level, *Raintree County* is literally a document of fragmentation, presenting Clift's two different faces through deliberately uneven camera angles. This visual muddle was the focus of contemporary expectations and receptions of the film, as Clift himself had accurately predicted: he feared people would flock to the cinema to guess "which is me before and after the accident."[26] This disturbing guesswork is not always as easy as audiences may have supposed: Clift's pre- and postcrash shots are often spliced together in the same sequence, offering an odd compound image, while in a key section of the film he wears a masking, conspicuously false beard. Nevertheless, the abundance of shots taken after Clift's return to the set, which show him looking changed, exhausted, and somewhat stunned, create an impression of the star as broken and lost.

Clift's face had not had time to heal properly yet, so it had a slightly swollen look in addition to its altered features and partial immobility; Edward Dmytryk decided to shoot him mainly in long shots, or from his less-damaged right profile, thus producing an odd portrayal of the

The 1956 Car Accident and a New Queerness

film's leading man. The face that had been immortalized in endless close-ups, lovingly lit and paraded on screen since *Red River*, was now often entirely avoided by the camera. In many of Clift's scenes with Taylor the focus is almost exclusively on her, while Clift is inserted in the two shots with a minimum of exposure: he is either seen from the back, or else his right profile is shown very briefly. Even with these precautions, however, Clift still presented a problem with his eyes, spared by the accident but now mostly bloodshot and glazed. Reflecting Clift's constant pain, his huge intake of pills, and the injections of codeine he gave himself in his dressing room, his gaze often hovered between vacant and frightened. Bob Surtees, the film's director of photography, was struggling to find a solution: "All we could do was give him a little softness and photograph him so that the camera never saw two eyes at the same time. The question about what to do about Monty's face came up a lot when we saw the rushes."[27] The film also sees the beginning of Clift's featherlight phase: a painfully skinny, emaciated look that clashed forcefully with his previously slim yet fit appearance. This was partly the result of Clift's starvation-style liquid diet, which continued to replace solid food as long as his healing jaws made eating difficult. However, Clift was also now indifferent to keeping his body in good shape, and in fact he would become increasingly unfit in the next few years: "He never went to Klein's gym anymore. His major exercise was walking up and down the stairs of his apartment. . . . His body lost muscle tone and grew sluggish."[28]

The physical and psychological changes Clift's accident triggered thus shape *Raintree County*; while the film was met with mixed reactions from public and critics, including Academy Award nominations for its costumes, music score, art direction, and Elizabeth Taylor as Best Actress, Clift's performance and sheer presence were often found disturbing. The *New York Times* lamented "the strange appearance and the ageing, husky voice of Mr. Clift," while the *New York Post* stated, "Montgomery Clift disturbs because he doesn't look quite as he did before his accident."[29] Reporting on the film's premiere, *Variety* described Clift as "curiously muffle-voiced," adding in bold characters that during the film's screening "Clift's hands, sensitive and thin, seemed to shake considerably."[30] The last remark is an example of the often-distorted perception of Clift's new appearance: his hands may well have been shaking, but they were certainly not thin. Despite his recent weight loss, Clift's hands were, as they always had been, disproportionately large and muscular for his slight built, and curiously out of place in his delicate image. Yet not all reviews of *Raintree County* treated Clift with gleeful pity or criticism: the *Los Angeles Examiner*, for example, warmly praised his performance, writing that, "There is no actor who can more clearly portray mental suffering and mental strength than Clift."[31] On December 30, 1957, *Film Daily* presented Clift with its annual award for "the highest achievement in the field of the motion picture."

These conflicting reactions to Montgomery Clift in *Raintree County* testify to the uneven, fragmented quality of his presence. Discrepancies and contradictions are not just the result of the film's mix of pre- and postaccident material; Clift, at one of the lowest moments of his life, still manages to leave a mark as an actor, exceeding his own representation as a destroyed human being. If he looks crushed in much of the film, he also impresses through his effort to conciliate the gaps, differences, and limitations in his own image. Faced with the vacuum created by the loss of his previous appearance, and by the huge energy drain caused by pain and drugs, Clift determinedly navigates a field of chaos; his performance is defined by the attempt to rearrange his identity into a perceptible presence. While that presence never achieves stability or coherence, it is nevertheless *there*, at times suggesting self-possession, substance, and even strength. Worn out as he certainly looks, John/Clift exudes a remarkable staying power as well as a sense of subjective agency that flashes, intermittently, through the dull fog of pain. This sporadic yet palpable force is highlighted by Clift's casting against Taylor, who plays with hysterical virtuosity a character defined by mental illness, childishness, and defeat; while she screams and cries through most the film, Clift's composure and fleeting intensity hint at subterranean reserves of power. According to his main biographer, for quite a while after the accident Clift imagined his face as a blank; he associated this mental image with the ancient statues he had seen in Rome, whose devastated features often lacked eyes and noses, yet had impressed him as still maintaining a strong presence. "It has something to do with dominating space," he had concluded, and had "set out to achieve that in his acting."[32] In *Raintree County*, Clift's performance is the willed manipulation of a self-perceived blank; it does not dominate

The 1956 Car Accident and a New Queerness

space yet, but nevertheless invades it, hinting at still unfinalized identities to come.

Based on a novel by Ross Lockridge, the film is set in Indiana in the fictional Raintree County, named after a mystical golden tree said to hide the secret of life. The plot spans approximately a decade, from 1859 to the American Civil War (1861–65) and its aftermath; it focuses on the relationships between John and two women, his childhood sweetheart Nell (Eva Marie Saint) and the Southern belle Susanna (Elizabeth Taylor). Literary minded, idealistic, and strongly abolitionist, John is enthused by the raintree legend and vows to find the magical tree; however, his youthful existence near the virtuous Nell is shattered by his passion for Susanna, a beautiful but mentally unstable woman who harbors dark secrets and a pathological fear of black people. Forced into marrying her by Susanna's claim that he has got her pregnant, John soon discovers that Susanna has lied; he resigns himself to his fate, trying in vain to stop his wife's descent into madness while knowing that the heartbroken Nell continues to love him. The birth of a son, Jim, does not improve John's domestic situation, and one day the increasingly wild Susanna runs away with the boy; as the Civil War is now raging, John decides to enlist with the Northerners, hoping to find his wife and child in his movements across the country. John's regiment is joined by his former teacher and mentor, Professor Stiles (Nigel Patrick), a philandering eccentric whom John had previously saved from lynching, by helping him flee the county after he had an affair with a married student. Reaching Atlanta after a series of horrific battles, John finds that Jim is alive, hidden and cared for by two of Susanna's ex-slaves; they tell John that Susanna always believed her real mother was Henrietta, a slave she loved passionately and who died in a fire with Susanna's parents. Susanna's insanity stems from her delusion that she was responsible for these deaths. The war ends; John is wounded and badly limping, but still determined to find Susanna, and he finally discovers her confined in a mental asylum. He takes her home with Jim, but her mental state worsens, and she eventually commits suicide by drowning herself in a swamp. Jim, who had run away in search of his mother, is also feared dead, but he is found asleep in a field near the place where she drowned. Consumed by grief for Susanna, yet overjoyed at still having his child, John begins a new life with Nell at his side.

CHAPTER 4

Motivated by a pattern of loss and renewed hope, *Raintree County* muddles its narrative through chaotic developments and characters defined by external actions rather than interiority. A major gap in the film's structure of meaning is between the erotic weight narratively placed on Clift and the exhausted, sexually absent quality of his performance. The hotly contended object of two women's desire, John/Clift is singled out as an erotic signifier through a series of actions, none of which is explored or explained; he begins by giving Nell a book of Byron's love poems, which the chaste girl condemns as "immoral." Next, he falls prey to an overwhelming sexual passion for Susanna and makes love with her on a beach in full daylight, without a thought for Nell. Indeed, he never informs his sweetheart of his infatuation for Susanna, until Susanna comes back to announce that she is pregnant. Through John's sexual activity the plot thus acquires a transgressive strand, and the real motivation for the whole story: without a ready excuse to trick John into marriage, Susanna may simply disappear off screen, and most of the film's catastrophes would not take place. But John's eroticized role extends beyond his own liaisons, reinforcing his connection to unbridled sexual desire. His firm defense of Professor Stiles, the seducer of young married women, places him literally in the firing line of the rifle-touting locals. John bravely defies the keepers of the town's morality, while saving Stiles's life by helping him to hop on a passing train; the close bond between the two men is reaffirmed later in the film, as they go together through the trauma of the Civil War. These are all narrative pointers of John's connection to sexual license, but they clash quite sensationally with Clift's looks and demeanor. Suffering, vacant, or just deadly tired, Clift tackles his love scenes with Taylor and Saint without a trace of erotic involvement. The confusion arising from this incongruity is matched by the difference between John's alleged youth and Clift's appearance. Even before the car accident, Clift's casting as the twenty-year-old John was short of extraordinary; although he had played a man younger than he was in his last film, *From Here to Eternity*, as Prewitt he had such a solid persona as to make age irrelevant, and he was himself still only thirty-two. In *Raintree County*, however, Clift is expected to play "a boy of twenty," described in the first scene with "shoulders square over the wide chest . . . his legs in the tight pants are long and muscular."[33] Clift was nearly thirty-six, and even before

The 1956 Car Accident and a New Queerness

A publicity still for Raintree County: *The left side of Clift's face is kept partly out of sight. The Kobal Collection.*

the crash he could not pass for a man barely past his teens, even if his face did retain a certain boyishness. As it happens, the film's very first scene, in which John is shown among his classmates and then alone with Nell, is clearly shot after the accident: Clift looks frail and spent, the very opposite of a muscular twenty-year-old. The film's stubborn clinging to Clift's boyish image heralds a new phase in his career, where the conflict between "man" and "boy" will develop in more meaningful ways. Clift's former youthful looks had only been one aspect of his es-

CHAPTER 4

tablished representation as a "boy"; as previously discussed, Clift's boyishness had entailed a deviant, unsettling version of masculinity, linked with, but not identical to his age and physical beauty. Clift's star persona had channeled a nonnormative gender and sexual identity through the "beautiful boy'" image, even when he had ceased to be very young, as in, for example, *A Place in the Sun*, when he was around thirty. In *Raintree County*, the discrepancy between John's initial student-like characterization and Clift's age and looks produces a visual disturbance as well as narrative confusion; at the same time, it aids the establishment of a tension between "man" and "boy" that partly rests on Clift's new appearance. His physical frailty and evident mental bewilderment may suggest aging, yet they also highlight Clift's childlike vulnerability, his ambiguous relation to traditional masculinity, and his uncomfortable fit to concepts of adult "normality." Clift's unorthodox erotic persona, which had already expressed not only deviation but also detachment from sexual initiative, will now develop into a more ambiguous identity; from now on, intimations of sexual "innocence" will play against his obvious maturity, producing a strongly disruptive, nonnormative adult image. Jostling conflicting elements from his own incarnations as "man" and "boy," Clift's presence will be structured into a new polysemy of unresolved tensions; this dynamic coexistence of present and past, experience and vulnerability, eroticism and asexuality, will define Clift's screen persona until his death. Indeed, he will be explicitly cast as a young man (and called "boy") in his next two films, *The Young Lions* and *Lonelyhearts*, despite his increasingly visible aging.

In *Raintree County*, the opposing facets of Clift's evolving image are especially marked in his role as Susanna's husband. At once protector and sacrificial victim, John is initially seduced by Susanna as a boy is by a temptress. Sexually and otherwise, John is innocent and inexperienced, a poor match for the knowing, manipulative woman who wreaks havoc with his life; indeed, Nell forgives his erotic escapade as she believes he was defenseless against Susanna's allure. At the same time, John soon emerges as the rock to which his unhinged wife needs to cling, a beacon of strength and sanity against her delusional world. The physical appearance of Clift and Taylor plays into their fragmented characterization; Susanna's ruthless pursuit of John denotes Clift as a priceless erotic object, yet he appears virtually asexual next to her. Taylor is only twenty-four years old, in the full bloom of her beauty: her hourglass figure bursts out of her tight bodices, oozing voluptuous sex appeal. Clift, on the other hand, mostly wears a puffed-up shirt and breeches that emphasize his extreme thinness; he looks dramatically ethereal, almost ghostly, and certainly not like a randy young man initiated to furious lovemaking. While Susanna/Taylor remains a picture of radiant sensuality, even as she sinks into despair and death wish, John/Clift acquires maturity and age, notably in his role as a father. *Raintree County* is the only film in Clift's career to provide him with a child of his own, as *The Young Lions* ends just before he can finally meet his daughter. As Jim's father, Clift exudes a sense of responsibility, marked by his physical behavior toward the child: he carries him in his arms or on his back in most of their scenes together, at times plodding exhaustedly through swamps amid flying bullets, as if Jim was a precious yet heavy burden. This protective and self-consuming attitude is similar to that toward Susanna, a child herself, who on their wedding night astonishes her husband by adorning their bed with her collection of dolls. Clift eventually tells her to "get rid of those damned dolls," yet his authority is mostly shown through a patient, steady perseverance in guarding Susanna from harm, even as the effort is destroying him. John's mixture of strength and fragility is most evident in the war sequences: sporting an increasingly long beard, Clift looks older and almost wasted, his eyes expressing infinite exhaustion. However, his unflinching determination to march on, fighting on the right side and looking for his family, constitutes the only plot development expressing positive vitality. There is something eerily strong in the sight of his stubborn, waiflike figure, doggedly making his way through battlefields strewn with bodies. The postwar sequences, which carry the film through its end, see John again expressing contradictory qualities. Back home with his wife and child, and working as a teacher, he presents a mature, gentlemanly appearance: the beard has given way to a smart moustache, he wears glasses when marking his students' work and uses a walking stick because of his heavy limp. This middle-aged look, however, vanishes in the film's last scene, when John is desperately looking for Susanna and Jim. Here Clift wears again the loose white shirt, breeches, and tight trousers he wore at the beginning, when he was meant to be a young student. Unlike in those early scenes, however, he now does convey a strong impression of youth: with his hair ruffled and his light clothes in disarray, he rapidly crouches by the dead Susanna, bending his slight frame in uncoordinated movements resembling those of a toddler. Rather than a grown man, he looks halfway between a distraught child and an elf, a disturbing and touching figure among the burly locals who have found Susanna.

Fragmentation and confusion thus define Montgomery Clift in *Raintree County*; he remains a partial blank, an unsettling presence both in what he expresses and what he lacks. Out of this broken representation, however, a solid image will again emerge; the next phase of Clift's career will see him as a powerfully deviant presence, bringing to the screen a complex and fascinating range of queer identities.

Alienation, Defiance, Self-Cripping: *The Young Lions*

The first film Montgomery Clift chose to make after his accident, *The Young Lions* sees him as Noah Ackerman, a heroic Jewish soldier battling discrimination in the US army in World War II. The film premiered in New York on April 2, 1958; as soon as Clift's image appeared on the screen, a woman in the audience let out a scream and fainted. All around, people were likewise shocked, whispering incredulously "is that *him*?" After the screening Clift was besieged by reporters, asking him to comment on the audience's reaction; as he ignored them, he was bombarded with questions about his postaccident condition, the amount of pain he still felt, and whether he was able to cope.[34] This combination of horror and pity encapsulates popular receptions of Noah, Clift's beloved among all his roles, and the one he most obsessively labored to create. The main cause of the audience's consternation was not, however, the damage the crash had inflicted on Clift. The star's changed appearance had already been visible in scenes of his previous film, and amply publicized; in fact, *Raintree County* had often shown Clift at his worst, with his features still swollen in the aftermath of the crash. What spectators now saw in *The Young Lions* was not just Clift postaccident; it was a face radically altered by Clift's deliberate intervention on it, an image meticulously crafted to express alienation and pain. Clift's external inspiration for his vision of Noah had been a photo of Franz Kafka, which had so impressed him that he had started

The 1956 Car Accident and a New Queerness

to carry it around with him. Taken shortly before his death of tuberculosis, the photo shows the writer looking gaunt and ravaged by illness, with a feverish expression in his eyes; Clift set out to emulate this look not only through his performance but also by a literal reconstruction of his own face. To replicate Kafka's features, he made his ears stick out very prominently, framing his head in an almost horizontal line; he wore a prosthetic nose that was longer than his real one, and starved himself to become even thinner, shifting his weight from 150 to 130 pounds. He thus distorted his image in a profoundly disturbing way, outdoing any physical alteration caused by the accident; though inspired by Kafka, the result was a frenziedly twisted version of himself, looking rather extraterrestrial with his odd features and wasted-looking body. This self-transformation was an extraordinary step for Clift to take. At this time he was devastated by the loss of his beauty, hunted by a press who decried his appearance, and mourned by fans as a ruined sex symbol; yet he had willingly made himself not simply worse looking, but so unsettlingly different as to seem explicitly alien. As a final touch, Clift chose to wear oversized, nonmatching suits in his scenes as a civilian, thus appearing even thinner and stranger. The contrast with his costars, Marlon Brando and Dean Martin, paragons of virile stardom and both big and beefy, was simply huge.

Clift's creation of Noah did not just rest on his attraction for Kafka; it was also a projection of his self-perception onto the role, of his sense of affinity for a character he saw as an outcast hero. Indeed, after the film's premiere Clift broke down in convulsive sobs, telling friends, "Noah was the best performance of my life—I couldn't have given more of myself."[35] To the journalists he had said: "I'm thirty-seven and Noah is twenty-five, but our characters met in this movie. Strange, isn't it? It's impossible to explain, but I couldn't have played Noah ten years ago."[36] Clift's words, in fact, may contain a key to what he found impossible to articulate. Ten years before *The Young Lions* he had been twenty-seven, a rising star courted by Hollywood and worshipped by fans; he had also, of course, been exceptionally beautiful. By the time he embarked on Noah as a project, Clift had just started to emerge from the accident trauma; he carried a heavy burden of physical and mental pain, and his status among Hollywood stars had suddenly declined. Constantly reminded of his lost beauty, he was often described

CHAPTER 4

by the press as an abnormal, messed-up individual. Clift must have approached Noah knowing the scrutiny he would be subjected to, and aware that the role was a chance to again make his presence count in Hollywood. These pressures only added to the mental distress he was already experiencing, and most likely turned *The Young Lions* into a matter of life and death for him; indeed, when shooting started in Paris in May 1957, Clift's reaction was to go missing. He disappeared and was not found for days, until he was eventually located in southern Italy, in a brothel, drunk to unconsciousness.[37] When finally on the set, Clift devoted himself to his acting with even more than his usual obsession; the notes he made on the script, extremely precise and detailed, ranging from Noah's inner feelings to his wardrobe, testify to his total commitment.[38]

He was, however, dealing with increasingly unmanageable issues: dead sober while on the set, he would often drink himself into a stupor after filming and spend the early mornings vomiting and taking pills. Equally gripped by pain and a painkiller addiction, he carried on set a flask containing a mixture of bourbon, narcotic pain relievers, and fruit juice;[39] walking became painful as he developed phlebitis in both legs, and difficult because of a balance problem which belied a thyroid condition. As a result, he began to acquire the uncertain gait and off-kilter posture that would characterize him from now on, making his appearance increasingly unsettling. Carlo Fiore, Marlon Brando's acting coach on *The Young Lions* set, said on meeting Clift there for the first time: "I thought he was a spastic. . . . His movements were so uncoordinated. He'd have a weird posture, slouched; his pelvis would be thrust forward, hands in his back pockets."[40] Dean Martin nicknamed

A frenzied alien: Noah in The Young Lions.

The 1956 Car Accident and a New Queerness

Clift "Spider" because of the odd way he moved, and even got him a cast chair with an image of a spider on it.[41] In this context of increasing distance from his former image, and enduring physical and mental pain, Clift took control of his own appearance by making it deliberately, sensationally different. Already marked by changes in his face and body, he did not try to counter his separation from notions of male attractiveness, or his public perception as a disturbingly strange individual. Instead, Clift immersed himself in alienation, channeling his own experience into a deviant portrayal of Noah, and forcibly directing the audience to it; physical self-construction was matched by a performance combining remoteness with frenzy, producing a deeply unsettling character. As a dramatic strategy, Clift's self-recreation on screen challenged standards of "normality," affirming a personal identity that subverted canons of Hollywood leading men. Crucially, of course, Clift expressed a changed relation to his former status as sex symbol, de-normalizing his own image as much as accepted tenets of physical norm. As Noah, Clift's disruptive presence is also informed by gender and sexual ambiguity, enhancing his strong quality of nonalignment, and further marking his contrast with the film's other male protagonists. The result is a strikingly queer figure, upsetting the normalizing plot *The Young Lions* overtly presents; in a narrative pushing for unqualified ethnic integration, social conformity, and the development of "boys" into "real men," Clift's Jewish hero resists normative identifications, facing the audience from a position of intentional difference.

Based on the novel by Irwin Shaw, *The Young Lions* starts just before the onset of World War II and follows the intersecting lives of three men prior and during the conflict. Christian Diestl (Marlon Brando) is a German ski instructor turned Wehrmacht officer, who comes to question and ultimately reject the Nazi doctrine he is called to defend. Michael Whiteacre (Dean Martin) is an American showbiz star, an amiable coward reluctantly drawn into the army, who will finally mature into a selfless soldier. Montgomery Clift is Noah Ackerman, a New York Jew and a loner, without family or friends, who meets Michael at the draft office; his apparent timidity gives way to savage resistance once his army company bullies him. The men's personal journeys in World War II are traced alongside their relationships with women, each one through a vastly different narrative. Michael is linked to the

CHAPTER 4

glamorous Margaret (Barbara Rush), who had enjoyed a fling with Christian before the war, but whose democratic views had made her recoil from his Nazi sympathies and later pressure Michael into active fighting. Christian has a sexual fling with the beautiful but shallow Gretchen (May Britt), the wife of his Nazi captain, while falling in love with a spirited Frenchwoman, Françoise (Liliane Montevecchi), whom he decides to leave as he feels the guilt of his Third Reich association. Noah, terribly shy of women and sexually inexperienced, meets Hope (Hope Lange), a pretty and demure girl from Brooklyn; unlike Christian's and Michael's liaisons, defined by eroticism and glamour, the love story between Noah and Hope is tender, romantic, and ends in marriage, although Noah has to overcome her father's anti-Semitism. The film unravels by showing Noah's vicious bullying at the hands of the US army, where Michael is his only ally; fearless and recklessly determined, Noah fights his persecutors one by one, despite his physical frailty, and is ultimately victorious. Meantime, Christian is increasingly troubled by the reality of fighting in the German army and is repelled by his Nazi superiors. A succession of dramatic climaxes brings the three soldiers to the same place, a concentration camp in France that the Germans are fleeing; before that, however, Noah swims through enemy lines to rescue one of his former tormentors, with Michael joining in the effort. The two friends then take part in the liberation of the camp, just hours after Christian has stumbled upon it by accident. As he grasps the meaning of the Nazi final solution, Christian is overcome by horror, throws away his gun, and runs in the nearby fields; a few steps away, Michael is patrolling the area with Noah, who is still greatly distressed by the sight of the camp. They spot Christian in the distance and, unaware that he is not armed, Michael shoots him dead; the war has now ended for all three men. The film's last scene sees Noah returning home to New York, to embrace Hope and their child he has still not met.

The Young Lions underwent significant changes in its screen adaptation, as the script was rewritten three times to gain the Pentagon's approval; accordingly, the film dilutes and contains the US army's anti-Semitism, and Noah's Jewishness is barely touched upon. In addition, Marlon Brando insisted on his own changes to the original text, vastly improving and humanizing his German character. Despite these omis-

The 1956 Car Accident and a New Queerness

sions and alterations, which greatly upset both Irwin Shaw and Montgomery Clift,[42] the film convincingly paints a multiple account of male identity; of the three protagonists, it is Noah who offers a radical challenge to orthodox representations of masculinity. Underpinned by an ambiguous sexual persona, which disrupts the normative social trajectory of his character, Clift's creation of Noah is shaped in every frame by his alienized face and body. In a production openly capitalizing on its star appeal ("Brando and Clift together at last!" announced the film's publicity), Clift's manipulation of his looks subverts notions of desirability, even of normality, constructing a powerful discourse of queer difference.

According to Eve Kosofsky Sedgwick, the concept of queerness functions importantly at a subjective level: it can be concretized by an affirmative act on and about oneself, by an intervention in self-articulation. "Queer," she argues, "never can only denote; nor even can it only connote; a part of its experimental force as a speech act is the way in which it dramatizes locutionary position itself."[43] In *The Young Lions*, Clift's radical operation on his appearance can be read as an experimental act, dramatizing his own position of externalized difference. Performing his role by literally reproducing himself, Clift's move is the visual equivalent of a speech act, a highly eloquent statement of deviancy. In Sedgwick's view, "queer" comes into being through "a person's undertaking particular, performative acts of experimental self-perception and filiation . . . there are important senses in which 'queer' can signify only *when attached to the first person*" (Sedgwick's emphasis).[44] In this light, as queer makes sense as a self-description, achieved through acts of creative self-conception, queer can then be meaningfully invoked in relation to one's history of Self. While obviously Clift did not, indeed could not, refer to Sedgwick's contemporary notion of queerness, his practice in *The Young Lions* can be fruitfully analyzed in relation to it. By deliberately creating a self-representation that subverts his former image, Clift is queering his own meaning in several ways: he is first subverting external identifications by imposing a disturbingly crafted look onto evocations of his past appearance. The stunningly beautiful Montgomery Clift, the self-displaying erotic object of multiple sexual fantasies, is now superseded by a violently different presence, at odds with both this cherished image and popular ideas of masculine appeal.

CHAPTER 4

At the same time, Clift is also literally queering himself; drastically intervening on his own flesh to reshape form and sign, he reveals new implications attached to his persona—indeed, *attached to the first person*.

This display of a shift in self-perception is also linked, just as in Sedgwick's model of queer enunciation, to an act of filiation. Brought up by anti-Semitic parents, Clift held instead a personal mythology of Jewishness that strongly idealized the Jews, whom he saw as superior to other people.[45] His identification with Noah rests partly on his belief in "the Jewish genius for survival," in his empathy for him as a hero of "persistence";[46] in his script notes, Clift writes, "Tenacity—as appropriate to stubbornness / The diff—receptivity / invaluable quality."[47] Likewise, under an unreferenced review of *The Young Lions* that claims that Clift must be Jewish after all, as he played Noah so convincingly he deserves compliments, Clift adds: "the greatest compliment."[48] While it is unclear if he is correcting the quote or simply commenting on it, his preservation of it and his words show his self-connection to a specific idea of Jewishness. Clift's creation of Noah is thus an act of subversive self-reinvention, hinged on a vision of Jewish identity that is both heroic and outcast.

To better identify the queer implications of Clift's approach to his role, it is useful to consider notions of "crip theory" and "cripping." As discussed in chapter 1, recent developments in disability studies have stressed their connections to queer theory through their shared challenge to prescriptive tenets of normality. Established notions of able-bodiedness and heterosexuality are mutually dependent, merged in a paradigm of "natural" functionality rooted in the denial of difference; likewise, dominant notions of "health" and "beauty" rest on a narrow set of ideal qualities, on the illusory stability of bodies and their associated identities. The continuity between "queer" and "crip" has been expanded upon in *Crip Theory*:[49] in this seminal text, Robert McRuer argues that social hegemony is based on a system of mandatory physical and sexual conformity. Highlighting how "the system of compulsory able-bodiedness, which in a sense produces disability, is thoroughly interwoven with the system of compulsory heterosexuality that produces queerness,"[50] McRuer posits "crip" as indissolubly overlapping with "queer." He thus acknowledges a field of critique encompassing "abnormalities" not necessarily linked to traditional signs of disabil-

The 1956 Car Accident and a New Queerness

ity. Indeed, as a critical strategy, "cripping" aims precisely at exposing the fantasy of physical perfection and wholeness, as much as that of a monolithic and "natural" heterosexuality; just like "queering," "cripping" uncovers the myriad deviations underlying and constitutive of all identities. At the same time, there is a crucial self-reflexive function associated to notions of crip: in a parallel with the homosexual closet, the crip experience can be often hidden, masked, or denied, which produces the possibility for an individual to "come out as crip." Both externally targeted and potentially self-affirming, the concept of crip can be meaningfully applied to Montgomery Clift in *The Young Lions*. Since his 1956 accident, Clift had been increasingly turned by the press into an object of pity and even disgust and was now facing a vaguely hostile cinema audience; however, he was still carrying a baggage of powerful star appeal, a strong association with his former erotic allure and with Hollywood glamour. In other words, Clift straddled two sides of his own star image; he remained a good-looking man, and he might have easily chosen to emphasize this. In building himself up as Noah, he could have equally used make-up, prosthetics, and body training to improve and correct his appearance, opting to stand firmly in the realm of traditional leading men. By doing exactly the opposite, deliberately increasing the faintly alien quality of his changed looks, Clift forced spectators to deal with his self-experience in a wildly uncomfortable, in-your-face manner. Through Noah, he effectively comes out as crip, as a nonbeautiful Clift, traumatized yet defiant, irremediably at odds with the requirements of the star system. It is a sensational statement, a radical self-representation that Clift will not attempt again; it is anchored to a moment of personal stocktaking, where the effects of the accident were still overwhelmingly present. After *The Young Lions*, Clift will deal with his changed condition ambivalently, holding himself in tension between past and present; while in a 1963 interview he will claim he emerged from the car crash "exactly the same,"[51] his last performances will rely heavily on the expression of physical and mental difference. Equally, he will continue to articulate subversion on screen through performative and narrative means, rather than by bodily deviation. *The Young Lions* represents a unique stage in Clift's career, a deliberate and bold reaction to traumatic change and external judgment; it seems no coincidence that he felt so close to Noah, and that he held him up as

CHAPTER 4

a hero. As the literal embodiment of a personal self-declaration, Noah stands out among Clift's roles as the most uncompromisingly deviant. According to McRuer, crip identities are constantly facing an implied social question, even in supposedly accepting environments: "Yes, but in the end, wouldn't you rather be more like me?"[52] In *The Young Lions*, this external query is conspicuously hanging over Noah/Clift, who replies with a resounding "No," despite and against the film's normalizing plot. Indeed, Clift here wouldn't even be more like himself as far as his factual appearance is concerned; the cripping of his identity reveals it as far more alien than it would otherwise look.

In an early version of *The Young Lions'* script, Noah's Jewish background is emphasized, being in fact the context through which he is introduced on screen: his first scene sees him at his father's deathbed, performing religious rituals.[53] Clift made lots of annotations for this scene, which was evidently cut out at an early stage, as it is not present in the shooting script. However, Noah's dual characterization as a Jew and a hero was very significant for Clift, and remains a frame through which he articulates Noah's misfit status; it is also an apt vehicle for his cripping strategy of de-normalization. Carrie Sandahl points out that "sexual minorities and people with disability share a history of injustice"; so, of course, do the Jews, and Sandahl's crip notion of a "critique of hegemonic norms"[54] is suitably channeled through a defiant character, marginalized by default, and further isolated by his lone position in society. When he first meets Hope's father, Noah must listen not only to his self-confessed anti-Semitism, but also to his proud boast of his family's established place in Brooklyn, where they have been buried in the same plot for seven generations. Noah replies: "I don't have a family plot—I don't have a family." Prior to the meeting, Hope had told her father that Noah was a Jew, and that he was alone in the world; thus located twice outside a "normal" social environment, the film lays the ground for Noah's persecution in the army. Although none of his fellow soldiers refer to the fact that he is Jewish, Noah is inexplicably bullied from the very beginning: he is forced to wash windows, derided for his New York origins, while the James Joyce book he is reading is confiscated and described as "filth." Shortly afterward, his savings are stolen; when he reacts, he is sadistically beaten. While anti-Semitism is implicitly at work, the enmity toward Noah is chiefly externalized through a physical and verbal hatred of his body: when one of the bullies says, "I saw someone who looked like Ackerman," another retorts "nobody looks like Ackerman!" to the company's raucous approval.

While his suffering at the hands of the army is obviously evocative of *From Here to Eternity*, there are huge differences between Noah and Prewitt, tough and resilient as they both are. Prewitt looked the picture of the soldier, and his sense of belonging to the army vastly shaped his identity; Noah's appearance is that of an emaciated, nervous alien, dropped into an environment he does not understand or care for. His heroism at the front, when he risks his life to save another soldier, is proof of his courage and humanity, not of his adherence to military codes. Prewitt's posture was straight, his movements skilled and confident, his expression strained in self-control; Noah is hunched, uncoordinated, with an uncertain walk and a frenzied gaze. The impact of these physical traits is vastly dependent on Clift's manipulation of his looks; although his initial scenes take place outside the army, in situations that don't yet trigger Noah's latent wildness, there is no denying the shock of his entrance. *The Young Lions* has been running for twenty minutes by the time Clift appears on screen; up to this moment, the audience has been shown first Brando, manly handsome as a well-built ski instructor, and then Martin, stripped to the waist while being assessed for the draft, displaying an ample chest complete with medallion. The camera then cuts to Noah/Clift in a long shot, getting progressively closer as he meets the draft committee and then Michael/Martin. In contrast with Brando's sportive attire in the snow, and with the seminaked muscularity of Martin and the other men being drafted, Clift is fully dressed, swamped by oversized and unstylish clothes; he had personally chosen these, and his handwritten notes on that scene's wardrobe memo state, "maybe odd pants" then changed to *"very* odd pants."[55] The effect of the extralarge jacket combines with his tense, hunched-up shoulders, giving the impression that he has no neck; more striking than anything, however, is the sight of his extremely protruding ears. Together with his wide-open eyes, at times almost unblinking, his nose changed to no recognition, and his slightly unbalanced gait, Clift makes for very uncomfortable viewing; it is impossible to exaggerate the effect of his appearance and its contrast with the solid virilities of Brando and Martin. As they are being assessed for their fitness to

CHAPTER 4

fight, Noah and Michael are automatically compared, and their shared inclusion in the army is, at this stage of the film, somewhat surprising. When Noah is later introduced to Michael's girlfriend, Margaret, she asks him whether Michael was classified as 1A, the military code for "fit to fight." The script had Noah simply replying in the affirmative, but Clift changed it to "we were both 1A,"[56] as if anticipating that Margaret (and perhaps the audience) may expect him not to be.

The meeting with Michael also establishes Noah's ambiguous sexual credentials; as they leave the draft office together, Michael's head turns in the direction of two passing girls, whom Noah instead ignores. Michael says: "Sometimes I think I give off a scent or something—you know—rouses the female." Noah's spaced-out reply is, "Huh?," making Michael insist, "Those girls!" and quickly conclude: "You are sick." Noah does not defend or explain himself, but when Michael next asks him if he has ever had a girl, he fumbles, nervously laughing and repeating "Have I ever had a girl?" The result is Michael's prompt invitation to a party he is giving, where girls can be found, followed by a firm "Let's not discuss this topic any longer." On one hand, this brief scene presents Noah's indifference toward the opposite sex as caused by inexperience, a solvable problem requiring simply the exposure to a roomful of girls. This is indeed the film's preferred meaning, formalized by Noah's eventual marriage and fatherhood and reinforced by the difference in age between him and Michael: the script describes them respectively as "in his twenties" and "in his thirties."[57] When Hope first tells her father about Noah, she stresses that he is "not just a man—he's a boy." On the other hand, Michael's impression of Noah as "sick" seems disproportionate to his failure to spot two beauties amid New York's crowd and contains a hint of more radical implications. As the film progresses by charting Noah's heterosexual trajectory, connotations of a queer sexuality remain, undeveloped, below the surface of the narrative. His relationship with Hope shows romantic love and tenderness yet exhibits a distinct lack of erotic passion—an ambiguous mixture, prompting Noah to summarize their first date as "a very confusing night—I don't think I've ever been through anything so confusing." On hearing this odd declaration, Hope kisses him, eliciting "I love you, I love you" from Noah, who nevertheless looks completely bewildered. As a man who "is also a boy," Clift here expresses the ambiguity that is

The 1956 Car Accident and a New Queerness

a constant of his star persona; this time, however, his ambiguous image is devoid of any erotic charge, maintaining a mysterious sexual identity that, before 1956, he had only possessed in *The Heiress*. Yet unlike Morris the dandy, Noah/Clift is clearly not presented as an erotic prize, and is emphatically not fashioning himself as one. In the context of *The Young Lions*, Noah's nonnormative sexuality is not only expressed through performance but also signaled by his physical appearance and reinforced by Lange's pretty yet studiously unsexy looks. Together, they make a striking contrast to the film's other main couples. The Brando-Britt and Martin-Rush pairs are not only glamorous but also statuesque; Clift and Lange are small, frail, and very plainly dressed, with Lange's blond hair providing the only spark in their almost severe joint appearance. The sequence in which they meet is cut first with a shot of Martin and Rush, kissing passionately in full evening attire; the film then cuts back to Clift, looking clumsy and nervous as he takes Lange home. The action next moves to Berlin, showing Brando's seduction at the hands of Britt: a lengthy scene highlights the erotic tension between them, showcasing Brando's masculine beauty and Britt's bombshell figure. Oozing sex appeal, and dominating the frame with their powerful physical presence, they are diametrically opposed to Clift and Lange, who of course share no comparable scene. At the film's very beginning, Brando and Rush cavorting in the snow had also exuded erotic vibes; interestingly, the only exception among Brando's voluptuous lovers is Françoise, who is small and average-looking, and who remains an unsexualized fantasy of love. Their union is impossible, and while Françoise's presence emphasizes Christian's redeemable side, the film leaves no doubt that Christian is Brando, a sex symbol and a magnet for glamorous women. As for Noah/Clift, his only passionate scene with Hope takes places as he leaves for the war, and it is not an erotic moment: he squeezes her face hard while kissing her mouth, visibly trying not to cry, giving an impression of frenzied yet nonsexual emotion. This very brief scene also hints at the full revelation of Noah's character, at his physical manifestation of latent feelings. Once he faces bullying in the army, he will turn into a raging figure; his deviant strength will be expressed through the resilience of his waiflike body and the disfigurement endured by his already faintly anomalous face.

The scenes where Noah fights his tormenters are among the film's

CHAPTER 4

most disturbing sights. The notion of someone so frail engaging in a brutal punch-up is unsettling; unlike in *From Here to Eternity*, Clift here lacks both muscles and body weight, and his taking on four burly soldiers looks reckless and unnatural. Indeed, Michael tries hard to dissuade Noah from fighting, calling him crazy, asking him how much he weighs, then starting: "If I were you," but Noah interrupts him: "You're not." Thus changing from wallflower to wild creature, Noah seems to direct an abnormal energy to his body, and while he is viciously beaten in most fights, he credibly wins the last one. When playing Prewitt in *Eternity*, Clift had eventually required a double to do most of his punching, despite weeks of training; in *The Young Lions*, however, he refused a stand-in and was coached by ex-boxing champion Johnny Indrisano. Even so, the fight scenes took four days to film[58] and are very painful to watch; retrospectively, they are only made more disturbing by the knowledge that every punch Clift gives on screen is his own. Wearing a military uniform, more fitted and revealing than his oversized civilian suits, Clift shows most clearly the result of his deliberate self-starving: he looks virtually skeletal, with no recognizable shoulders, chest, or buttocks shaped under his clothes. A physical fraction of every other man on screen, he lacks the obvious signs of bodily masculinity, to say nothing of a soldier's ideal appearance. Despite his unvirile looks, however, Noah/Clift displays a fearless indifference to physical harm; savagely beaten and almost whipped in the air by the others' blows, he seems oblivious to pain, his odd-looking face remaining set to feverish determination. While he appears badly hurt from the first fight, Noah's physical damage is shown in its full extent before his last round; sitting in the doctor's surgery to get his wounds cleaned, he presents his most disturbing look yet. One of his eyes is so swollen it is virtually closed, his mouth is disfigured, and both eyelid and lip are held together with massive stitches; there is a clear resemblance to Frankenstein's monster. His appearance, already self-manipulated to express difference and pain, reaches here a higher stage of alienation; with parts of his face grotesquely emphasized, he acquires a veneer of horror that completes the unnatural feel of his presence. In a film dealing with World War II, it is notable that Clift in this scene, out of active combat, provides the only shocking physical sight. It is true that Maximilian Schell, playing the Nazi Captain Hardenberg, ends up entirely

The 1956 Car Accident and a New Queerness

cast in plaster with only his eyes showing, having lost several limbs; but Schell is literally dehumanized by his plaster entombment, rendered invisible and only nominally himself. Clift, instead, is intensely alive, as well as eerily recognizable, and that is why his appearance is so unsettling. De-naturalizing physical prowess as well as physical norm, the monstricized Clift is calm and unfazed while the doctor treats him, a look entirely at odds with the pain he must feel and the frenzy he shows while fighting; his only comment, or self-explanation, is "I like to fight." Yet when victory comes, Clift again subverts notions of virility through his behavior and appearance. Getting hold of his opponent by encircling his waist with one arm, he furiously hammers punches into him with his free hand; when the other falls down and does not get up, Clift looks around him with a pained and vacant gaze, showing no trace of satisfaction. Framed in a close-up, Clift's thin, almost triangular face is bruised and bloody, edged by his terribly protruding ears; his mouth is ripped, his hair wildly unkempt, his expression uncertain. Staring in apparent disorientation, his eyes are big and wide open, the only beautiful feature in his disturbing image.

Noah's dual status as hero and deviant outsider is emphasized in his last spoken scene, set in the concentration camp he has helped liberate. After entering the camp, Noah is very visibly affected, and Captain Green (Arthur Franz), one of the company's former bullies, tells him to go for a walk outside with Michael. In one of the film's rare acknowledgments of Noah's Jewishness, after the two friends briefly mention the gas chambers, Noah says, "My father's brother died in one of those," adding, "Did I tell you about my father?" But when Michael replies that he didn't, Noah abruptly shifts the subject to the newly rehabilitated Green, who is working to restore dignity to the camp's ex-inmates. "Once this war's over, Green's gonna be running the world," he tells Michael; suddenly, a change comes over him, and he rapidly goes from looking calm to looking beside himself. With a savage countenance to his face, that more readily suggests alienation than hope, Noah shouts: "There are millions of him! They are human beings! They will rule the world! Millions and millions!" His voice is croaky, and his words are accompanied by a violent swinging of his arm in the air; at some point he even beats Michael in the chest with his fist. It is extremely disconcerting behavior, pointing to an alternative system of feeling, to a painful experience that, like the story of his father, he is not expanding upon. Small and skinny next to Michael, with his conspicuous ears sticking out under the army helmet, Noah the outsider, the Jew, the hero, looks decidedly different from everyone else. His words confirm his remoteness: "they" will rule the world, hopefully for the best, but he will not. Opting out of the mainstream, outside the masculine system of power, Noah reclaims an identity away from normative structures; through him, Clift unsettles the norm of the system he himself inhabits, subverting his own image with powerful crip significations.

Shame, Perversion, Unnatural Sex:
Lonelyhearts and *Suddenly, Last Summer*

Montgomery Clift did not repeat the radical self-transformation of *The Young Lions*; his next two roles, in *Lonelyhearts* and *Suddenly, Last Summer*, are not centered on bodily difference, or on the literal distortion of his image. Nevertheless, both narratives are heavily concerned with issues of "normality." As the films' protagonist, Clift is defined by empathy with aberrant social identities, aligned with sexual proclivities and situations deemed abnormal or humiliating. In *Lonelyhearts*, these deviant configurations are also at times linked to physical anomalies, ranging from blindness to disfigurement. While very different in style, the two films present a striking continuity in their articulation of transgression; focusing on difference and unnaturalness, they construct a queer discourse hinging on the subversive reclamation of shame. Through his performance and presence, Clift adds one more layer of ambiguity to intricate plots, where the motivation to do good blurs with the embrace of forbidden morals.

The disruptive relation between queerness and normative ethics has been discussed by Sally R. Munt in *Queer Attachments: The Cultural Politics of Shame*.[59] Referring to the established meaning of perversity as "the intention to wilfully deviate from what is good, proper and reasonable," Munt conceptualizes queer interventions as perverse acts, "reworking of norms, attempts to create livable lives on the wrong side of the blanket."[60] *Lonelyhearts* traces a deliberate journey to the wrong side of normal, driven by the protagonist's effort to revaluate outcast identities. This subversive quest seems doomed to fail in the

The 1956 Car Accident and a New Queerness

film's dominant text, with a plot introducing deviation only to follow it with a panicked return to conformity. Yet despite a heavy normative coating, the film cannot fully contain its subtextual disruption; through Montgomery Clift's character, *Lonelyhearts* intermittently allows the legitimacy of difference by reclaiming perverse configurations as queer attachments.

Based on a novel by Nathanael West, the film sees Clift as Adam White, an idealistic young man thrown in the corrupted world of popular journalism. Almost a Christlike figure, instinctively siding with social misfits, Adam is cast by *The Chronicle* as agony columnist under the pen name of Miss Lonelyhearts; against a cynical work environment headed by the bitter Mr. Shrike (Robert Ryan), Adam is overwhelmed by empathy for his readers. His colleagues are both amused and disgusted by the letters sent to Lonelyhearts, pathetic stories spanning an assortment of human misery: victims of horrific accidents; loners incapable of forming relationships; people marginalized by social transgression, poverty, physical or mental illness. Explicitly or implicitly, the thread linking these lives is a distressing experience of sex, which is either unobtainable or stigmatized. Angered by the sneering attitude of the *Chronicle* staff, Adam is soon consumed by his readers' anguish, feeling that "he would rather die than laugh at them"; sharing their pain as if it were his own, and obsessed by the compulsion to reach out to them, he puts all his energy and time into replying to their letters. This symbiotic approach to his correspondents, whom Shrike defines as "rubbish from the rubble," is also strongly criticized by Adam's girlfriend, Justy (Dolores Hart). A prim young woman living with her father and teenage brothers, Justy clings in equal measure to her squeaky clean lifestyle and her boyfriend, trying to control his altruistic excess. The only person sympathizing with Adam is his boss's wife, Mrs. Shrike (Myrna Loy). An image of suffering herself, being constantly abused by her husband for a past episode of unfaithfulness, she is smitten with Adam and driven to tears by his plight. All the while, Adam is hiding a shameful secret: his father murdered his mother many years before, when he surprised her in bed with another man, and is spending his life in jail. Things come to a head as Shrike defies Adam to meet one of his readers, to put his compassion to the test. Choosing a letter writer at random, Adam contacts Fay Doyle (Maureen Stapleton), who had

CHAPTER 4

described herself as the unhappy wife of a disabled man, and who immediately invites herself to Adam's flat. Unattractive and predatory, Fay has however a suicidal story to tell and breaks down in sobs relating that her husband is impotent, and she has lost the will to go on. Adam tries to comfort her, deeply upset by her suffering, when she suddenly kisses him; he then instantly, irresistibly, kisses her again passionately, as the film cuts on what is clearly a prelude to sex. The next scene sees Adam in a cab next to Fay, who has changed her manner and is openly brash, vulgar, and insistent; Adam looks lost and detached, unwilling to see her again. What follows is Adam's deepening crisis: as he gets drunk for the first time in his life, he is approached by a distressed-looking man (Frank Maxwell), who ignoring Adam's identity reveals himself as Fay's husband. He complains that his wife has written to an agony column, inventing stories about him. Shocked by the encounter and the man's words, Adam moves to the next bar where he finds the *Chronicle* journalists; they greet him by telling jokes about his readers' sexual plights. Outraged by their attitude and completely drunk, Adam hits one of his colleagues. When he is finally nursing his hangover in bed, he is visited by Justy, who breaks off their relationship once he confesses all that happened. The film's climax sees Adam at night in his office, getting ready to leave town; as Justy arrives on the scene wanting to make up, Fay's husband also appears, determined to shoot Adam in revenge for his wife's betrayal. He crumbles, however, letting Adam take his gun off him, and goes home to Fay; Adam and Justy, happily reconciled, go away together. In the empty office, a repentant Mr. Shrike wraps up some flowers to take to his wife.

Adapted by Dore Schary, the *Lonelyhearts* script has none of the savagery of West's original text, which exposes America as an unmitigated hell of corruption, unfit for the protagonist's dream of inclusiveness. The novel also emphasizes Adam's sexual activity, notably through an affair with Mrs. Shrike. But the script's most incongruous change is its happy ending; instead of being killed by Fay's husband, as in West's novel, the visionary Adam is reinstated to the "normality" of life with Justy. These alterations were a great disappointment to Clift, who had read all of West's novels, and for whom Adam's obsessive identification with his readers was "the element which attracted [him] initially—the element he wanted to drown in."[61] Yet despite the script's limitations,

The 1956 Car Accident and a New Queerness

Clift does achieve immersion in his role, lending Adam dramatic pathos through his presence, and a troubling performance centered on the gaze. Still handsome enough to be cast as a leading man, Clift however looks frail and sickly, his eyes reverberating with pain: this appearance informs Adam's descent into people's despair, while complicating his role as sexual adventurer.

Clift's biographers concur on his precarious state of health in *Lonelyhearts*. His consumption of alcohol and assorted pills had reached "unbelievable proportions," making him so fatigued he would forget his lines and fall asleep by 2:00 p.m.; the film crew struggled with his erratic behavior, which included naked night walks he did not remember the next day, while friends simply worried that he might die of an overdose.[62] Ironically, Adam is introduced in the first scene as a nonsmoking teetotaler, and it is to Clift's credit that his reaction to his single drinking episode, a mixture of shock and repulsion, is entirely believable. Yet if Clift successfully conveys naïveté and inexperience, his casting as a man in his twenties only increases the tensions in his image, which the film's narrative brings to the fore. Looking all of his thirty-eight years, with his thin body hunched and his face drawn, Clift does not fit his frequent appellations as "young man" or "little boy blue," or Fay's boast to her husband that her lover is "young and strong." Likewise, though Clift's frequent look of bewilderment suits his role as passive object of desire, it also enhances the ambiguity of his volitional sexual transgression. The encounter with Fay is the only implied sex in the film's diegetic present, and while initiated by her, it is met by Adam's immediate response, pointing to eagerness on his part. At the same time, this is sex wrapped up in his powerful need to give of himself, shifting the focus from eroticism to a self-explaining logic of total availability. Adam's sexual agency is thus both crucial and undeveloped, constructing an ambiguous persona suggestive of a deviant sexuality. Clift's performance hints at erotic feelings for just a few seconds, the screen duration of his passionate kiss with Stapleton; his overall motivation in the film, however, is the implicit validation of sexual outcasts, and his connection to his readers hinges on sexual identification. The multiplicity of Adam's image is completed by the pointedly unsexy glasses Clift wears while typing (anticipating his real-life look a few years later), and by his unflinching referring to himself as "Miss Lonelyhearts." From all these

CHAPTER 4

clashing elements there emerges a triangle of desire, formed by Mrs. Shrike, Justy, and Fay, with Adam at its center. His ambivalent crisscrossing of paths of connection creates the film's structure of meaning, which rests on the social experience of shame.

The subversion of Adam's character is expressed through his multiple rule breakings, which pervert established norms of "normality" and "decency." His first infraction is to disobey the law of popularly sanctioned journalism, which prescribes both emotional detachment and moralistic judgment. He instead desperately connects to his readers' pain and to the shame of social deviancy his job is meant to exploit; while his colleagues delight in people's disgrace, Adam's immersion in it smashes the boundaries of propriety, as his empathic kindness turns into the sharing of perversion. Of course, Adam is no stranger to shame, as his parents' secret is both sexual and criminal; his bond to the Lonelyhearts readers, however, is crystallized by having sex with Fay, an "unnatural" act taking place in a forbidden context. The adulterous side of this sexual encounter, which befits the film's emphasis on women betraying their husbands, is in fact a minor factor in its perversity. The shameful connotations of Adam's escapade stem from Fay's pariah quality: she is an overweight, loutish woman from an inferior class stratum, who breaches standards of dignity by parading her sexual misery to a stranger. As a contemporary reviewer put it, Fay is presented as "pitiable but repellent,"[63] yet Adam is seduced by her on the spot. To the humiliation of sex with a socially repulsive partner, the protagonist adds a more unsettling quality, the symbiotic and nonsexual trigger of his action. Adam makes love with Fay because he is indiscriminately available, because the excess of his empathy has wiped out the specifics of choice; doubly subverting normative patterns, his act takes place in a framework of boundless yet generic compassion. At the same time, Adam has sex with Fay because he wants to, as he will himself confirm afterward: he is satisfying his need for a sexual meeting that, contrary to Fay's later expectations, suffices to itself and is not classifiable. An attraction where erotic pleasure is born out of pity and emotional pain, this socially inexplicable event is, on Adam's part, a queer attachment based on the free exchange of bodies. As Patricia MacCormack argues, queerness posits the liberation from traditionally meaningful sex, always tied to the logic of profitable erotic

The 1956 Car Accident and a New Queerness

expenditure; embracing perversity instead, queer interaction does not seek "a pay-off object such as orgasm or partner," as queer seduction aims "to create a unique hybrid beyond any sexual narrative."[64] Adam's acceptance of Fay's seduction falls in this queer rubric, unfettered by standards of attractiveness, relationship patterns, or the avoidance of social disgrace. The "unique hybridity" he seeks presupposes the loss of boundaries in a sexually and socially ambiguous context where, as he will firmly admit to Fay's husband, he *is* Miss Lonelyhearts.

In order to better understand the queer implications of Adam's conduct, it is important to consider the disruptive potential of shame. The social ignominy ascribed to deviancy, according to Sally R. Munt, belies a "queer latency," an inherently possible radical outcome. By evoking a divide between norm and subversion, shame can effectively enable the reclamation of difference. Munt calls it "a separation between the social convention demarcated within hegemonic ideals" and distinguishes between guilt and shame: while feeling guilty means to believe one has done wrong, feeling ashamed is the experience of disgrace caused by the breaking of social laws.[65] Although often merged together, guilt and shame are not equally useful in the assertion of transgression, and it is shame that Munt sees as contributing to identity formation. As a practical illustration of her thesis, Munt refers to Charles Darwin's work on the effects of shameful feelings, where he describes the visible break in connection separating ashamed individuals from the defied social order. Darwin observes that "an ashamed person can hardly endure to meet the gaze of those present, so that almost invariably casts down his eyes or looks askant."[66] As Munt argues, this averting of the gaze effects and reflects a rupture, the potential affirmation of a distinct queer identity. Shame, therefore, can lead to queer outcomes in two ways: on one hand, the disconnection it causes entails the prospect of a new, oppositional configuration. On the other hand, shame may instead be shared between individuals, leading to queer bonds centered on the recognition of joint difference. *Lonelyhearts* articulates its queer discourse through Adam's relation to a structure of shame, as he forms, breaks, and reestablishes key belongings at both ends of the "normal" spectrum. Because Clift's performance highlights nonverbal communication, especially by his use of the gaze, a close reading of crucial scenes reveals the enactment of alignments and separations.

CHAPTER 4

Adam's route in and out of perversity is chiefly shown through his interaction with Fay and Justy, polar opposites signifying incompatible moral registers; between the two camps is the fallen woman Mrs. Shrike, equally partial to Adam's good looks and his compassionate zeal. The shadowy world of *The Chronicle*, including its staff's corrupted worldview as much as its readers' transgressions, stands in opposition to natural, healthy living, as hinted by the film's beginning. As the initial credits roll on the screen, the camera shows assorted scenes from the town's main thoroughfares, presenting a clean-looking America cheerfully going about its business. This view changes suddenly when Adam appears, walking into a dingy side alley, then entering a dimly lit bar frequented by journalists, where Mrs. Shrike is drinking alone; they sit together, waiting for her husband to arrive to discuss a job for Adam. The narrative then moves forward to Adam's increasingly ambiguous position, pulled between empathic suffering for his readers and the normative demands of life near Justy. All the while, the plot has been building toward his encounter with Fay, the film's pivotal moment and the concretization of Adam's perversity. In her first-ever screen appearance, Stapleton is breathtaking as the needy, manipulative woman who turns up at Lonelyhearts' place; the powerful chemistry between her and Clift is evident, as their different styles complement each other's in an unrelenting connection. Far from effecting a separation, the inherent disgrace of Fay's meeting with Adam cements their shared deviancy, aiding a queer alliance ratified by their gaze. The scene starts with Adam walking firmly to the door, to let Fay inside; she greets him as "Mr. Lonelyhearts" yet appears hesitant, lingering on the threshold in acute embarrassment. As she nervously mentions the impropriety of the situation, Adam's eye contact with her is rock steady, remaining so after she explicitly says she is ashamed. Utterly focused on her, he asks her if she still wants to proceed with their talk, to which she greedily answers that she does, as only he can hear her story. She begins a hysterical tale of sexual unhappiness, breaking and reestablishing their eye connection as if to test Adam's involvement, and his permission to humiliate herself. His look, however, is so intensely fixed on her he hardly blinks. Fay's admission of shame to Adam is effectively a self-description, causing a separation not between them, but rather between both of them and the established social system. Adam,

The 1956 Car Accident and a New Queerness

who has shifted his empathy from anonymity to a real-life exchange, now entirely shares her shameful identity; he acknowledges this by his attitude of total immersion, forging an intimate bond through their mutual distance from normality. Clift's performance seals Adam's commitment to Fay's world of shame. Even when he gets up and briefly moves away, to ease Fay's intense mortification, he then irresistibly looks back at her; walking around her in circles as she talks, he appears deeply absorbed by what he hears, moving very close to her when she starts crying. He first places a hand on her shoulder, next he kneels on the floor at her feet with his arms on her lap and waist; he has thus eliminated most of the physical distance between them and is staring intensely into her eyes. Fay pleads, "Tell me what to do," and he replies, "I don't know, I don't know"; they stand up again, now shot in a profile close-up, as she suddenly says, "Softly just once, let me feel your lips." Clift does not stir or say a word, his eyes glued to hers as she touches his mouth with her fingers; after she kisses him, his only reaction is to visibly gulp, suggesting both shock and arousal, and a stunned concentration. She says slowly, "You are a gentle . . . man," and they kiss again, as he grabs her passionately in a tight embrace.

The abnormality of Adam's meeting with Fay is completed by its reversal of established gender patterns: against traditional male behavior, he does not instigate sex, responding instead to her need with emotional and physical empathy. The disruptive quality of their encounter, however, is short-lived, as Fay breaks their queer bond with a violent switch to convention. Once Adam takes her home, she drops shame and pathos to become ordinarily rapacious, trying to lock him in a predictable affair he does not want; the troubled alienation she triggers in him is again visible in Clift's use of his eyes. He first looks at her steadily, but as her pushy vulgarity increases he averts his gaze, looking down in obvious humiliation; this time his shame separates them, marking their diverging identities and relation to established social mores. Fay tells him angrily: "You're not a very appreciative fellow. Love 'em and leave 'em, is that it?," to which he replies with effort, "Mrs. Doyle, I didn't call you . . ." But she bursts out: "All right, what did you call me up for? Who are you kidding? Listen, you wanted a sad story, you heard a sad story! You also wanted some action! And so did I!" The original script ended their dialogue here, but Clift added Adam's reply, "You're right,"

CHAPTER 4

Adam is first perfectly still as Fay advances toward him...

...but then he kisses her back with passion.

The 1956 Car Accident and a New Queerness

and Fay's last shot: "You're damn right I'm right!"⁶⁷ Clift's additions emphasize Adam's awareness of his idiosyncratic desire, and of its inevitable reduction to the banality of a selfish man seducing a woman. Imposing her normative narrative on his perversity, Fay is shifting onto everyday territory, denying their queer attachment by demanding "a pay-off object": sex ought to lead to more sex, and to a commonly illicit relationship. Adam's feeling of shame is caused by her breach of their unspoken contract, by the discovery that she exploited suffering for conventional ends. When he later tells Shrike that Fay is "a fraud," he means she is not the aberrant individual she made him suppose; just as importantly, her emotional dishonesty has tainted him too. "People are fakes and frauds—and you know what—I lead the parade," he says in anguish; it is now that Adam admits to feeling the "iron grip" of guilt, for the first and only time in the film. The reasons for his guilt, however, remain unsaid and unclear, casting more ambiguity on his eventual return to Justy. There is a sense that Adam's remorse is centered on his self-betrayal, on his wildly misplaced compassion; even when confronting Justy he will express shame rather than guilt, with no admission of wrongdoing in his encounter with Fay. Adam's oblique relation to normative ethics is confirmed by his words to Shrike, when he tells him: "All I want to do is to heal a wound I gave to myself—before it festers." It is Adam's unorthodox belief system that has been ruptured, and while he clearly wishes to be with Justy, he is not denying his identification with the Lonelyhearts world. Indeed, as much as Fay is part of the queer connections he pursued through his column, Adam's alignment with his deviant readers is unbroken; his raging attack on his colleague, in the bar, leaves no doubt as to whose side he is on. Although he expresses deep regret at having hit a man, he is obviously repelled by what the journalist represents. Adam's emotional clinging to his readers is a reaffirmation of queerness, as is his admission that he wanted to have sex with Fay. In her account of the dynamics of shame, Munt claims that "shame may be relinquished *reluctantly*" (Munt's emphasis),⁶⁸ being often a source of pleasure and fulfillment. While Munt explicitly refers to sadomasochistic practices, her point is equally applicable to the rest of her argument: if shame can lead to self-affirmation, then its relinquishment would entail a very unpleasant identity loss. In *Lonelyhearts*, Clift/Adam never lets go of his shameful yet gratifying

CHAPTER 4

associations, as shown by his anger at his colleagues and by his changes to the script. As well as the addition of "You're right" to Fay's claim that he was eager for sex with her, Clift also altered his lines in the film's last scene, the confrontation with Fay's husband. Stressing his personal investment in their sexual encounter, Clift adds: "I met her because she asked to see me, she stayed—I wanted her to stay—I asked her to stay," later slightly changed to "I met her because she asked to see me. I asked her to stay. She stayed. I wanted her to stay."[69]

Adam's self-definition through the power of shame, however, is most obvious in another key scene, his meeting with Justy after the Fay interlude. Here Adam/Clift lies in bed feeling ill, as Justy arrives and stands at some distance from him; he looks upset and distant, making no attempt at physical contact. When she asks him why he disappeared for two days, his reaction is overwhelming shame: he averts his gaze from hers, then pointedly raises an arm to cover his face, remaining in that position. The camera frames him in medium close-up, so that his arm over his eyes is the most prominent feature on screen; almost entirely hidden from view, Clift slowly says, "I didn't call . . . because I was ashamed to call you." He then takes his arm off his face, making sporadic eye contact with Justy while he mentions his drinking, and his fight with a colleague, but as he prepares to tell about Fay, he looks away again, saying "Not only that . . . ," turning his whole face toward the opposite side of the room. "A woman," prompts Justy, to which his only reply is to keep looking away, not speaking to her; his silent admission highlights a severe break in connection, an ashamed separation from Justy and the normative values she stands for. The radical potential of this moment, however, is quickly reined in by the film, which next sees Shrike's arrival and Justy's departure, with Adam running after her; the following scene shows him going to great efforts to see her again. It is notable that Justy is the only main character immune from shame and the only woman in the film who has not committed adultery; as Adam's empathy is directed to Fay, to Mrs. Shrike, and to his own dead mother, who have all betrayed their husbands, Justy poignantly marks the field of normality and decency. Yet while Adam constantly oversteps this field, the limits of his transgression remain undefined as he maintains an essential ambiguity until the very end. In the last scene, surrounded by Fay's husband, Justy, and Mr. Shrike, he is quick to own his perverse identity; he not only stresses he wanted Fay, he also firmly tells her husband, "I'm Miss Lonelyhearts." At the same time, he has just reconciled himself with Justy and is about to leave with her, in plain commitment to a life "on the right side of the blanket." Still, when the husband demands to know if Adam will see Fay again, Clift closes his eyes, without speaking, slowly shaking his head in the negative; it is a strangely muted reply at this crucial moment, suggesting again shame and its latent possibilities. Munt notes how shame can be sometimes turned into pride, providing an identity model based on the strict opposition of ashamed and proud;[70] this neat binarism, however, is strikingly absent in Lonelyhearts. Clift/Adam retains at all times a distance from pride, while navigating seemingly oppositional fields; such ambiguity is completely in line with Clift's star persona and a truer expression of queerness than an identity based on exclusion. Montgomery Clift saw Adam White as a fractured personality, a man often steered by another self inside him;[71] this fracture comes across as multiplicity through his performance, as a dualistic nature negotiating belongings in excess of his own division, open to the unforeseeable possibilities of queer.

A 1959 poster for *Suddenly, Last Summer* shows Elizabeth Taylor on a beach, kneeling on the sand; stunningly sexy in a flesh-revealing swimsuit, she is looking up with a troubled expression. A menacing bird is hovering above her, and at the top of the poster her face is shown again, next to costars Montgomery Clift and Katharine Hepburn; the huge caption warns, "These are powers and passions without precedent in motion pictures!" Locating a heavily eroticized Taylor at the core of a disturbing narrative, these images were matched by reviews asking of her character, "Was she mad, or was her shame more horrible?,"[72] while the film's trailer promised to show "a woman's strong wants and a man's strange needs" in its adaptation of "the world's most provocative play." Such lurid implications in the film's publicity greatly contributed to its box-office success; the "shame" at the heart of the plot, however, visualized on the posters by Taylor's sexual allure, was more complex and sensational than her image alone could suggest. Tennessee Williams had converted for the screen his original one-act play, arguably his most deliriously brilliant, a story crammed with thinly veiled allusions to homosexuality, sodomy, rape, incest, and cannibalism; Gore Vidal collaborated on the script, which was granted a special license from the Motion Picture Production Code Office. The reason for the censors' lenience was their belief that the film, despite its controversial content, expressed unconditional revulsion for the aberrations it depicted; while it is hard not to ascribe this view to a certain degree of self-delusion, a literal reading of *Suddenly, Last Summer* confirms its apparent exposure of the horrors of sexual deviation. The film is haunted by a never-seen but much-described figure, the implicitly gay Sebastian Venable, who meets a monstrous death as a consequence of his sexuality; along the way, he also inflicts tragedy and grief to those near him. Yet against this surface normative plot, the film's subtext plays subversively with notions of sanity and perversion, producing a parallel narrative that turns "normality" upside down. As in *Lonelyhearts*, shameful secrets are reclaimed and queer identities are validated. If Elizabeth Taylor's character, Catherine, is central to the film, it is Montgomery Clift who directs textual and subtextual developments in his role as Dr. Cukrowicz. In *Lonelyhearts*, Clift/Adam was swept away by emphatic queer self-sacrifice, and by the very events he triggered; as Dr. Cukrowicz, Clift possesses instead authority and control, engineering the "coming out" of closeted narratives against an oppressive dominant context. Clift's motivating agency is all the more remarkable in the light of his performance, the most outwardly passive and verbally spare of his career. In this film Clift speaks even less than he does in *I Confess*; this is partly due to his lines being cut by director Joseph Mankiewicz, when he found that the heavily drugged-up Clift could not remember them.[73] Yet at the same time, the role of Dr. Cukrowicz is essentially one of measured, poignantly quiet interventions, demanding a maximum of active listening and understated command, qualities that Clift exhibits in abundance. Despite an all-time low in his psychological and physical health, he gives an arresting performance that catalyzes the film's development; his scenes with Katharine Hepburn are layered with signification, but his strong chemistry with Elizabeth Taylor literally creates the film. In the role of intuitive facilitator, Clift assists the flow of communication between them, giving rise to a privileged level of meaning; in tune with each other's performance and linked by emphatic complicity, Clift and Taylor weave a queer web that structures *Suddenly, Last Summer*.

The 1956 Car Accident and a New Queerness

The film is set in New Orleans in 1937, where the brilliant neurosurgeon Dr. John Cukrowicz works at the chronically underfunded state asylum for the insane. Frustrated by the place's primitive equipment and conditions, he is about to return to his native Chicago when the asylum is offered a huge sum of money by Mrs. Violet Venable (Katharine Hepburn), a wealthy local widow. Mrs. Venable's offer, however, is conditional to Dr. Cukrowicz performing his specialty, lobotomy, on her niece Catherine Holly (Elizabeth Taylor), who allegedly went insane the previous summer. Hospitalized ever since, she has lost her memory and is classified as violent. Strongly pressured by the asylum director, Dr. Hockstader (Albert Dekker) to comply with Mrs. Venable's request, Dr. Cukrowicz however waits. From his first meeting with Catherine he suspects she has suffered a terrible trauma, and that in order to get better she needs to remember, not to be lobotomized. Meantime, the bizarre Mrs. Venable, who grows carnivorous plants and claims her dead son Sebastian saw the face of God, tells Dr. Cukrowicz that she sees herself as Sebastian's widow because of the perfect love that united them. She reveals that her son died in Catherine's company, when the two were in Spain the previous summer; in fact, the girl's insanity dates from the day of her cousin's death, ascribed to a heart attack by the local authorities. Realizing that Catherine was declared insane because she spread "unspeakable" rumors about Sebastian, Dr. Cukrowicz sets out to discover what happened during their summer together; Catherine, however, cannot remember. While Mrs. Venable hinders his efforts, the doctor soon develops a close relationship with Catherine; against the asylum's rules, his unorthodox treatment for her consists in unlimited sympathy, removal from the patients' ward into the nurses' wing, and the permission to smoke and wear her own clothes. All the while, Dr. Cukrowicz is focused on Catherine's fragmented memories as an unsettling picture begins to emerge: she tells how Sebastian used both her and his mother as bait to procure himself "contacts" when traveling, and admits that she loved her cousin although he could not return her feelings. She also reveals that prior to their summer abroad, she was raped at the Madrigal's ball and plunged into a severe depression as a result. Catherine's rape is confirmed but dismissed by her family, who are united in pressing the doctor to lobotomize her; indeed, Catherine's mother and brother (Mercedes Mc-

CHAPTER 4

Cambridge and Gary Raymond) are impatient for the money promised to them by Mrs. Venable, which is conditional to Catherine's operation. Increasingly protective of his patient, Dr. Cukrowicz does not operate, requesting instead a meeting in the Venables' house garden, which was Sebastian's favorite place. He hopes that there Catherine will recall the whole truth. He prepares her for this ordeal with a sedative injection and asks her to trust him; she responds by kissing him passionately and follows him into the garden where her family and Dr. Hockstader are waiting. In a dramatic crescendo of emotion, Catherine at last retraces the events of the previous summer, with the doctor prompting and reassuring her at every step. She tells how Sebastian forced her to wear a see-through swimsuit in Spain, so that she could attract young men and then deliver them to him; once he grew tired of the local flavor he planned to go north, seeking a diversion in blond men. Before they could leave, however, one day they were surrounded by a large gang of boys, hostile and threatening; the boys made a terrifying noise with primitive musical instruments, prompting Sebastian to flee in panic. He fled in vain, as the evil-looking crowd raced him to the top of a hill, when they attacked him in front of the horrified Catherine; Sebastian disappeared from view, submerged by the raging, animalistic mob. When she finally reached him, he lay dead and naked on the ground, with parts of his body missing; it looked as if he had been eaten. By this point in her narration Catherine is screaming in cathartic grief, while Mrs. Venable, her mind clearly gone, serenely addresses Dr. Cukrowicz as Sebastian, and rambles on about their life together. The doctor does not contradict Mrs. Venable and sees her off indoors; as the rest of the company, deeply shocked, follow them inside, Catherine is left alone in the garden. Not for long, however, as Dr. Cukrowicz quickly returns for her, anxiously checking how she feels. She smiles at him with relief, and holding hands they go back to the house.

With its evocation of apocalyptic horror linked to barely disguised homosexuality, and to hints that Sebastian might have participated in incest and even child abuse, *Suddenly, Last Summer* packs this overt narrative with the supposed terrors of sexual deviation. As the film unfolds, however, the uncovering of Catherine's truth complicates the aberrations it supposedly denounces; the identities of both cousins are freed from oppressive representations, de-naturalizing the system of

The 1956 Car Accident and a New Queerness

meaning that held them captive. If the film's initial motivation rests on the unutterable nature of Sebastian's sexuality, the recovery of queer shame unmasks a coercive, homophobically driven depiction: the casting of Catherine as a lunatic to be silenced, and of Sebastian as both a gay monster and the lover of his castrating mother. The climax of Catherine's grief-ridden narration shows the real horror of Sebastian's death, which lies not in his queerness but in his murder by a homophobic crowd; likewise, Mrs. Venable's hiding of her son's sexuality confirms her as the film's genuine monster, the planner of Catherine's virtual obliteration. In his quest for the truth, Dr. Cukrowicz subverts established morality and patriarchal medical power, liberating shame from its destructive function and making insanity and sanity swap places. If Catherine's testimony is the key to the film's queer disruption of the "norm," Dr. Cukrowicz provides the agency that makes disruption possible; aligned with Catherine's repressed desire to speak the unspeakable, he implicitly empathizes with her shameful connections, acknowledging her complicity in Sebastian's lifestyle and her unrequited desire for him. By leading Catherine and the dead Sebastian out of their closets, Cukrowicz/Clift is the master of a complex queer discourse, channeled through a "cure" that allows perversity and shame without judgment.

Befitting the film's dualistic structure of overt normativity and subtextual deviation, Clift's queer intervention rests on parallel planes of ambiguity. As Dr. Cukrowicz, he is obliquely inserted in the sanitizing, normalizing system threatening Catherine; while his first appearance on screen sees him perform a lobotomy, he soon breaches psychiatric conventions, placing his medical authority on the side of social transgression. Introduced by the film as a leading light in neurosurgery, the doctor is curiously skeptical about his own field. When Mrs. Venable enthuses about the healing powers of lobotomy, he is quick to express doubts on the operation's lasting benefits, and to point out his extreme caution in using it. On being told that Catherine's diagnosis is "dementia praecox," he retorts that the term is "meaningless," an assessment he will later amplify in conversation with Catherine: "Insane is such a meaningless term." From the very beginning, the film's visual text anticipates a rift between the asylum's archaic system and the doctor's enlightened compassion, suggesting that he is upsetting the status quo

CHAPTER 4

from the inside. The building that hides Catherine's shame is a veritable closet, as well as a place of horrors. As the initial credits roll on, the camera shows a seemingly endless brick wall, entirely filling the frame, bearing a plaque announcing "Lion's View-State Asylum for the Insane." A cut to the interior reveals a Victorian-like dungeon, where distressed female patients offer a sight of gruesome desolation; next, the visibly frustrated Cukrowicz/Clift is shown in a decaying operating theater surrounded by failing electricity and crumbling plasterwork. Clift wears a surgical mask throughout the scene, but his darting eyes and irritable manners express conflict. The film's spoken narrative aids the doctor's status as insider-outsider: he is presented to medical students as a specialist from Chicago, and his first words are a venting of anger at the primitive conditions around him. Indeed, in his outrage he tells Dr. Hockstader that he intends to return to Chicago; this challenge to the asylum's director will be followed by clashes over Catherine's treatment, as Hockstader will disparage Cukrowicz's methods as "unorthodox" and "not a lot to do with neurosurgery." As a lobotomy expert who saves an unruly woman from lobotomy, allowing her instead to reveal and mourn her relationship with a gay man, the doctor holds a contained yet subversive power; his presence means controlled sabotage to the machinery of propriety, decency, and normality.

However, if the medical ambivalence of Cukrowicz/Clift helps to validate queer identities, his disruptive relation to heteronormativity rests on his own characterization. Clift's appearance and performance, untypically masculine and sexually ambiguous, unsettle the patriarchal connotations of his role; Cukrowicz's often-noted resemblance to Sebastian, from the same blue eyes to a preference for the same chair, to Mrs. Venable's final blurring of the two, casts further doubt on his "normality." Because his rescue of Catherine rests on his transgressive relation to the film's main axes—pathology, sexuality, and the aberrant Sebastian—Cukrowicz/Clift emerges as the only viable, yet deviant, alternative to oppressive male identifications. Against the chauvinistic Dr. Hockstader, Catherine's unseen rapist, her greedy brother, and the homophobic representations affixed to her cousin, the doctor stands by the heroine in a queer alliance; their relationship de-naturalizes heterosexuality and horror at the same time.

The interaction between Dr. Cukrowicz and Catherine is shown,

The 1956 Car Accident and a New Queerness

from the very beginning, to go well beyond traditional doctor-patient relations. A few minutes into their first meeting, he breaks hospital regulations by allowing Catherine to smoke; later he expels the presiding nun from the room, while holding the distressed Catherine in his arms. The ritual giving of cigarettes is a symbol of the doctor's closeness to his patient, and of their shared defiance of orthodoxy; he offers her a smoke whenever they meet, even giving her his own cigarette packet, and ensuring she has tobacco handy if she is particularly upset. When Catherine's mother and brother come to visit, Dr. Cukrowicz's first move is to rush to light Catherine a cigarette, oblivious to her family to whom he does not offer any; his frequent eye contact with her, over and above what is being said in the room, strengthens the feeling that they share an intimate world, inaccessible to the others. Clift's performance is key to their wordless communication: if his face looks tense and still in this film, at times almost ravaged by the effects of substance abuse, his remarkably eloquent eyes take center stage, expressing a powerful range of insights and emotions. Cukrowicz/Clift looks at Catherine/Taylor with total absorption, his expression rapidly shifting in response to her every word and mood; his gaze is empathic to the point of pain, but also quickly alerted by any new meaning in Catherine's story, any possible clue to the cause of her suffering. Clift obviously felt that his character was linked to Taylor's by a privileged knowledge. In his copy of the script, next to a scene with Catherine's family where he exchanges no words with her, he writes, "C & C eyes lock" and draws a shut padlock and a key on the page.[74] As it already happened in *Raintree County*, there is a tension in *Suddenly, Last Summer* between Clift's vulnerable, wasted-looking appearance and his reassuring authority over a helpless, hysterical Taylor; even more than in *Raintree County*, however, Clift's role is complicated by his sexual ambiguity, as he allows Catherine's advances without either rejecting or reciprocating them. Dr. Cukrowicz is an object of desire for both Catherine and her aunt, who throughout the film attempt to eroticize him. However, while Mrs. Venable often touches him and flirts with him, her efforts remain self-contained, as she never connects to the doctor; Catherine, on the other hand, shows a strong passion for him through her frenzied kisses and expresses her feelings in the context of their mutual liking. "Hold me, hold me," she tells him, "I've been so lonely,"

167

CHAPTER 4

Dr. Cukrowicz is utterly focused on his patient Catherine.

and hold her he certainly does, yet without any obvious erotic involvement. While physically affectionate toward her, and never surprised or put off by her desire, Clift is once again sexually uncommitted to the beautiful woman he is paired with. When Catherine impulsively kisses him for the first time, she immediately worries: "Oh, I shouldn't have done that"; totally unfazed, Dr. Cukrowicz casually remarks: "Why not? It was a friendly kiss, wasn't it?"—a cryptic comment unlikely to lead to their jumping into bed together. In the final sequence, when Catherine frantically embraces the doctor and covers him in kisses, the script's directions for Cukrowicz are: "For a moment he wavers; then he responds with equal intensity."[75] Clift, however, does nothing of the sort; he lets himself be kissed, holding her close even as Dr. Hockstader interrupts them, yet without exuding clear erotic interest.

The sexual ambiguity Clift brings to his role is further complicated by other meanings, associated to him and Taylor both together and individually. By 1959, any intimate scene between them would be laden with associations: it would first conjure up the media speculation on their relationship and impending marriage, which had continued on and off since their joint appearance at *The Heiress* premiere, in 1949. Another, equally powerful reference was their iconic love story in *A Place in the Sun*; as D. A. Miller comments, "the very alignment of the stars would bring this couple under the sway of romance."[76] At the same time, Montgomery Clift was still a bachelor as he approached his forties, and his aura of sexual uncertainty had only increased with time. In September 1959, three months before the release of *Suddenly, Last Summer*, a fire broke out at his New York home, and firemen surprised him in bed with his male lover; the incident made front-page news the next day, with reports of Clift having been with an "unidentified male companion."[77] Elizabeth Taylor, on the other hand, was an undisputed symbol of heterosexual appeal, yet in the film she is closely associated with queer men and their narratives,[78] causing an indefinite suspension, a nondevelopment of her erotic image in favor of ambiguous but strongly felt attachments.

The conflicting meanings attached to Clift and Taylor strengthen the film's uncertainty over the Cukrowicz-Catherine coupling, increasing the de-normalization of male heterosexuality. By siding with Catherine and helping her to remember, the doctor brings to light her rape by a married man and the devastation it caused to her life, yet unlike every issue connected to Sebastian, this horrific event is treated by Catherine's family with complete indifference. The exposure of Catherine's dual ordeal, her rape and the lack of importance ascribed to it, points to the potential horror of normative male sexuality and to the complicity of the social order in its lethal deployment. Similarly, Catherine's first diagnosis of insanity was reinforced by allegations that she had sexually harassed the asylum's gardener. Dr. Cukrowicz argues that, on the contrary, the man had molested Catherine and then lied about it. Heterosexual horror is visibly represented in a scene when Catherine, walking through the asylum at random, accidentally enters the men's section; she looks down from the gallery into a pit of lecherous, ferocious-looking patients, who violently attempt to grab her legs through the railings. The asylum's authorities will later describe the episode as "a riot" and will implicitly blame it on Catherine for exciting the men with her presence. Male heterosexual desire, and its personal and social consequences for the heroine, is thus cast in a wholly terrifying light; conversely, the sexually ambiguous closeness of Dr. Cukrowicz is literally life saving. The uncovering of a positive queer narrative, partly resting on the doctor's relation to Catherine and Sebastian, also gradually redeems Sebastian from his casting as a villain; in another striking resemblance to Cukrowicz, he is described by Catherine as "bringing

CHAPTER 4

her back to life" by taking her abroad after her rape ordeal. Indeed, Catherine claims that Sebastian was essentially "gentle and kind," again an apt definition for the doctor himself. However, it is the truth about Sebastian's death, the climax the film's plot has been inexorably leading to, that ultimately frees him and Catherine from homophobic silence and pathologized representation.

The narration of what happened the previous summer, told by Catherine with the doctor's assistance, seems to initially coat its drama in a veneer of queer horror. Catherine's account of her exploitation by Sebastian, of his capricious attitude, and of his forcing the see-through swimsuit on her for his own sexual ends, conveys a strong sense of cruel selfishness; similarly, his abominable death suggests not only the revenge of the boys he used but also a repulsive queer cauldron in which like kills like. Yet at the same time, the vicious nature of Sebastian's conduct is never ascertained; there is no clue that the boys he lured were minors, or that they were coerced into sex, or even that they were involved in sex at all. As for Sebastian's recourse to a female decoy to attract them, it seems plausibly the result of social prohibitions, of his having to hide his shameful identity. In the documentary *The Celluloid Closet*, the scene of Sebastian's chase by the gang of boys is compared to that of Frankenstein's monster fleeing his killers: it is a strikingly effective comparison, but its power lies in the perception of both "monsters" as hunted victims. This meaning is latent in the film's visual rendition of Sebastian's death, when his frail arm and hand emerge from under the mass of his attackers, in a last, vain gasp for life; even more poignantly, Catherine's grief-stricken narration, mixing sobs and tears with horrified screams, suggests her enduring love for her cousin. Given that Catherine has been the focus of audience identification throughout the film, her mourning for Sebastian disrupts his representation as a monster, shifting the horror onto his murderers. It is notable that Elizabeth Taylor saw this scene as one of devastating loss: she played it by summoning up her grief for the recent death of her husband, Mike Todd, killed in a plane crash.[79] Sebastian's murder thus highlights his being undeserving of such horror while showing his lasting place in Catherine's affections; it also clarifies that her mental breakdown was not caused by his sexual activities, which she had known all

The 1956 Car Accident and a New Queerness

along, but by witnessing his barbaric and probably homophobic killing. Sebastian's death has the sacrificial value of purging him not of his queerness but of his superimposed identity as a queer monster; this is crucially helped by Dr. Cukrowicz's nonjudgmental stance about him, effectively bringing him back from demonization to normality. At the same time, the circumstances of his death reinscribe Catherine's cousin in a very queer narrative, counter to both homophobic queer horror and patriarchal values.

Some of the scholarship produced on *Suddenly, Last Summer* appears obsessed with spotting allegories of sodomy in the film. Kevin Ohi sees lobotomy as a "sodomitical reenactment" as it consists in "boring a hole into the skull," and suggests that the very first scene, in which a railing in the medical students' gallery breaks down, places audiences in uncomfortable alignment with the operating table below, the lobotomy taking place on it, and thus the act of being sodomized.[80] D. A. Miller argues that the gorgeous sight of Elizabeth Taylor on the beach, kneeling down in her scanty swimsuit, is really drawing attention to the imagined male buttocks of a gay fantasy, as her breasts are nothing but a "mimicking" of the "original, but outlawed offer" of sodomy.[81] The usefulness of such creative musings is questionable, as the film's obvious symbol of literal, gay sexual consummation coincides with its most crucial piece of information: Sebastian was brutally killed in an act of cannibalism. As Ohi rightly mentions, sodomy and cannibalism are related not only by being infractions of established laws, but especially by their "nonregenerative, self-consuming, and self-reflexive" nature.[82] To be eaten and to be sodomized are both passive acts, and their overlapping meanings in Sebastian's death point to his being raped before being killed. As the implicit stage of his killing is a sexual act willingly and pleasurably undertaken by gay men, the sacrificial value of Sebastian's death confirms his sexual identity yet redefines it, revealing him as a gay martyr while separating him from his monstrous killers.

Sebastian's queer recuperation through sodomitic death can be usefully framed by Leo Bersani's classic text, his discussion of homophobic narratives in *Is the Rectum a Grave?*[83] Bersani argues that the AIDS crisis crystallized a series of well-established representations of gay men, based on notions of male-to-male sex as sick, contagious, and potentially homicidal. Crucially, these images relied on ideas of homosexuality as perversely unmanly, through its relation to a passive sexual role that ought to have been the exclusive (and compulsory) domain of women. Writing in the mid-1980s at the height of the AIDS tragedy in the West, Bersani asks if the homophobic hysteria generated by the HIV virus has indeed made "the rectum a grave" and concludes that the discourses pertaining to male anal sex have the potential for non-patriarchal, queer-affirming identifications. Advocating the subversive celebration of "abnormal" male passivity, he writes that if the association with shameful nonvirility turns the rectum into "the grave in which the masculine ideal (an ideal shared—differently—by men and women) of proud subjectivity is buried, then it should be celebrated for its very potential for death."[84] Applied to the conflicting representations of homosexuality in *Suddenly, Last Summer*, Bersani's theory shows how Sebastian's death undergoes a positive transformation thanks to Dr. Cukrowicz's exposure of the "cannibalism" hidden by the alleged heart attack. Through his homosexual and homophobic murder, Sebastian is not only victimized but also feminized; he is associated with a passive sexual role both in life and death, and thus further linked to Catherine, the female coprotagonist of his queer existence and the other rape victim in the film. The associations brought forth by his murder shatter his homophobically determined identity, what Bersani calls "the murderous judgment" against gay men;[85] they also blot out Sebastian's connotations of patriarchal mastery over weaker others, be they men or women, as well his mother's reinvention of him as her straight, Oedipal partner. While Sebastian's sexual preference may have been his own, well-deserved grave in the eyes of the Catholic Legion of Decency, who supported the censors' passing of the film, it becomes instead the burial of his fictional self, freeing him from oppressive identifications. In other words, Catherine and Dr. Cukrowicz kill the illusory Sebastian by allowing the truth about his death. As he now only lives in representation and memory, Catherine's final speech validates his recuperation. This speech, however, is directed by Dr. Cukrowicz and delivered as a duet; although the presence of the film's main characters makes it a public revelation, it is essentially a dialogue between Catherine and her doctor. Without Dr. Cukrowicz, Catherine is unable to even get up from her chair and walk to the garden, and she only

The 1956 Car Accident and a New Queerness

manages it when he tells her to stand up, promptly holding her in his arms in case she should fall. Once she begins her narration, the doctor is clearly in command: he tells her where to start from, forbids interruptions from the others, and sits very close to her, guiding her with his questions. Her story is punctuated by his gentle yet relentless interventions, so that their voices follow each other and become part of the same narrative. When she loses courage, he begins the next sentence for her; when she stops, he repeats "Go on" until she speaks again, and if she is unsure about a word he clarifies it for her. Clift's whole body is turned toward Taylor in tense concentration, and he never stops looking into her eyes; the force of their connection is palpable. At times her face is partly shown in extreme close-up, next to flashbacks of the events she is recounting. While the doctor is not visible at these moments, his off-screen voice continues to prompt her, retaining control of her process of remembering. The film's last image, showing Dr. Cukrowicz and Catherine happy together, points to a narrative closure sealed by their shared experience of her story; through his intimate participation in her shame and grief, Cukrowicz/Clift inscribes both of them and Sebastian in a queer narrative, legitimizing their deviant and now liberated identities.

FIVE

The Final Period
"Abnormality," Asexuality, Asynchrony

Straight Queerness, Gender Subversion, Near-Sameness: *Wild River* and *The Misfits*

A key scene of *Wild River* shows the protagonists Chuck (Montgomery Clift) and Carol (Lee Remick) lying on the muddy ground after a gang of thugs has assaulted them. Chuck has proved no match for the mob of hostile men and has been hopelessly beaten up; Carol, however, has aggressively and fearlessly attacked their enemies and has been finally knocked down. After a pause in which the two look uncertainly at each other, Chuck says quietly, "I wish someday I could win maybe one fight," quickly adding, his voice warming up, "You were wonderful out there. "Carol replies, "I don't care if you never win a fight." Chuck's reaction to these words is to blurt out: "Marry me. I know, I'll probably regret it, and sure you'll regret it, but . . . " Carol's face slowly relaxes into incredulous happiness. This scene is the culmination of the complex, unconventional relationship that has developed between the protagonists; shaped by Montgomery Clift's performance as Chuck, the film's love story offers a striking example of "straight queerness."

CHAPTER 5

As discussed in chapter 1, the "straight queer" is a contended yet much-embraced concept among queer theorists. It rests on the view that heterosexuality is neither monolithic nor easily definable, even when presented as such to serve dominant fantasies of "normality." In fact, scholars argue that so-called heterosexuals constantly fail to conform to normative straight rules; to queer hetero identities means to validate the deviations, contradictions, and possibilities inherent in relations between men and women. Heterosexuality can thus be reclaimed as subversive, as part of the nonessentialist discourse underpinning queerness; reveling in "the productive failure to master the terms of identity, anxiety, and desire," the straight queer is someone who dares to risk "identity's incoherence."[1] This gambling, profitable failure to self-cohere is remarkably present in *Wild River*, which dramatizes heterosexuality's queer potential more than any other of Clift's films. The complete narrative centrality of Chuck's relationship with Carol identifies him as a straight lover, yet it also highlights Clift's sexual ambiguity and evolving erotic persona. While each postaccident film had shown both continuity and shifts in his image, *Wild River* brings these tensions absolutely to the fore: Clift's portrayal of Chuck mixes visible aging with boyish connotations, and powerful feelings for Carol with very uncertain sexual directions. Chuck's obliqueness in his heterosexual liaisons, of course, is a sign of continuity in Clift's star persona. Clift's affairs with women had always been high profile and subject to media speculation, as gossip columnists expressed bafflement at his unorthodox or nonconclusive relationships; equally, they also pondered endlessly on his frequent lack of girlfriends. The perennially unresolved tensions in Clift's private life had informed his public image and shaped the ambiguous sexual aura he brought to his screen roles; at the same time, as discussed throughout this book, Clift's performance at times had been characterized by a distance from open eroticism, or even by the apparent suspension of sex drive. This disorienting erotic identity had both underpinned and clashed with his heartthrob status, and indeed Clift himself, early on in his career, complained of his marketing as a sex symbol by saying "I don't feel particularly sexual."[2] While this multiplicity of meanings had been evident since Clift's first films, after 1956 his overall performance became dramatically less sexualized: *Raintree County* and *The Young Lions* see him focused on romance rather

The Final Period

than sex, and erotic uncertainty shapes his bonds with women in *Lonelyhearts* and *Suddenly, Last Summer*. This shift to a markedly erratic or absent sexual presence paralleled the trajectory of Clift's private life. His biographers agree on his decreasing, if fluctuating interest in sex, and on his privileging platonic or semiplatonic relationships. On one hand, it is easy to relate this change to Clift's worsening physical and mental state. Patricia Bosworth tells how "Monty was often impotent, and sex became less important to him. His deepest commitments were emotional rather than sexual anyway,"[3] while Robert LaGuardia states that Clift became "incapable of sexual pleasure."[4] On the other hand, there is certainly no evidence that Clift ever turned completely asexual, and accounts of the last phase of his life do make reference to erotic encounters, or at least to attempts in that direction; speaking after Marilyn Monroe's death, for instance, Clift said they had "fooled around a lot," and they had once tried to make love but were both too drunk.[5] Just prior to starting *Freud*, when his health was worse than it had ever been, Clift outraged John Huston by spending the night with a male journalist he had just met, under Huston's own roof.[6] Whatever the details, objective health issues may well have contributed to Clift's variable yet decreasing libido; however, a presupposition of this book is the ultimate impossibility, indeed the undesirability, of "explaining" and much less pathologizing, any shift in individual sexuality. It seems more useful to acknowledge how, in a society dominated by the sex therapist's dogma that "the goal is to be sexual,"[7] Clift's changing patterns of sexual consumption ran squarely against notions of "normality." This diminishing focus on sex coincided with Clift's new level of deviancy on screen, as his characters' ambiguity suggested alternative interpersonal contracts, or nondeveloped sexual configurations. In *Wild River*, Montgomery Clift radically undermines conventions of the male lover; inserted in a narrative of seemingly normative coupling, he subverts established models of male sexuality and normal adulthood, constructing his straight role as remarkably queer.

Wild River is set in the 1930s, in rural, racially segregated Tennessee. The narrative takes place in the context of the terrible river floods that, at the time, had caused widespread fatalities in the area. Montgomery Clift plays Chuck Glover, an agent of the newly created Tennessee Valley Authority (TVA), in charge of supervising the opening of a dam

CHAPTER 5

that will harness the river and prevent more deaths. Before the dam's gates can be opened, however, the surrounding area must be cleared and people relocated; Chuck has been sent there with the specific task of persuading a stubborn old woman, Ella Garth (Jo Van Fleet) to allow her house to be demolished and to move elsewhere. Chuck immediately becomes the target of the locals' hostility, as his pressing for Mrs. Garth's relocation is accompanied by his decision to employ black workers at the same pay as whites. Harassed and repeatedly beaten up by the town's thugs, Chuck still persists in his mission, while beginning an affair with Mrs. Garth's young widowed granddaughter, Carol (Lee Remick); as their relationship deepens, Chuck also meets Carol's fiancé, Walter (Frank Overton), a timid and well-meaning figure. Instead of relating to each other as rivals, the two men rapidly become friends, and Walter acts as Chuck's protector in his struggle against the local rednecks. Meantime, Chuck feels increasingly troubled about having to evict Mrs. Garth from her home; when her sons decide to have her declared mentally incompetent in order to move her out, he reacts with indignation and rushes to warn her of it. He must then reluctantly proceed with her eviction and the demolition of her house and is heartbroken when the old woman dies shortly afterward. In the midst of all this, the relationship between Chuck and Carol quickly intensifies, providing the film with its main focus: she falls passionately in love with Chuck, soon asking him to marry her and take her away with him, with her two children. Chuck, however, takes a decidedly passive role, and while displaying a desire to bond with Carol emotionally and physically, he does not express sexual passion, nor does he try to take her away from Walter. The film's climax sees Chuck violently attacked by the gang of thugs, and Carol, in a neat gender reversion, fearlessly fighting back on Chuck's behalf. Only after this does Chuck make his odd marriage proposal, acknowledging doubts but following a strong impulse; the film ends on a sexually ambiguous, yet hopeful, note as the new family flies away to a life unknown, based on kinship and love.

Through its narrative and visual texts, and rich subtext, *Wild River* builds a complex discourse, which belies the almost biblical clarity of its plot. While the film is ostensibly about good men fighting evil and harnessing nature's power, to bring safety and progress to all, this narrative is however subordinated to another one, created by Montgom-

The Final Period

ery Clift's problematic portrayal of Chuck. Bringing a deeply subversive quality to his role as government agent, man, and lover, Clift also builds a highly unorthodox relation with his female love interest; the close interplay of these two strands of meaning carry the film's structure of feeling.

The film begins with Chuck's arrival at his new job in Tennessee, taking possession of his TVA office; he is met with the incredulous stares of his all-female staff who, when quizzed by Chuck, admit they had thought "they'd send an older man." Chuck is thus immediately presented as someone who confounds expectations, and who may not fit conventional notions of authority and power associated with the US government. This impression is soon confirmed by his inept fiddling with his chair, which nearly causes him to fall on the floor; by his expressed belief that Mrs. Garth may be won over by a new approach based on dialogue; and by his reception by Mrs. Garth's sons, which follows shortly. As Chuck tries to quietly reason with the group of big burly men, explaining why the land needs to be vacated, one of them effortlessly picks him up and throws him in the river. Without showing anger or the desire to retaliate, Chuck walks off, frail-looking and soaking wet. The protagonist is thus singled out as a misfit in the masculine system he is meant to belong to; too young to be in charge, too physically weak to command respect, he is however presented to the audience as the locus of reason and moral authority, as well as of New Deal progress. A narrative of ambivalence is set in place whereby Chuck/Clift will straddle boundaries between traditional manhood, with its connotations of maturity, of social and sexual power, and perceptions of boyhood, linked to innocence and inexperience, as much as to erotic ambiguity. As in all his film roles since *Raintree County*, Clift again holds in tension his different facets, being at the same time man and boy, object of desire and sexual enigma; if his physical appearance denotes age, his character is invested with the tenderness and uncertainty of youth. Clift's conflictive persona is especially evident in *Wild River*: while his face looks healthier than in the recent past, due to his compliance to Elia Kazan's request that he avoid alcohol during the shoot, he is, however, older looking than before. His hunched body is exceptionally thin, and when he walks his movements are stiff and difficult, like those of an elderly man. He was suffering from leg cramps and muscle

CHAPTER 5

twitching, and from severe problems with his balance and spatial coordination; Kazan found that "there was strain everywhere in him—even, it seemed, in his effort to stand erect."[8] Indeed, just after completion of the film Clift was diagnosed with a rare metabolic disorder, "spontaneous hypothyroidism"; the illness was responsible not only for his motion problems but also for his developing cataracts, an extraordinary affliction for a man of thirty-nine. Clift had started to lose his hair too, and while shooting *Wild River* he would creep into the make-up room early in the morning to have his bald patch covered up.[9] Yet despite his aging physical state, Clift's interpretation of Chuck has strong nuances of the "boy"; if this is partly a reflection of his star baggage and of his obvious vulnerability, it is also a direct result of his performance. More in command of his acting than in his last two films, with no problems in remembering lines, Clift painstakingly crafts a layered portrayal of Chuck: his speech is inflected with sudden enthusiasm as much as with hesitation, his eyes are alternately wide open and elusive, and his body language shows anxiety and desire. While these boyish connotations are best expressed in Clift's love scenes with Lee Remick, where they inform Chuck's characterization as a man who is not a "real man," they are also crucial in marking the TVA agent as an outsider, ill fitted to the demands of conventional masculinity. Clift's rendition of Chuck as different from the other men, by virtue of being more of a boy, is given expressed acknowledgment in the film, from its first scene at the TVA office; later on in the narrative, when the drunken Chuck has fallen asleep on the ground, Mrs. Garth observes him and comments on how small he looks. Elia Kazan (who was fifty years old when directing *Wild River*, thus hardly a father figure for Clift) remarked on the problems he had with him on set: "despite all, I felt tender toward him. He was just a boy."[10]

The queerness Chuck/Clift expresses is then rooted in gender disruption; while very much an adult in age, and by virtue of his job, he is however strongly associated with notions of the "boy" and effectively feminized by his dysfunctional masculinity and narrative development. Physically vulnerable, repeatedly humiliated and hurt by other men, Chuck is also strictly aligned with the film's female subjectivity: his sympathies lie firmly with the two women protagonists, Carol and Mrs. Garth, despite the latter's antagonism to his plans. In a key exchange with the old woman, just before collapsing drunk at her feet, Chuck tells her emphatically: "I understand you—I know *exactly* what you are fighting for—your dignity!" But Chuck's "boyishness" goes much further than this; the condition of being "not a man" continues to imply Clift's sexual ambiguity, now shaped by the postaccident changes in his image. With no trace of erotic self-display, indeed wrapping eroticism in affection and passive acceptance, Chuck/Clift still makes himself available to male and female desire through his relationships with Walter and Carol. Allied with Walter in a homosocial pact, which marks them both as different from the town's normative masculinity, Chuck is able to relate to Carol in a nonpossessive, sexually ambivalent way, indifferent to institutionalized coupling; open to modes of connection which defy the "norm," and which are powerfully felt but undetermined, Chuck is at the center of a deeply queer discourse.

In *Wild River*, Walter is clearly linked to Chuck as the only other male misfit: as Carol's official "fellow" and one of the town's resident males, he is patently, almost painfully, failing to meet expectations. Although as physically robust as any of the locals, Walter is unwilling to fight, and his decision to side with Chuck against the thugs is an act of moral rather than physical courage. Scorned by the others for his acceptance of Chuck's "theft" of his girl, Walter befriends the man who should be his rival; at their first meeting, he tries in vain to warn Chuck about the town's worst redneck, Hank Bailey (Albert Salmi), and when he finds Chuck beaten and bruised he takes him out drinking. The film's elliptical narration does not show what happens next, but it presents the two at the end of the night, obviously close and relaxed together. Later on, during the fight between Chuck and the locals, Walter first intervenes as Chuck's protector; when it is all over and Chuck and Carol are lying on the ground, Walter casts a desiring gaze toward the couple. This unspecified longing finds a practical expression in his last gesture: he rescues the bag containing Chuck's belongings, which the thugs had taken and thrown away, and carefully places it by its owner before leaving the scene with a last yearning look. A homoerotic subtext thus underpins the relation between Walter and Chuck, and the latter's characterization as a deviant male and lover; this deviancy, however, finds its fullest expression in the love story between Chuck and Carol. While clearly drawn to Carol by feelings of affinity and attraction, Chuck doesn't think of claiming her for himself; instead, he builds with her a relationship counter to dominant gender, sexual, and societal structures, providing a striking example of straight queerness. The two meet, become lovers, get married and form a family, yet all this happens in opposition to established notions of heterosexual coupling, and even of "normality." Most importantly, Chuck's sexual identity remains fluid and ambivalent, disrupting the equation between men-women relationships and heteronormativity.

The film's plot rushes the couple along, as they rapidly become very intimate; the exact configuration of their intimacy, however, is constantly called into question by Clift's performance. Clift's behavior as Carol's lover is suitably amorous and tender, and indeed Judy White argues that much of the film's power rests on the credibility of this screen romance;[11] if Carol is the one who initiates their affair, Chuck is soon turning up at her door again, taking her in his arms and kissing her. Afterward, however, while Chuck's behavior remains affectionate and very physical, the extent of its erotic motivation is uncertain. In a scene where they are kissing in his car, Carol tries in vain to extract a declaration of passion from him, eventually saying, exasperated, "You can't get enough of me. Tell me! Tell me!" Chuck compliantly tells her, but in such muted tones as to leave unclear whether he is overcome with desire or simply basking in comfort. Throughout the film, Clift's behavior toward Remick is physically insistent, but oddly composed at the same time, resulting in a portrayal of strong yet undefined desire. For the first time in his postaccident career, Clift here expresses a powerful infatuation for his female partner; this same display of strong feelings, however, calls attention to his sexual incongruity, to his lack of a correspondent sexual passion. Indeed, at the time of the film's release, he was berated for not being predatory and "virile" enough, and his portrayal of Chuck Glover was perceived as an unmitigated sexual failure. The first person to be unhappy with Clift's performance was Elia Kazan. The director had initially hoped to get Marlon Brando to play Chuck and now felt that Clift's passive approach to the love story was expressing sexual inadequacy: "in their love scenes she [Lee Remick] was dominant and Monty seemed sexually uncertain. He was. [. . .] in one scene Monty, at the instant of arousal, slumped to the floor. I cursed him under my breath as a limp lover."[12] There is no doubt

The Final Period

that Kazan saw Clift's behavior as resulting from the "wrong" sexual orientation: "he was terribly uncertain with girls—like a homosexual is."[13] Reviewers were hardly kinder to Clift's style as a lover, seemingly expressing indignation on behalf of "real men": "[Clift's] incapacities are almost indecently flagrant in the scenes in which the full-bloodied Lee Remick tells him she loves him."[14] The *New York Herald Tribune*, specifically commenting on the film's love scenes, also found shortcomings in Clift's heterosexual performance: "Clift always seems to me a bit pained, even under circumstances that would leave most people happy." While the *Hollywood Reporter* wrote: "the film comes undone with Clift's performance. . . . His diffident, tentative style is the antithesis of the character he should be playing." Lee Remick, however, saw that Clift's interpretation of Chuck had resulted in a radically alternative model of relationship: "insofar as Monty was incapable of being the dominant partner in a male-female relationship . . . the film showed a very different kind of relationship than what one usually sees."[15] In the light of Clift's deeply ambiguous, unorthodox performance as Carol's lover, Chuck's bizarre marriage proposal becomes especially suggestive; it reads as the statement of intention of a queer man. Whether Chuck is ultimately a "gay" or a "straight" queer man, or anything between the two, is never established and not important. Obviously concerned by the impossibility of fulfilling normative expectations of "the husband," Chuck is, however, ready to marry someone he has come to cherish; it is a relationship where nothing is guaranteed, apart from the desire of being together. It is notable that the proposal scene was not

A queer wedding: Chuck marries Carol.

in the original script, but was entirely improvised by Clift and Remick during rehearsal.[16] Clift's own notes show a first version of his speech, stressing even more forcefully the apparent incoherence of his offer: after "Marry me," he writes "I know it's insane," and later changes it to "I'll probably regret it."[17] The scene of this impulsive wedding is also fittingly unusual: as they are pronounced man and wife, Carol looks in front of her, with a beatific expression on her face, while Chuck gazes intently at Carol, at once loving and bemused. Once they are married, the new couple does not exchange a kiss; instead, Chuck takes his wife by the hand and quietly leads her outside.

Montgomery Clift's interpretation of Chuck thus posits a fluid gender identity and an ambiguous sexual orientation; these qualities are also informed by other elements, inseparable from Clift's persona and performance, that expand and reinforce the film's queer discourse. As already mentioned, a dissonant element in *Wild River* is the suggestion that Chuck's desire for Carol may not be especially sexual. But Clift's physical behavior toward Remick, which is constantly affectionate yet cool at the same time, contains at least a hint of another possibility: that sex, understood as erotic need and pleasure based on genital satisfaction, may scarcely be present in Chuck's life, or even not present at all. In the arrangement the couple share, symbolically ratified by their low-key wedding, a full-blown sex life may not be included, or it may be subordinated to other needs; conversely, Carol's sexual attraction for Chuck may perhaps be fulfilled, but not reciprocated. A crucial factor here is again Clift's performance: as Chuck, his physical ambivalence toward Carol is not countered by open erotic desire for Walter, or for any other person. A reasonable implication of Clift's overall behavior in the film is that Chuck (and/or Clift himself) may simply not be interested in sex. Notions of asexuality, or of a "dormant" sexual drive, are of course radically incompatible with dominant representations of masculinity. Likewise, orthodox views of loving, intimate commitments between two people, let alone a married heterosexual couple, are indissoluble from the presence of sexual activity. From a queer perspective, compulsory sex appears as oppressive as compulsory heterosexuality, being the function of an idea of "normality" imbedded in patriarchy and heteronormativity. Commenting on her own nonsexual lesbian relationship, Leslie Raymer argues: "I now refuse to allow myself to measure the value of any of my relationships by such male values as how often I 'get some'".[18] If, as Adrienne Rich claims, heterosexuality is the instrument of patriarchy,[19] then *Wild River* constructs a strongly antipatriarchal discourse; it denaturalizes the hetero "norm," yet it recuperates relationships between the sexes by subverting mandatory sexual patterns. One of the ways in which these patterns are disrupted is by constructing a male subject whose sex life may be absent, scarce, or irrelevant. As in all queer configurations, the suggestion that Chuck may be uninterested in sex remains highly ambiguous; a feasible but unuttered intimation, it may denote a temporary or lifelong situation, it may be partial or total, but the crucial element is its nonabsolute value. Lack of sexual action does not automatically turn a person into a nonsexual being; Chuck's distance from notions of sexual prowess, of whatever orientation, coexists with the presence of desire. It is the nature of male desire that, in *Wild River*, is ultimately queered and queer, being undetermined and unclassifiable. The suspicion that Chuck may be unconcerned with sex adds an extra layer of subversion to the film, placing its protagonist even deeper at odds with established concepts of the male lover; just as importantly, Chuck's possible chastity goes against accepted notions of "normal" adult development. A departure from "'normality" in a variety of ways was, of course, an integral part of Clift's persona by 1960, and it is telling that the ever-sententious Elia Kazan could declare: "Monty's sexuality was that of a child waiting for his mother to put her arms around him."[20] To the publicized notion that Clift was becoming physically and mentally impaired, his screen presence had added an unsettling image: his freakishly altered looks in *The Young Lions*, the identification with social and sexual perversion in *Lonelyhearts* and *Suddenly, Last Summer*, had all shaped him into a strongly deviant figure. In *Wild River*, Clift's aberrant quality is articulated through a heterosexual love story, whose surface convention is turned upside down by his "productive failure to master identity's coherence." While ostensibly contained by the film's dominant text, Clift's subversion is in fact ultimately validated in *Wild River*; as Chuck, he is affirmed not only as the protagonist but also as the lover, the object of the heroine's devotion, and the bearer of moral and practical progress. Both "man" and "boy," Montgomery Clift constructs a powerful straight queer subject, open to the potential and possibilities of nonnormative relationships.

The publicity for *The Misfits* gave equal billing to its three stars, Clark Gable, Marilyn Monroe, and Montgomery Clift, despite Clift's briefer presence on screen; in fact, Clift's first appearance takes place forty-five minutes into the film, well after that of all the other characters. Yet even in this smaller role, Clift is pivotal to *The Misfits*; against a main narrative of alienation and failed communication between men and women, he stands out as the film's alternative to oppressive patterns of misconnection.

The action is set in Reno, Nevada, where the beautiful Roslyn Taber (Marilyn Monroe) has gone to get a divorce from her cold, insensitive husband, Raymond (Kevin McCarthy). Distressed and lonely, she is comforted by Isabelle Steers (Thelma Ritter), an older woman who has settled in Reno after multiple divorces; they meet Guido (Eli Wallach), a widower, drifter and spare-time pilot, and his friend, Gay Langland (Clark Gable), an aging cowboy and fellow drifter, devoted to rodeos and womanizing. Both men are immediately smitten with Roslyn, vying for her attention and pressing her to stay in Reno, to share their life of casual work and rodeo society; their apparently laid-back existence, however, belies disorientation and lack of belonging. Equally lost, and generally pessimistic about men's facile attraction for her, Roslyn still falls for Gay's charm; she settles with him in a house belonging to Guido, who begrudgingly accepts her choice. They are all soon on the move again, driving to a rodeo with Isabelle; on the road they come across Perce Howland (Montgomery Clift), a younger cowboy who is traveling around with no fixed plan. Despite a record of horrific injuries from past rodeos, Perce readily joins the group and is likewise greatly struck by Roslyn's beauty; his admiration for her is evident, although he does not show the sexual rapacity of Gay and Guido. Perce also agrees to a desert expedition, to help the two men capture mustang horses. He does so reluctantly, even as he shares the others' interest in any alternative to a steady job. On their arrival in the town holding the rodeo, Isabelle spots one of her ex-husbands with his wife and leaves abruptly to spend time with them. Perce goes in for the rodeo and is instantly thrown off a horse; undeterred by his bad fall, he tries again with a bull, this time being knocked unconscious and seriously hurt on

The Final Period

his head. Roslyn, horrified by the rodeo's violence and Perce's ordeal, cries hysterically until he returns from getting first aid, drugged-up and heavily bandaged. During the evening spent in the town's bars, Gay and Guido resent the growing bond between Perce and Roslyn and appear increasingly depressed; despite the rodeo's festive atmosphere, a sense of social disconnection and lack of purpose hangs over them. Things get worse when Gay's estranged children arrive on the scene, only to leave him again without saying goodbye; meantime, Roslyn has followed Perce to a quiet corner outside, where they share an intimate talk. Perce tells Roslyn how both his mother and his girlfriend let him down, and that he feels abandoned and confused; Roslyn empathizes with his isolation, and their affinity and closeness are palpable. Interrupted by Gay, they rejoin the group, and after a brief rest they all drive off to the desert, with Guido joining them aboard his plane. Roslyn is deeply shocked by the brutal capture of the horses, which are to be sold to be turned into pet food; becoming terribly distraught and hostile to cowboy culture, she calls the men "murderers" and vainly begs them to give up the mustangs. While initially perplexed by Roslyn's tearful rage, Gay and Guido quickly dismiss it as female hysterics; only Perce shows respect for her feelings and looks increasingly troubled by his own part in the expedition. When Gay tries to rally his enthusiasm for the horses' capture, Perce blurts out: "I don't know, Gay—to tell you the truth, I don't even know about rodeos anymore." Guido then tells Roslyn he will free the horses if she agrees to move in with him, while Gay opts to simply ignore her presence; she reacts with indignation to Guido's proposal and is devastated by Gay's refusal to comprehend. Suddenly, Perce gets in the truck next to Roslyn. He drives to the horses and cuts their ropes free, one by one, under the astonished gaze of his friends. As the last mustang is liberated, Gay rushes to capture it again, engaging in a dangerous fight with the animal; he finally manages to subdue the horse, but then he immediately lets it go. Although impressed by Gay's last gesture, Roslyn seems wholly alienated from him; Gay himself appears bewildered and sad, Guido is clearly unable to understand what happened, and the party breaks up in a defeated mood. Perce exchanges the briefest goodbye with Roslyn, who is then left alone with Gay. Their mutual unease gives way to tenderness and reconciliation, and they drive away together into the night.

CHAPTER 5

Heavily resting on dynamics of heterosexual attraction, *The Misfits* places its protagonists in a paradoxical structure. If on one hand they are lost, at the margins of the familial, economic, and professional status quo, their lack of a clear belonging is not compensated by freedom. Still caught in a web of prescribed gender and sexual roles, they struggle to find meaning in behaviors that have none left and in modes of interaction that fail to connect them to others. Gay's change of heart about the horse signals a breach in his macho self-definition; as a last-minute conversion, however, and preceded by a desperate show of virile power, it leaves his future development uncertain. Guido never breaks free from futile normative patterns, and his anguished question to Roslyn, "How do you get to know someone, kid?" is clearly bound to remain unanswered. Roslyn and Perce, instead, inhabit all the time a border zone, hovering between fixed social models and uncharted paths to self-reinvention. As the outsider among outsiders, the stray character flitting into the plot, Perce/Clift is marked as a potentially different man, obliquely related to the stubbornly patriarchal Gay and Guido. Immediately feminized by his rodeo failures, and by his strikingly vulnerable body, Perce is best shown as a deviant male through his unique bond with Roslyn. Against the film's dominant structure, their relationship falls outside heteronormative schemes. These overlapping strands in Perce's characterization—aberrant masculinity and unorthodox heterosexuality—are most openly dramatized at the end of the film, when Perce sides with Roslyn and personally frees the horses, against any logic in the cowboy world. In *The Misfits*, Clift follows naturally from his role in *Wild River*, again inflecting men-women relations with gender and sexual subversion; this time, however, Clift's portrayal of straight queerness acquires a special resonance through his extraordinary affinity with Marilyn Monroe. Generating empathic chemistry on screen, and linked in real life by a much-publicized intimacy, Perce/Clift and Roslyn/Monroe posit a union based on near-sameness, further destabilizing heteronormative rules.

The late introduction of Perce in *The Misfits* serves his character's function, as he irrupts into a narrative where "normal" masculinity has been clearly established. Guido is the first male protagonist to appear, sharing the film's initial scenes with Roslyn and Isabelle. In a marvelous performance, Eli Wallach shows Guido as an insinuating, sex-struck

The Final Period

man who can barely contain his greedy craving for Roslyn. Next, Gay is presented on screen as he says goodbye to a woman, and expertly fends off her pleas for a promise to meet again; his status as a womanizer is immediately confirmed by Guido, who has observed him at a distance and now asks him, "Which one was that?" These early scenes define the sexual conquest of women as men's prize activity, achieved through the mastery of laborious, preestablished behavior; as Guido admits to Gay, weighing the odds against his own scoring with Roslyn, "when I think of all the useless talk you gotta do, I get discouraged." As the narrative develops, its representation of masculinity emphasizes the two men's assumptions about gender roles. When Guido describes his much-loved dead wife, he boasts proudly "She stood behind me 100 percent, uncomplaining as a tree"; as Gay later prepares breakfast for Roslyn, he stresses that it is a special treat, and that he had never before cooked for a woman. Dominating the film's structure, this patriarchal virility is both acknowledged and questioned in *The Misfits* as audience sympathy is directed toward the suffering, hugely attractive Roslyn/Monroe. Against Guido's praise of his wife for being patiently mute, Roslyn's immediate retort, "Maybe that is what killed her," rings disturbingly true. To Roslyn's ongoing conflict with the imperceptive Gay and Guido, which points to a basic problem within orthodox gender relations, the film adds the ghostlike presence of her husband. Only fleetingly seen outside the divorce court, she describes him in the very first scene as a "cruel" man who "wasn't really there." The film's mounting evidence of the failures of masculinity is further confirmed by Isabelle, the divorce veteran, who acts as Roslyn's sympathetic guide. Cheerfully pragmatic, Isabelle unquestionably accepts the doomed fate of heterosexual relationships, mocking Gay and Guido for their predatory attitude and virile posturing; she thus highlights their adherence to a default, unhelpful male identity, which, however, she does not question. Indeed, her assessment of Gay and Guido is that "cowboys are the last real men left in the world." In this context of fixed gender patterns, seemingly bound for endless repetition and disappointment, Perce's arrival instantly strikes a discordant note, not matching the established criteria for "cowboy and real man."

Despite a suitably rugged appearance, and faultless rodeo attire from his boots to his Stetson hat, Perce/Clift enters the narrative through an emotional phone conversation, signaling his potential distance from traditional virility. After a rapid exchange of greetings with Gay and Guido and a polite introduction to the ladies, Perce rushes to a nearby phone booth, where he must take a long-distance call; the group waits for him inside the car. As the phone call is entirely filmed on Perce's side, and his interlocutor is never seen or heard, the conversation turns into a monologue; attentively listened to by the others, it becomes Perce's self-presentation to both the protagonists and the audience. Unlike Guido and Gay, Perce is not introduced as a sexually frustrated, women-hungry male, or as a confident playboy enjoying his success; instead, in this very first scene, he is defined by emotional and physical injuries. Perce's call is to his mother, and his words to her reveal a conflictive, distressing relationship. His voice is initially enthusiastic, expressing childlike delight in announcing he won a rodeo belt buckle with his name on it; however, it soon changes to a melancholic, self-defensive tone. By the time he makes some diffident comments about his stepfather, it is clear that Perce is alienated from the maternal home and that he is hurting from long-standing neglect. Clift's performance, so pitch-perfect it required only one take,[21] informs his brief speech with multilayered suggestions of loss. He is first smiling while he talks, yet showing tension by constantly shifting his position inside the booth and fidgeting with the door. From the grin that accompanies "You proud?" as he speaks of his rodeo win, he quickly moves to a somber expression referring to a recent stay in hospital: "My face is fine, all healed up, as good as new," he says as he wearily passes his hand over his face, "you would too recognize me." As the conversation moves on to his stepfather, Clift's body stiffens up, his voice becomes low and hurt only to regain hope for a moment when he mentions the possibility of a trip home. At the end, when the operator has already cut him off, he does not let go of the dead receiver, and in a bitter tone he slowly says into it "God bless you too." This scene establishes two sides of Perce's character, which lead to crucial identifications. Although never sentimental, Perce's words and attitude frame him as a son longing for his mother's love, in obvious contrast to standard notions of "real men"; thus singled out as a boy, Perce is also importantly linked to Roslyn, who had earlier summarized her loneliness with the tearful admission, "I certainly miss my mother." Suggesting deviancy

The Final Period

from "normal" adult maleness, these implications are strengthened by Perce's other revelation, the reference to some terrible past damage to his face. No matter how much Arthur Miller, who wrote the film's script, may have denied he created Perce with Clift in mind,[22] intentional or not, the evocation of a smashed face inevitably merges Perce with Clift, defining his character as wounded, vulnerable, and "not quite right." Perce's body will be further de-virilized by his defeating rodeo injuries, but the key factor is that physical battering is part of his history; on joining the others in the car, he tells how in rodeos he has broken his arm three times in the same place, eliciting Gay's comment that he is "a natural born fool." If Perce's manhood is called into question by his disaster-prone body, the script's obvious remainder of Clift's physical odyssey blurs star and role into one; with his own public image projecting a less and less secure masculinity, Clift turns Perce into a decidedly ambiguous male.

Perce's relationship with Roslyn crystallizes his disruption of normative, straight male identity. His attitude toward her resembles that of the others for only a few seconds, when he first meets her. Almost stunned by her beauty, Perce takes his hat off as he greets her, in a conventional gesture that does not hide his amazement. Some minutes later, as they briefly talk during Gay's absence, Perce and Roslyn exchange a look of great intensity, yet unlike the flirting glances she shares with Gay and Guido. Staring confidently into each other's eyes, their gaze hints at a mutual recognition, at some level of connection beyond the trivial words of their introduction. With their link silently established, Perce gets in the back of the car, constantly leaning forward to be nearer to Roslyn, who is in the passenger seat; while his movements show a desire for physical closeness, they are also very relaxed and spontaneous, with no trace of erotic anxiety. Throughout the film, Perce looks supremely comfortable in Roslyn's presence, untroubled by the sexual coveting or the mental bafflement Guido and Gay show. The difference in Perce's behavior is made explicit through the trope of dancing, the one physical activity that all three men share with Roslyn. Gay and Guido dance with her in a possessive, overtly sexualized manner and are wholly concentrated on her body. Perce's style is exactly the opposite, as he launches into a playful, joyful ball with Roslyn, clearly focused on having fun together and not on erotic designs. This appar-

CHAPTER 5

ent sexual serenity, or suspension, is, however, complicated by other elements in Perce's characterization. In a narrative devoid of homoerotic subtexts, Perce is an ostensibly heterosexual man, and indeed he makes reference to a past girlfriend; more significantly, his powerful interest in Roslyn is explicitly articulated through an exchange between him and Gay. While both men are busy preparing for the rodeo, Perce spots Roslyn and Guido in the audience, and exclaims, "There she is!" with obvious delight; immediately, however, he corrects himself by saying, "I mean, there they are," and turns uneasily to look at Gay. His next words are effectively a request for Gay's permission to pursue Roslyn: "Gay, I wouldn't—wouldn't want to move in on you—unless of course you didn't mind," to which Gay forcefully replies, "Boy, I'd mind!" This brief scene appears to frame Perce's desire within orthodox gender patterns, as he defers to a patriarchal order that gives Gay exclusive rights to Roslyn; likewise, Perce's manly negotiation about Gay's woman defines him as Gay's potential rival and labels his attraction for her as appropriately sexual. This moment of straightforward virility, however, is later reversed by Perce's intimate conversation with Roslyn, which stands out as a key narrative knot and the film's longest scene.

Just as Chuck/Clift had done in *Wild River*, burying his face in Carol's shoulder in a pose halfway between relief and excitement, Perce/Clift here exudes an intense longing for Roslyn; the sexual implications of this longing, however, cannot be easily established. In addition, Perce's time with Roslyn is shaped by contextual issues; it is his brief, only chance to be alone with her, and he chooses to prioritize concerns that have nothing to do with sex. It is a scene of striking yet disorienting intimacy, where camerawork both follows and shapes performances. Shot in a series of close-ups, it presents Perce and Roslyn in a desolate backyard: she sits on the ground and he lies flat on his back, with his head in her lap, yet constantly turning and raising himself up to talk to her. Her summery dress, short and sleeveless, allows the camera high above her to offer a full view of her bare legs; her feet are sexily clad in pointed, high-heeled shoes. Monroe's rounded, exposed shoulders are visibly heaving as she breathes, evoking the movement of her breasts; however, not even a glimpse of her cleavage comes into view. Her face and hair occupy the right half of the frame and are visually disconnected from her legs by Clift's body, which lies in the middle; her

The Final Period

arms and hands lie inert, outstretched around Clift as if ready to hold him should he falter, yet hardly touching him. Holding this static pose throughout the scene, Monroe suggests yet simultaneously evades erotic allure. The result is an ambivalent, composite female body; part sex object, part soft pillow, it cradles the wounded Perce/Clift in perfect stillness, as a protective harbor for his restless movements. Clift also presents an ambiguous picture. On one hand, with his heavily bandaged head, a large wound on his nose, and his nesting position against Monroe, he seems vulnerable and childlike next to her voluptuousness. At the same time, the close-ups reveal him to be a mature man by showing the wrinkles on his forehead and neck, and even the rough texture of his skin; as he constantly turns toward Monroe, his expression shows deep pleasure in their contact, and his face is so close to her it almost touches her breasts. Clift's elfish yet rugged appearance, his passionate eyes, and his insistent body language invest Perce with an undefined intensity; overriding his head concussion and painful wounds, Perce's keen awareness of the moment points to a motive behind his energy, to a latent yet present erotic force. Camera angles and framing increase the scene's ambiguity by deliberately obstructing the view of Clift's hands. While his gestures often seem to indicate he is caressing Monroe, his lower arms are cut out of the screen, as are also Monroe's hips and part of her arms, leaving their faces in close-up as the natural focus of the viewer's gaze.

In this sexually unclear context, Perce injects further uncertainty through his words to Roslyn. "I don't like to see the way they grind up women up here," he says, adding a little later, in a voice suddenly broken by emotion, "Don't you—don't you let them grind you up here." Far from leading to erotic developments, Perce's fear for Roslyn's freedom marks their bond of spiritual affinity, of shared vulnerability; in a series of reverse shots, they now disclose their common loneliness and isolation. As Perce tells her how his girlfriend and friends abandoned him, after he was badly wounded in a rodeo, Roslyn winces in pain; looking dejectedly in front of her, she is, however, attuned to Perce's every word, reflecting his sorrow in her eyes. Perce goes on, recounting how his mother betrayed him, and then asks her, "So what I want to know . . . what I want to know is: who do you depend on?" Roslyn's reply is the saddest, most painfully intimate self-revelation she

CHAPTER 5

makes to anyone in the film: "I don't know. Maybe all there really is—is just the next thing. The next thing that happens. Maybe you're not supposed to remember anybody's promises." At her last words Perce leaps up saying, "You can count on mine!" immediately adding, "I trust you, Roslyn—I think I love you!" Roslyn smiles tenderly at him and replies, "You don't know me." "I don't care! Roslyn . . ." says Perce, moving even closer as if about to kiss her, but stopping abruptly with a groan of pain, holding his head. As she bends down to hold him in her arms, Gay enters, putting an end to this private scene; with their kiss remaining an unexplored possibility, Perce and Roslyn are left in an ambiguous, incestuous alliance of nonidentical twins. Half-children, half-adults, they are virtual orphans as well as virtual lovers; framed by a comfortless world that both oppresses and abandons them, they are ultimately connected only to each other. Unlike Gay's relationship with Roslyn, based on the "natural" attraction of fixed gender oppositions, Perce's link to her is built on connective similarity; it is a socially deviant attachment, disrupting "straightness" through the subversive appeal of near-sameness.

The ambiguity of the relation between Perce and Roslyn is increased by their off-screen personas, in an exceptional fusion of star and role; if there are clear echoes of Montgomery Clift in Perce's character, Marilyn Monroe is inextricably linked to Roslyn, a role created for her by her then-husband Arthur Miller. In an interview given long after her death, Miller goes as far as accepting *The Misfits* as a documentary on Monroe, and says: "she was so much like Roslyn . . . that kind of person, who cannot get connected."[23] Miller was not alone in *The Misfits'* crew to equate Roslyn with Monroe; in his script notes, Clift adds some playful lines between Perce and Roslyn, writing on a blank page "you know what—what—I could swear you were M. Monroe."[24] The link between Roslyn and Monroe is most evident in Roslyn's innocence and vulnerability, traits that were part of Monroe's image and a huge factor in her popularity. Like Clift, she had a much-publicized history of unhappiness and health problems and was perceived as a fragile being in need of protection. The needy, easily broken persona they both projected helped Monroe to appear hyperfeminine, while in Clift's case it only increased his sexual and gender deviation; their public and friends saw two strikingly similar persons whose drama-ridden

The Final Period

Very close: Montgomery Clift and Marilyn Monroe in a candid moment, during a pause from shooting The Misfits. *Eve Arnold, Magnum Photos.*

lives naturally converged. Frank Taylor, *The Misfits'* producer, thought that "Monty and Marilyn were psychic twins. They were on the same wavelength. They recognized disaster in each other's face and giggled about it."[25] Arthur Miller also stressed their shared fragility: "Neither of them was capable of dealing with the situations they were in. They were terribly sensitive people," while press agent John Springer commented: "You should have seen them together. They were like two babes in the woods."[26] The perception of Clift and Monroe as twins separated at birth has fueled the mythology of *The Misfits*, as accounts of the shoot endlessly relate their massive addiction to prescription drugs, their chronic insomnia, and their constant sharing of tips about medications. Even before the film's release, however, publicity photos by the Magnum agency showed them meaningfully together: both fragile-looking, usually holding each other, they are caught exchanging looks of tenderness and complicity. The impression that Roslyn was Monroe, and that Perce was Clift, added extra complexity to their screen relationship; if Clift's sexually ambiguous image brought more uncertainty to their interaction, the publicized rumors that they were having an affair complicated things further. Estranged from Arthur Miller, and waiting for the film to be finished to announce their divorce, Monroe was also the only person Clift spent time with off set; surprised together by paparazzi in a club near Reno, and overheard discussing Monroe's marital problems, they were declared by various fan magazines to be seriously in love.[27] To determine what exactly happened between them is of course impossible, as well as irrelevant; it is more significant to consider how Clift appeared to blend their screen roles with real life, and how he saw an incestuous potential in their profound similarity. Discussing the film's ending, Clift merges reality and fiction, leaving unclear whether he is referring to their relationship on or off screen: "Arthur wanted him [Gable] to keep Marilyn because he wants to himself. But their marriage is over, and he might as well face it. My character represented something new, the future—Marilyn's future. Maybe Marilyn and I would have gotten together one day if we weren't so much alike. As it is, it's too much like brother and sister getting together."[28] What is left recorded on film, in *The Misfits*, is their obvious joy in each other's presence, as much as their extraordinary closeness as actors, something Clift was to mention again and again:

The Final Period

"When I look into her eyes, it sparks everything. To another actor, that's a joy. And it's so rare. So goddam rare."[29] The creative empathy between Clift and Monroe shapes their characters' affinity, yet it was not the first time Clift had shared a deep bond with a woman actor and friend: his screen interaction with Elizabeth Taylor is clearly underpinned by mutual love and complicity. With Marilyn Monroe, however, Clift went a step further, reveling in a closeness of performance that verged more on communion than on communication; likewise, the strong link between him and Taylor did not entail a resemblance in their images. Already in *A Place in the Sun*, before addictions and accident took their toll, Clift exudes a vulnerability that does not define the adolescent Taylor; indeed, Taylor's star persona always remained one of strength, even toughness, regardless of her film roles and personal tragedies.

The subversive implications of attraction through sameness are central to *The Misfits*, whose patriarchal order is disrupted by the queer link between Perce and Roslyn. As Leo Bersani discusses, queer sameness entails the linking of different configurations through deep similarities rather than by the exact reproduction of illusory models of "normal" identity; queer affinity opposes the fantasy of same-sex equivalency, where sameness is the quality of being identical as much as that of oppositional heterosexual attraction, where the sameness of men and women is deemed impossible. The result of these queer connections is a range of unorthodox relationships, resting on both kinship and difference. That is why Bersani prefers the term *near-sameness*, which he detaches from fixed homo- or heterosexual identities. Expanded on the wider scale of an ideal queer society, the near-same mode of relating to others generates a web of unique associations, conceptualized by Bersani as "a network characterized by relations of inaccurate replication. Accurate replication—the perfect identity of terms—is an attempted human correction of these correspondences, a fantasy of specularity in the place of correspondence."[30] In *The Misfits*, the relationship between Perce and Roslyn is based on correspondence and inaccurate replication, away from the fallacy of matching sex with gender, and gender with sexual orientation, which still entraps Gay and Guido. The strong yet ambiguous bond Perce and Roslyn share has no place in the film's larger context, as the queer network envisaged by Bersani is entirely

CHAPTER 5

absent in *The Misfits*; indeed, the film's discourse of alienation rests on the narrative denial that such a network may exist. While all the protagonists are variously confused and helpless—Gay and Guido mostly cling to sterile models of interaction—Perce and Roslyn do achieve an alternative connection, yet this remains completely undeveloped. However, although Perce and Roslyn do not end up together, nor do they formalize their attachment in any way, this very lack of closure points to the freedom and complexity of their interaction. Steeped in sexual ambiguity and acute emotional empathy, their relationship signals the potential outside normative patterns; the identification of Clift and Monroe with their roles strengthens the multiple meanings of their closeness. Talking about Marilyn Monroe after her death, Montgomery Clift said: "Working with her was fantastic . . . like an escalator. You would meet her on one level and then she would rise higher and you would rise to that point, and then you would both go higher."[31] Clift's language is remarkably erotic, offering a description of mounting excitement and pleasure, yet he is talking about acting, something he took very seriously indeed. The complex strength of Clift's link with Monroe is evident in these words, and as he only ever worked with her in *The Misfits*, it is impossible not to link his statement to his experience of the film; his memory of Monroe seals the Perce-Roslyn connection, positing affinity and attraction beyond categories.

Disrupting Time and Meaning: *Judgment at Nuremberg* and *Freud*

Montgomery Clift was to live only five years after *The Misfits*. The period between 1961 and 1966 is marked by his dramatically worsening health and by his consequent blacklisting in Hollywood, where he was deemed unreliable and uninsurable. Fluctuating between illness, unemployment, and two stunning film performances, in this phase of his career Clift shows both fragmentation and continuity. Although Clift's altered appearance had been part of his image since 1956, after *The Misfits* his looks took an unprecedented turn for the worst: he now gave an alarming impression of precipitating illness. Exhausted by his struggle with pain and addictions, Clift was aged, skeletal, and lined, while his hands often shook like those of an old man; if his features never lost a certain handsome quality, he seemed infinitely remote from the perfect beauty he had oozed in the past. This extremely changed appearance was highlighted in his next films, though in very different ways. In a small part in *Judgment at Nuremberg*, cast as a psychologically damaged man the Nazis had sterilized, Clift's distressed looks were inevitably linked to his role; combined to his devastating, Oscar-nominated performance, they made his fourteen minutes on screen memorably unsettling. One year later, Clift played the lead in the biopic *Freud*: looking frail and worn out, with a feverish and pained gaze, he seemed an extraordinarily odd choice for a thirty-something Sigmund Freud. Clift's performance was idiosyncratic and powerful, but his air of extreme vulnerability seemed hardly fit for an icon of rational thought. In any case, the notion that something was very wrong with Clift had been publicized before *Freud*'s release, when the film's studio, Universal, had sued him. The studio blamed Clift's ill health for the delays and extra costs in production; the trial was going on when *Freud* opened, drawing further attention to Clift's physical deterioration. Although he eventually won the suit, Montgomery Clift would remain an outcast in the film world, and after four years of unemployment he agreed to star in the inferior thriller *The Defector*. It was a desperate move, aimed solely at demonstrating his fitness for work. Released after his death, this film shows him wasted and ghostlike, yet still somehow attractive despite his terminally ill looks. If Clift's appearance in his last years seemed wildly distant from what it had been, it also informed the continuity of his sexually ambiguous, visually asynchronous persona. Clift's subversion of normative identities, which run as a thread throughout his career and included his own fragmented image, progressed to a deeper disruptive function. His screen roles and performances, public and private life coalesced in a newly found deviancy, posing a challenge to some established foundations of meaning. In order to conceptualize Clift's presence in this period, and its link to his overall star trajectory, it is useful to refer to temporal queer theory.

As mentioned in chapter 1, heteronormativity is dependent on a parallel chronological structure, where time is understood as both a function and a cause of "normal" development. Heterosexual rules posit a narrative that, prescribing marriage between the sexes followed by reproduction, also crucially defines the temporal element of this progression: there is a "right" age to get married, a "right" age gap

CHAPTER 5

between husband and wife, and a "right" age to have children. While these norms may change and evolve in different contexts and generations, they remain cardinal referents for socially accepted identities. Equally, sexual activity is not just directed toward the opposite sex, it is also expected to take place within certain age limits and with certain patterns and frequency; bodies are meant to show specific characteristics at different ages and to be able to function in specifically different ways. Mental and emotional life is drastically organized along timelines in accordance to rigid notions of childhood and adulthood. In this straight, chronologically ordered existential path, the past and the present are clearly marked and separated, while the future is made possible by a productive use of the present. Queer time, or queer temporality, is the disruption of this normative progression, the de-naturalization of linearity in favor of temporal hybridity. By drawing attention to the glitches, anachronisms, and asynchronies disturbing "normal" time, queer exposes "the fiction of a time fully present to itself and accessible as such."[32] Temporal hybridity is significantly centered on the body, and indeed Elizabeth Freeman coins the term "erotohistoriography" to define the queer take on a crucial temporal issue, the individual's relation to the past. Rather than the wish for a return to the past, or the inscription of the past in the present, she posits the *encounter* of the past in the present, in an acknowledgment of hybrid time. The body, she claims, can be used "as a tool to effect, figure, or perform that encounter."[33] While Freeman concentrates on the body's erotic positioning toward an external past, the hybrid encounters of queer time can be found in a range of configurations, which include the body yet are not necessarily erotic. By not being "fully present" to one's current physical situation, and to one's socially allotted temporal station, the queer subject is produced and located across time coordinates.

Montgomery Clift obviously fails to conform to dominant temporal norms. Clift's most dramatic departure from normative time is his 1956 accident, when he was visibly and functionally torn apart from his current self; without any sense of progression, Clift's present suddenly ruptured, revealing itself as the past. Yet this elapsed present did not fully recede, becoming instead an integral part of Clift's image; a physically and temporally composite figure, Clift from then on literally embodied notions of asynchrony. As the accident both fueled

The Final Period

and accelerated his deviant trajectory, Clift seemed increasingly out of step with the chronosexual expectations placed on him; from his plethora of old-man illnesses to his childlike emotional needs, from his growing alignment with a gay lifestyle to his waning interest in sex, his breaching of "normal" male adulthood reached its peak in the 1960s. Yet at the same time, temporal incongruity had always been part of Clift's persona. Clift's sexual ambiguity and aberrant masculinity were linked to his relation to time, to his total avoidance of the basic steps along the heterochrononormative route: engagement, marriage, and fatherhood. Equally unsettling were the relationships Clift flaunted in public, perhaps none as much as his love affair with Libby Holman, which started in the late 1940s and continued on and off for years; their bond remained one of the most important in Clift's life. Holman was fourteen years older than Clift, not particularly good looking, with a sensationally murky past, and active in the civil rights movement. If the whole package appeared inappropriate for a rising Hollywood star, the real shocker was her age. Not only the paparazzi but also Clift's friends were puzzled and disturbed by their union, as one of them recalls: "the idea of this young god in bed with an unattractive older woman seemed repulsive."[34] The press never let go of the issue; as late as 1957, *Photoplay* gloomily reported that Clift "turns up escorting Libby Holman around town again. . . . You want to know what's with Montgomery's love life? So do we, pal, so do we." In March 1959, after Clift had been spotted on an intimate holiday with Myrna Loy, who had played his boss's wife in *Lonelyhearts*, an article in *Picturegoer* asked incredulously: "What does he see in older women like Myrna Loy and Libby Holman?" Meantime, the rumors about Clift's closeted homosexuality became gradually louder as he got older; impossible to dismiss as a youthful phase he would outgrow, same-sex relationships were a permanent and crucial side of his life. Clift's noncompliance to the convention of the sham Hollywood wedding (unlike, for example, Rock Hudson) sabotaged any chance of his insertion in "normal" temporal narratives. At a more mundane level, Clift had always been capable of wildly anachronistic behavior. On one hand, his peers revered him for his mature approach to acting, defined by rigor and lucid control in every aspect of his performance. This side of Clift's personality never fluctuated, regardless of his health and personal problems, and indeed he worked

CHAPTER 5

on the script for *The Defector* with methodical devotion.[35] On the other hand, Clift regularly displayed attitudes that were socially unacceptable for an adult; for example, he had a lifelong dread of being alone at night and went to extreme lengths to avoid being in that situation. When still in his twenties, he regularly shared the matrimonial bed of his close friends Jeanne and Fred Green, driven by a neediness that was entirely nonsexual.[36] As Clift's alcoholism got worse, his nights usually ended in unconsciousness, but until that moment he could not bear to be abandoned: "The worst thing in the world was for anyone to leave him alone before he would pass out."[37] If everything else failed, Clift would call friends on the phone in the middle of the night and keep them talking to him until he was sufficiently reassured to fall asleep. Neither a child nor a senile old man, Clift stunned those around him with his range of childlike behaviors, as when the unsuspecting Joseph Mankiewicz invited him for dinner: "Mankiewicz was appalled at the sight of a grown man reaching for food on the plates of others, throwing it around, blurting things out to strangers, eating with his hands, and engaging in other acts of embarrassingly infantile behavior."[38] Likewise, the "grown men" around Clift were acutely disturbed by one of his defining traits, the tendency to burst into tears at the slightest provocation. If institutionalized temporality is, as Freeman believes, mastered by the subject in order to become one, through learning "the cultural norms of withholding, delay, surprise, pause, and knowing when to stop,"[39] then Clift's social or arguably antisocial peculiarities placed him outside temporal norms; in so doing they assisted his perception as an incomplete, abnormally developed subject.

As the master of his temporal contradictions, Clift stayed aligned with his own hybrid time, achieving subjective unity through the acceptance of his discrepancies; this is most evident in his relation to the past. While utterly devastated by the loss of his beauty, and presumably wishing for a return to preaccident times, he also used his new appearance with an ultimate sense of purpose. From his dramatic self-cripping in *The Young Lions* to his acting solely through his eyes in *Lonelyhearts*, to his deliberate physical incoordination in *Judgment at Nuremberg*, Clift expressed himself by inhabiting his new face and body. Yet if he may have seemed to live in the present and long for the past, this "normal" relation to time was subverted by Clift's most striking temporal attri-

The Final Period

bute: his literal encounter of the past in the present. Through his own physicality Clift merged old and new, visually and semantically; he revealed the hybrid quality of his subjectivity, the absence of a neat divide in his experience of time. As part of his increasingly deviant persona, Clift's factual carrying of his past threatened the temporal structure applied to him; the preaccident Clift constantly overlapped with the postaccident Clift in a "stubborn lingering of pastness" that Freeman sees as "a hallmark of queer effect."[40] Clift's growing distance from chrononormativity finds powerful expression in *Judgment at Nuremberg* and *Freud*, in two roles and performances defined by temporal subversion.

Judgment at Nuremberg is monumental both in length and scope; over three hours long, the film narrates the 1948 trial of four German judges, accused of assisting Nazi cleansing policies during the Third Reich. Almost entirely set in a courtroom, the film organizes its huge topic through the figure of Chief US Judge Dan Haywood (Spencer Tracy). Haywood grimly listens to the appalling testimonies of the witnesses, who are interrogated by the prosecuting attorney, Colonel Tad Lawson (Richard Widmark), and the defense lawyer, Hans Rolfe (Maximilian Schell). In this harrowing film, which incorporates concentration camp footage, narrative structure is built on a composite account of guilt and suffering; a stellar cast includes Marlene Dietrich, Judy Garland, and Burt Lancaster, deployed in key roles on both sides of the Nazi madness. Of all the famous names in the film's credits, Montgomery Clift has the briefest part: he plays Rudolph Petersen, a simple, possibly mentally disabled man, sterilized by the Nazis as part of their purges against undesirables. Making his entry fifty minutes into the film, Petersen is a key witness for the prosecution; in a shocking plot turn, he is introduced just as the defense has dismissed all sterilizations records, arguing they were not authenticated and consequently there was no case. A survivor where there was none expected, Petersen is soon revealed as a traumatized, inarticulate man, whose testimony unravels through agitation and horror. Questioned first by Lawson for the prosecution, Petersen relates the abuse suffered after the Nazi takeover, culminating in his sentence of sterilization; he tells how he tried to escape but failed and was then captured and forcibly sterilized. As defense lawyer Rolfe takes over from Lawson, the distressed Petersen is treated

CHAPTER 5

to a sadistic interrogation, aimed at proving his hereditary idiocy and thus the reason for his sterilization; the defense line is that the accused were simply carrying out their duties under Nazi law, which required the "mentally incompetent" to be sterilized. Rolfe's methods include forcing Petersen to take an "intelligence test" of linguistic comprehension, the very same he had failed when assessed by the Nazis; Rolfe also tries to make him admit that his mother was feebleminded. These demands cause Petersen's complete breakdown; seemingly unable to even understand the words of the test, he erupts in a horror-stricken frenzy, screaming at Rolfe in broken sentences. Watched by the court in stunned silence, Petersen next produces a photo of his dead mother and implores Judge Haywood to pronounce a verdict on her: was she feebleminded? As Rolfe then declares the witness not to be in control of his mental processes, Petersen screams back that he knows he is not and has not been since the day the Nazis took him. The last view of Petersen shows him coiling on himself like a wounded creature, before the camera moves on Haywood, who sternly declares the court adjourned.

This extremely upsetting scene, adding to the film's evocation of atrocities, is made especially disturbing by Clift's performance and narrative status. At a most basic plot level, Petersen is a living anachronism; a witness who was not supposed to exist, his appearance in the courtroom is that of a living ghost. Moreover, a sterilized and mentally disturbed male is a deeply unsettling figure, threatening "normality" and its related gender and sexual categories; these different aspects of Petersen's character, troubling as they are, become completely nightmarish through Clift's performance. To begin with, despite a lack of narrative and historical certainty, the overall impression Petersen suggests is that his sterilization means castration; yet in fact, according to the available evidence, Nazi-enforced sterilizations in the 1930s were carried out through vasectomy procedures.[41] Most scholars and critics, however, have read Clift's character as an unquestionably castrated man;[42] Judith M. Kass describes him as "the man from whom one of the essential functions of mankind has been cruelly taken,"[43] while Thomas Doherty calls Petersen "a man neutered by the Nazi."[44] As Doherty immediately adds that, as Rudolph Petersen, Clift appears "horribly scarred from his automobile crash of 1956," one wonders not only if

Doherty actually watched the scene but also if assumptions of Petersen's castration rest partly on notions of Clift as a physical freak, notions so strong as to override his factual, unscarred appearance. Indeed, a 1961 reviewer writes ambiguously, "Montgomery Clift is introduced tellingly as a stumbling, mumbling witness, victim of brutal sterilization."[45] More than his star baggage, however, it is the effect of Clift's performance that suggests castration. Projecting a broken, humiliated identity through a chaotic presence exuding trauma, Clift builds an image of unbearable personal loss; infantilized and confused, he readily evokes the barbaric anomaly of emasculation. To this perverted male figure, Petersen/Clift gradually adds a final disruptive meaning; his visible reencounter of bygone events gives them a tangible form, turning painful memories into a horrific meeting with the past. A temporally hybrid presence to himself, and to the diegetic and nondiegetic audience, Rudolph Petersen *is* what happened to him under the Nazis.

Petersen/Clift is first seen through an open door, walking nervously outside the courtroom; heeding the prosecution's call, he walks in but lingers on the threshold, looking intimidated. After these long and medium shots, the whole scene takes place in close-up, with Petersen sitting in the witness chair; he appears immediately odd, swamped by a huge, badly cut suit, which crumples so much on his arms as to give the impression the sleeves are empty. He also sports a rough haircut that, like the suit, had been Clift's personal choice for his role. As the interrogation begins, Petersen/Clift gives his answers in slow, hesitant words; he looks uncomfortable, constantly changing position in his chair. Clift's accident-damaged lip is very evident here, as he holds his mouth very tight, distorting it through jerky facial movements; his eyes are mostly dilated, expressing fear. Asked by Lawson to recount the 1933 assault on his father by Nazi thugs, Petersen hunches his shoulders in tension, so much as to make his neck disappear; he looks deeply upset, though still keeping some distance from his past suffering. As Lawson proceeds with the questioning, Petersen recalls how the Nazis asked him for the birth dates of Hitler and Goebbels: "I told them I didn't know and also that I didn't care," he tells the audience, who react with subdued laughter. Looking naively pleased by his success, Petersen smiles, then immediately lowers his eyes like a scared child. This fragile composure begins to crumble as he is shown the record

CHAPTER 5

of his own sterilization order: asked to read it aloud, he complies very slowly, looking dazed, while his hands visibly shake. Next, Lawson asks Petersen about his escape from home, return, and subsequent capture by the Nazis: Clift's voice falters as he replies, and his eyes move randomly around the room. Lawson presses him: "Were you in fact . . . sterilized?" but Clift does not utter a word; instead, after a pause, he nods twice and looks away. The camera briefly cuts to Judge Haywood, looking utterly absorbed by Petersen/Clift; indeed, from this moment onward, Clift's distraught face and restless body start to dominate the screen. Even in the next five minutes, when Schell gives a chilling performance as the interrogating Rolfe, it is Petersen/Clift who imposes his meaning on the scene. A seemingly poor match for Rolfe, who grills him by alternating suavity and cruelty, Petersen hears himself described as mentally deficient, and born that way just like his mother. Effectively, Rolfe is trying to normalize Petersen's brutally ruptured timeline by evoking a continuum where his "mental incompetence" is viewed through an ordered perspective. His sterilization happened in the past yet is linked to his family's timeless abnormality, and to his own. A glitch in the productive, normative temporality everyone else in the courtroom shares, Petersen's genetic stunting preceded the Nazis, who simply "took care" of it. Rolfe's key strategy is to bring the witness to reveal his condition *before* sterilization; to this purpose he asks him about his childhood, inquiring how long he attended school and if he was a bright pupil, able to keep up with the others. From Rolfe's first questions Petersen starts to tremble, looking increasingly disturbed; he often looks away, seemingly caught by some frightening vision. He cannot provide a coherent account of his early youth, and his replies are broken by pauses and time lags. When the issue of his brightness is mentioned, his hands shake more visibly, and with great effort he starts to say "It was a long while ago, I don't . . ." but cannot finish the sentence; his face looks scared and remote, while his body incessantly moves on the chair. Rolfe's next question, whether he kept up with the others, receives no answer. Unable to produce himself as a subject through temporal linearity, Petersen fails to appear as a subject at all, occupying instead the uncertain space outside normality; as Freeman points out, in "psychiatry, medicine, and law—having a life entails the ability to narrate it . . . in a novelistic framework."[46]

The Final Period

Petersen's lines were shortened and broken up by Clift's script revisions, which made his speech disjointed and undeveloped; though not all his changes appear in the final cut, they show Clift's intention to fragment Petersen's self-narrative. At times he achieves this by making his words clumsy and unclear, as when instead of saying that his mother "died of heart disease" he replaces it with "she died of her heart."[47] Other times, however, Clift radically cuts the original speech until there is no causal articulation, only a few pain-ridden syllables; for example, his defense of his mother turns from "My mother was a woman who worked hard all her life. It's not fair to say things about a woman like that. It's not fair" to just "Not true. Not true."[48] Likewise, it is Clift who changes his "Yes" confirming he was sterilized into a mute "nods his head."[49] On a blank page facing these lines Clift writes "slow burn," and indeed, Petersen's acute distress slowly erupts into a scattered, terror-driven rage. As Rolfe argues that his mother was feebleminded, and that Petersen shares the trait, the camera moves in on Clift looking terribly agitated; he violently swings an arm toward Rolfe, with his hand open as if shielding himself from a dreadful sight, and says "Not true, not true, not true!" Rolfe insists, and Clift shouts, "It was just something they said to put me on the operating table!" His terrified eyes are glued to Schell's face. With jumpy, uncoordinated movements Clift repeatedly grips the table near him, as if trying to steady himself.

At this point in the scene, Rolfe's drive to expose Petersen as subnormal is about to find its climax in the restaging of the Nazi test that determined the verdict of mental incompetence. Yet Rolfe's strategy has already backfired, as the effect of Clift's performance has been a growing materialization of past trauma. Rather than evoke a presterilization idiocy, Petersen has started to embody a specifically past abuse, a time of violence that is invading the courtroom through his presence. Now Rolfe orders him to take again the linguistic test: he must make a sentence out of the words "hare, hunter, field." On the verge of tears, Petersen/Clift clenches his fist in the air, while holding on to the table with the other hand; he says "hare ... hunter ... field ..." as his body jerks in the chair, then again grips the table with both hands. His face trembles and his mouth is distorted; a blank terror seems to possess him, while he repeats "hare ... hunter ..." and finally screams: "They had already made up their minds!" Through broken sentences

CHAPTER 5

Encountering past horrors: Rudolph Petersen on the witness stand.

he describes being held in the hospital, then covers his mouth with his hand; his eyes move away from Rolfe to a point in the middle distance. The awful disturbance of this scene lies in the impression that Petersen is not recalling, but meeting his past anew. Regardless of his inherent mental capacities, his barbaric abuse shatters Nazi chronology, bringing forth a tangible past that cannot be normalized into a corrective progression. Encountering in the present a distant horror, and the irrevocable change it caused, Petersen is constituted as a hybrid subject; he simultaneously inhabits life before, during, and after sterilization in a chaos of overlapping experience. The display of this deviant temporality is completed at the end of the scene, when Petersen's collision with the past shapes his relation to his dead mother. After shouting that what Rolfe said about his mother is not fair, Petersen reaches inside his huge jacket, extracts a torn, faded photo from it, and says "I want to show you—I have here her—her picture—I would like you looked at it." Carefully holding the photo with both hands, he turns it toward Rolfe; the camera cuts to Schell, whose face drops, expressing stunned disorientation. As Petersen reappears in the frame, it is evident that his mother's image has had a corporeal effect on him; he has at last found some coordination, and as he turns to face the judge his body is focused on holding the picture. In hesitant words he addresses Hay-

The Final Period

wood: "I would like you to judge—I want that you—tell me—was she feebleminded?" He looks several times at the photo, his voice rising to a shout as he repeats, "My mother! Was she feebleminded? Was she?!" Haywood remains speechless, not knowing how to deal with Petersen's time-bending request; as the witness encounters his lost mother in the temporality of the courtroom, Haywood cannot join in the encounter, yet he cannot avoid it either. The force of Petersen's anachronistic experience has turned it into a solid presence, which cannot be diluted by Rolfe's claim that he is mentally unsound; besides, Petersen/Clift is now expressing devastation, fear, and rage, to a level that goes beyond the recall of past memories. Clift's shoulders and neck are swerving, his face grimaces as he pulls his chin toward his chest, his wild eyes intermittently meet the gaze of the court; violent pain exudes from his every pore, and even his hair seems electrified. In a last distraught sentence, uttering one word at a time, he shouts: "Since that day—I've been half I've ever been!" In the petrified courtroom, Rolfe responds by saying, "The tribunal does not know what you were like before—it can never know—it has only your word." Yet by now the whole court, as well as the audience, know that Rolfe is lying. As Petersen collapses trembling in his chair, the horrific alteration forced on him by the Nazis is actually there, in the courtroom's present, a breach in the linear time shared by the prosecution and the defense. Through his performance, Clift has given Petersen the capacity to reveal temporal hybridity, exposing the fiction of a consequential time and its associated "normality."

Freud sees Montgomery Clift in his last big role, playing the lead in a fictionalized account of Sigmund Freud's early career. Although punctuated by delays, Clift's health problems, and John Huston's allegedly sadistic direction, *Freud* bears no sign of its unhappy production history; it presents the viewer with strong performances, arresting cinematography, and a tight narrative spanning five years of Freud's life. Specifically, the plot charts Freud's initial experiments in uncovering psychic repression and his revolutionary formulation of the Oedipus complex; despite its basic faithfulness to Freud's work, however, the film relates obliquely to the real-life Sigmund Freud, bringing an artificial focus on his interaction with one special patient. More ambiguously, through Clift's presence and performance, the emphasis on Freud's self-analysis highlights his incomplete fit to his own theories; already the agent of medical and temporal subversion, Freud/Clift adds an extra layer of disruption to psychoanalytic discourse.

The film begins in 1885 in Vienna, where Sigmund Freud is struggling against a reactionary medical establishment; his attempts to conduct experiments on patients with hysteria are opposed by Dr. Meynert (Eric Portman), the director of the hospital where he works. Freud travels to Paris to meet Dr. Charcot (Fernand Ledoux), who is using hypnosis to demonstrate the psychic root of hysteria; on his return to Vienna, he is publicly ridiculed by Meynert for endorsing Charcot's theory and is forced to resign when he starts to practice hypnosis. Freud's only supporter is Dr. Breuer (Larry Parks), a well-established physician, who offers to refer his hysterical patients to him; Freud begins to see a pattern in these new cases, the presence of past sexual fantasies that have been displaced from the patients' conscious mind. Freud's investigations turn to a young man, Carl von Schlossen (David McCallum), who has senselessly attacked his father with a knife; under hypnosis, Carl reveals that his father raped Carl's mother when she was a girl. Still in a trance, Carl addresses a clothes dummy as if it was his mother, caressing it and kissing it with clear erotic desire; Freud is shocked by this sight, and later has a nightmare in which he is tied to Carl by a rope, being pulled into a dark cavity in the earth. In the dream Carl moves downward, reaches Freud's own mother and kisses her; Freud then awakes in terror. Disturbed by his response to Carl's revelations, Freud leaves his research aside, until he is summoned to Meynert's deathbed; here his former director persuades him to continue his experiments and confesses that he has hidden his own hysteria from society. Freud resumes his research and identifies the repression of past sexual fantasies as the basis for all neuroses; the cure must lie in the lifting of repression, to allow the subject to face the past and to free libidinal energy, which will then organize itself fully in the present. Breuer resists this formulation, bringing the example of his own patient, Cecily Koertner (Susannah York), as a nonsexual hysteric; she is a young woman exhibiting baffling symptoms, ranging from the inability to drink to paralysis, blindness, and a false pregnancy. By using hypnosis on Cecily, Freud ascertains a first truth: her father died in a brothel in Naples, while he was on holiday with Cecily, who was forced to go to identify his body. On recovering this memory, which she had repressed, Cecily immediately regains her sight. From this moment, the relationship between Freud and Cecily dominates the film; handed over to Freud by Breuer, who cannot deal with the girl's heavy flirtation, Cecily soon transfers her attentions to Freud. For his part, Freud is untroubled by Cecily's sexual interest and equally indifferent to the jealous protests of his wife, Martha (Susan Kohner). Delving into Cecily's past, Freud discovers that as a child she developed an erotic obsession with her father, fantasizing about being one of the prostitutes he liked; at the same time, she nurtured a hatred of her mother. Freud also examines his own hysterical symptoms, which appeared after his father's death: about to enter the cemetery for the burial, he had found his legs refused to carry him farther, and had collapsed on the ground. Convinced that he too, like Cecily, suffers from the repression of past sexual feelings, Freud has another revealing dream in which he is again pulled into a dark vault; this time, however, the person who pulls him toward his mother is himself, as a small boy. Recognizing a childhood wish to be sexually close to his mother, and to kill his father whom he saw as a rival, Freud formulates his theory of the Oedipus complex; he now believes that infant sexuality, and its relation to one's parents, is the basis of adult neuroses. Breuer is repulsed by Freud's ideas and urges him to abandon them; undeterred, Freud announces his findings to Vienna's medical elite, who receive him with hostility and abuse. All the while he continues to treat Cecily, who slowly improves and is able to walk again; one night she runs away to Vienna's red light district, and Freud goes searching for her. He finds her provocatively dressed like a prostitute and openly offering herself to him; concerned for her mental state, but otherwise unfazed, Freud takes her back home. On his next visit, Cecily admits to Freud that she is in love with him; he calmly accepts her love "as a sacred trust," telling her she is trying to reach her father through him, but that she will move on to a love life unencumbered by her past. The film ends with Freud finally able to enter the cemetery; looking pensive and emotional, he walks to his father's grave.

As previously mentioned, *Freud* is marked by the discrepancy between two vastly different images, those of Montgomery Clift and the real-life Sigmund Freud. In terms of Clift's star trajectory, however, it is hard to imagine a more fitting performance, completing the discourse of queer transgression expressed throughout his work. The film provides continuity from *Suddenly, Last Summer*, as Clift is cast again as the facilitator of sexual truth; this time he places himself in the narrative he unearths, locating his sexual past in the symptomatic disruption of his present. Through this first-person involvement, Clift's role lends poignancy to Freud's idea of a temporally hybrid subject; likewise, the centrality of the closet is stressed in the film, with Freud inscribed in a twin process of coming out and "outing" others. Yet Clift's performance resists Freud's ultimate goal, the production of a fully accessible subject through unequivocal sexual resolution. On the one hand, Freud's empirical obsession is given a live energy by Clift's intensity: engrossed in deciphering sexual motives, Clift magnifies the act of thinking through his eyes, alert and shining with dramatic insight. On the other hand, this immersion in erotic narratives clashes with Clift's overall behavior, which is strikingly asexual, and with his disorientingly self-contained body. The result is a dualistic queer structure of meaning; Freud's radical take on sex and time is validated, but also deviated from, through Clift's rendition of Freud as sexually and temporally indefinite. Resting chiefly on Clift's performance, this open-ended portrayal is assisted by his star persona, by now an alliance of physical and mental ambiguity, sexual uncertainty, and acute vulnerability. Complicating Sigmund Freud's image of uncluttered reason, Clift adds further disruption with his fragile looks, a clear departure from what was Freud's well-known appearance in his thirties: strong, well-built, exuding solidity. Adding multiple queer possibilities to his role, yet supporting his narrative function with a dedicated performance, Montgomery Clift shapes Freud's biopic into his own film.

In its explicit text, *Freud* highlights the temporal subversion of Clift's character: Sigmund Freud sees time as a hybrid force, molding the subject by invading the present with the past, and thus causing bodily symptoms and anxiety. This past-infused present is further unsettled by the elusiveness of the unconscious, an uncharted chronotope pulling the subject along slippery coordinates; as Freud remarks to Cecily, "time does not exist in the unconscious." Freud's medical strategy, the bringing of past mental events to the mind's surface, reinforces a nonlinear concept of the subject, as the required experience of the present includes a conscious encounter with the past. Freud's investigations rest on what Freeman calls "erotohistoriography," the queer collision of body and time; in this case, it is a specific erotohistoriography of the mind, where meeting the past through the body informs psychological methodology. By watchfulness and analysis, Freud traces and decodes the body's encounters with the psyche's erotic past. The psychoanalytic process is thus rooted in time and physicality, and the film stresses this by immersing the protagonist in his symptoms: "I can feel it moving inside me like a snake," says Freud of his own repressed past. A sensuous and transgressive image, the snake recurs in the narrative, linking Freud's analytical function to sensory and temporal experience; in Cecily's recurrent dream about her father, a snake thrones in the medical emblem topping a tower, merging her childhood fantasies with her eroticized doctors, Freud and Breuer. A snake also features in one of Freud's nightmares and haunts him again when he is awake. Deliberately seeking his past, he borrows from his mother something he played with as a child, a coil bracelet shaped like a serpent. Freud/Clift turns the bracelet over in his hands, thinking, while caressing its curved surface with preoccupation. This continuum between physical sensations, mind, and time forms the structure of the film's representation of the closet. Neurotic bodily symptoms, the leaking of repressed sexuality into the present, are the manifestation of the active silence constituting the closet; asynchrony is thus the precondition for closetedness, as well as for "coming out" through encountering one's past. A telling account of the open secret of repression is given by Meynert, whose appeal to Freud to resume his research lies entirely on narratives of the closet. Admitting that he has always "suppressed his real being," Meynert pleads guilty to "silence" and to having lived "a sham life." Taking the established line that it takes one to know one, Meynert outs Freud as a fellow closet dweller: "Neurotics learn to recognize each other, as I did you," he tells him, adding later, "Break the silence—do what you set out to do: betray us!" The implications of Meynert's challenge are registered on Clift's face, shifting in expression from consternation to pained resolution; in his script notes for this scene, Clift writes only one word, "courage,"[50] suggesting the personal cost of lifting psychic repression.

Coming out of the closet is then Freud's method to achieve self-realization; while this process rests on a fluid concept of time, it leads

CHAPTER 5

Authoritative and fearless: Freud argues his controversial theory.

to a fixed notion of the subject, who is deemed to be fully explainable in sexual terms. Although Freud's research is initially fueled by Charcot's experiments, all dealing with nonsexual traumas, Freud's temporal theory sexualizes both present and past; the complete human being is a sexual being, brought forth by the recuperation of long-silenced libido. This utter emphasis on sexuality is crucial to the film's plot, which follows Freud's efforts against medical and social bigotry; his heavily sexual idea of "normality" is received as aberrant. The opposition between Freud and the Establishment is clear from the very first scene: confronting Meynert, to whom other doctors literally bow in submission, Freud is openly conflictive over the nature of hysteria. The power of this rebellious thread shapes the narrative and is enhanced by Clift's performance. Freud's defiance of the system is not expressed through emotive outbursts, but by displays of cold rage that resonate with authority. Freud/Clift never raises his voice when angry, yet his eyes dart ominously and his words fall sharp; warned that his use of hypnosis will be reported to Meynert, he says in slow, furious tones, "I shall tell him myself." As in many of his previous films, Clift complicates moments of direct confrontation, mixing fearless self-control with a vulnerable physical appearance; he suggests an inner strength behind a very brittle exterior. This effect is especially important in *Freud*, which is driven by the implicit force of the psychoanalytic argument, while showing Freud alone and helpless under virulent attack; in the key scene of his lecture on infant sexuality, Clift wears glasses for the only time in the film, projecting extra authority and expertise. Surrounded by a wildly hostile audience, who interrupts and insults him, Freud/Clift continues to read aloud his notes; he then takes his glasses off, surveying his listeners with a steely look of disobedience. Earlier on in the film, when Martha had expressed concern for his reputation, he had calmly replied: "People only whisper about me today—tomorrow they might stone me in the street."

This subversive, prophet-like persona is however problematized by Freud's ultimate goal: a temporal stability where the past, once met and recognized, must recede into history, leaving the subject in a fully accessible, equal-to-itself present. Paradoxically, Freud's drive is to rectify hybridity, but his way to do so is to acknowledge that time is hybrid. This was indeed the intellectual position of the real Sigmund Freud, whose vision straddled a routine dimension of psychic fragmentation and an ideal one of restored order through a whole, linear, sexually explainable subject. The smooth finale of Freud's journey inside the psyche, symbolized at the film's end by his ability to enter the cemetery, becomes undone through Clift's sheer presence; inserting a subtextual distance between theory and subject, Clift divides psychoanalytic narration from Freud's own self-production.

Freud/Clift initially follows his patients' pattern, tracing his physical symptoms to a distant sexual fantasy; recognizing the erotic longing he felt as a four-year-old, he effectively comes out and puts his past to rest. While reaching this stage, however, Freud's development varies greatly from that of Cecily, his chief respondent and metapatient, whose future trajectory he has also mapped out. As Cecily's repression gradually lifts, she becomes aware of her full sexual identity, paving the way for a libido wholly channeled in the present; her coming out is thus linked to an erotic continuum, positing her final incorporation in a sexually definable "norm." On the brink of adulthood, Cecily represents the human condition at large, a dimension of sexual immanence that is everywhere around Freud; from his wife's jealousy of Cecily to Breuer's fear of Cecily's seduction, to his many patients whose erotic fantasies he has let into view, the world Freud inhabits is a deeply sexualized one, in full accordance with his own theories. Yet

CHAPTER 5

Freud himself is only partly revealed through a sexual narrative; his only self-reference to sex points to his childhood, and nothing links his adult experience to a sexual identity of any description. Unlike Breuer, who is both troubled and attracted by Cecily's erotic charge, Freud/Clift is personally unaffected by it, nor does his behavior to his wife, or to anyone else in the film, contain a hint of sexual involvement. Separated by a gulf from Cecily's sex-laden character, and from Martha's conventional erotic awareness, Freud/Clift is equally distant from the film's male protagonists; his only felt similarity is for Carl, whose sexual identification rests on his infancy. Breuer, who as Freud's predecessor is also his most obvious comparison, reacts to Cecily's courtship by literally fleeing temptation; before that, however, he shows his erotic interest by calling her "a young deer," suavely praising her "lovely eyes," and wearing on his jacket the carnations she sends him. When Cecily's flowers start to be addressed to Freud, he does not touch them, yet glows with satisfaction at their psychoanalytic meaning; proving the transfer of her sexual fixation onto him, the carnations reveal that Cecily will allow him to hypnotize her. "Any day now she'll ask me," he tells Martha triumphantly, without a trace of embarrassment; as his shocked wife asks him if Cecily is in love with him, he replies uninterestedly, "You could . . . call it that." The sense that Freud's sexual detachment is a deviation from "normal" virility is confirmed by his looks: hunched, wafer thin, with the stamp of illness on his gaunt face, Freud/Clift is ghastly different from Breuer and Meynert, both supposedly older than he, and from the easily recalled presence of the real Sigmund Freud. While these other men are notably strong and masculine, therefore implicitly sexualized, the ethereal Clift is exactly the opposite, on a level with his nonsexual performance. Clift's scenes with Martha, who appears on screen before Cecily, are physically cold. Saying goodbye to her when leaving for Paris, he does not kiss or embrace her, limiting himself to a light peck on the cheek; he is equally cool in their wedding scene, kissing his bride with no visible thrill. In a later scene, after saying that his love for Martha may be linked to an image in his past, he kisses her on the neck, echoing Carl's Oedipal gesture; unlike Carl's, however, Clift's attitude totally lacks erotic feeling, suggesting that Martha's connection to his mother has been stripped of its original passion. Indeed, when Martha confronts him about his intellectual obsession with sexuality, she uneasily asks, "How can you—you of all men—be interested in such . . . things?" Her words can be easily read as a reference to his sexual indifference. If the implied dynamics of Freud's marriage cast doubt on his sex life, Freud's interaction with Cecily brings his erotic neutrality to the fore; the scenes between Clift and York form the film's narrative backbone, presenting them as accomplices on a psychosexual journey. Linked by the social transgression and shared discoveries of psychoanalysis, as well as by obvious mutual liking, Freud and Cecily are natural partners; this alliance, however, only makes their differences more striking. Susannah York is twenty-three years old in *Freud*, and looking much younger with her cherubic face and mischievous smile; pretty and curvaceous, she is ideally cast as a child-woman, framing Cecily through an artlessly sexy performance. Despite her medical afflictions, York/Cecily oozes awareness of physical pleasure; as she constantly recalls her father's embrace, his caresses, even how he undressed her and put her to bed, her expression is one of intense enjoyment. She talks breathlessly of her childhood dressing up as a courtesan, aimed at pleasing her father, and at times she hugs her body while absorbed in these memories. Although confined to bed or an armchair, and clothed in a demure white nightgown, in Freud's presence Cecily shows a marked degree of self-display: she moves eagerly in his direction, her face bent coquettishly on one side, looking at him sideways. Alternately smiling and pouting, she reaches for his hand and holds it; her gaze moves playfully over his face, intent on attracting him. Her clear excitement in his company is seamlessly carried to her masquerade as a prostitute, pointing to an instinctive, active erotic core; likewise, her furious piano playing indicates a passionate nature, expressed through any available means. Freud's view of Cecily as a wholly sexual being, a bundle of erotic energy needing an outlet, is entirely validated by York's rendition of her character; as a final proof of Freud's theories, however, she is contradicted by Clift's parallel yet opposite presence.

On an immediate level, Clift looks drastically aged compared to York. Emaciated and clad in dark suits, he clashes with the plump whiteness of her appearance, and the hand he places in hers is knotted like an old man's. His somber physicality is matched by his behavior, which grows only steadier as York's sexual obsession gets stronger. When

CHAPTER 5

she finds him indifferent to her prostitute attire, York/Cecily threatens to kill herself by jumping off a bridge; Clift/Freud, looking perfectly composed, tells her to step back on the pavement. Cecily complies, but such is her distress that she is unable to stand on her feet, leading Freud to delicately place his arm around her waist, supporting her as they walk together. She leans on him in the full seductiveness of her low-cut dress, yet Freud's reaction to her body is sexually blank, all the more striking as, a few minutes earlier, she had paraded her cleavage in front of him, telling him, "I never made love, you know—you will have to teach me . . . you can have me for nothing." Neither aroused nor embarrassed, Freud remains focused on her mental anguish, meeting her sexual onslaught with compassion and scientific attention. The ongoing erotic discrepancy between Freud and Cecily is enhanced by Clift's use of his body, completing his undoing of Freud's sexual theory. Never responding to an erotic stimulus, never reveling in self-display or physical pleasure, Clift's body is literally self-contained: he keeps hands and arms very close to himself, even if he gesticulates, and does not invite contact. Waiflike and lightweight, Clift occupies space but does not relate to it, nor to the bodies it contains, presenting himself through a visible but remote corporeality; his gestures denote feelings, but they are oddly self-referential. This is exemplified in two key but very different scenes, his first nightmare and the moment of his theoretical breakthrough. In the earlier scene he wakes up trembling with fear; in the latter he walks around the room, fired by enthusiasm. In both cases, his intense emotion is expressed by holding his arms in front of him, shaking his hands up and down, yet keeping his elbows attached to his body; like a convulsive puppet, he continues to move his arms stiffly once his hands have stopped. Distressing to watch, these are almost epileptic-like movements, fairly typical of Clift by this time; they suggest an alien physicality following its own mysterious laws. Even more troublingly, his gestures bear an uncanny resemblance to those of Charcot's patients, whose hysterical shaking was unrelated to sexual issues; this motile connection emphasizes Freud's neurosis while casting doubt on its primarily sexual cause.

Yet if Clift's overall performance obliterates eroticism, it maximizes Freud's mental activity and the extraordinary focus of his intellectual engagement with life. Clift's face, whether tense with concentration or enraptured by insight, shows a total involvement in the mechanisms of the psyche; his eyes respond instantly to every change in Cecily's voice, to an unexpected word, to a possible new link in the chain of her narrative. Staring wide-eyed, observing, analyzing, Clift's gaze imparts excitement to Freud's exploration of humanity, producing a character defined by the emotive experience of reason. While Clift's body looks fragile and detached, it is also rarely still, reflecting the powerhouse of Freud's mind. Working out his theories, Freud/Clift is often shown walking the streets at night, deep in thought. If he is indoors, he shifts position all the time, standing up and pacing the room, sitting down only to get up again; Breuer and Martha, the usual witnesses to his thinking, are static by comparison. Freud too, like Cecily, is a bundle of vital energy, but his energy is devoid of visible sexual content; as a subject working on his self-production, he remains not fully explainable through sexual discourse. Yet of the main characters affected by repression, Cecily, Meynert, and Freud himself, only Freud is presented as a successfully produced subject. The removal of his single neurotic symptom, the inability to walk to his father's grave, points to the resolution of his unconscious crisis. As the film rests on Freud's belief in a temporal route of the psyche, leading to self-realization in the present via stages of erotic desire, Clift's sexual inscrutability puts in question Freud's location in time. Freud's unrepressed present, achieved through his encounter with the past, is not a clearly sexualized present; it follows that Freud, as a fully realized subject, inhabits a time that is sexually undefined and thus not entirely revealed as the present. The obvious consequence is that both time and subject must be irrevocably hybrid. Subversive as Freud's role is in the script, Montgomery Clift makes it more so, stepping out of Freud's own rewriting of human chronology; the result is an extra layer of queer possibilities, a subject who will not be linearized or regulated in a fully accessible present. At the same time, the sexually enigmatic Freud/Clift challenges the ontology of sex itself; if psychoanalytic success depends on sexual resolution, the successfully unrepressed Freud may indeed be a sexualized subject, but in ways that completely elude recognized understandings of sex. In Freud's last scene with Cecily, he lays out his vision for her psychic progression: "Our work is only beginning, Cecily—it will take time to put your past in order—there'll be relapses—but the day will

CHAPTER 5

come when you'll be able to face life on its terms." Cecily's life terms have been clearly defined as the reordering of libido in the untroubled fullness of her present; Freud's own life configuration, however, remains ultimately unsaid, leaving him open to a queer temporality yet to be known.

Epilogue

Following the making of *Freud*, Montgomery Clift went through the bleakest phase of his life. An outcast in Hollywood, where a growing reputation for mental instability sealed his uninsurable status, Clift was now unable to work as an actor. Although he recorded Tennessee Williams's *The Glass Menagerie* for Caedmon Records, in 1964, and narrated a television documentary on William Faulkner in 1965, he never once appeared on screen, or indeed on stage. Acting had been Clift's life since he was thirteen, and this new situation plunged him into a severe depression; mental distress exacerbated his physical condition, by now a critical mixture of spontaneous disease and self-induced damage. Constantly affected by acute back pain, a legacy of his car crash injuries, and by leg cramps and phlebitis, Clift injected himself with ever-larger doses of Demerol, a narcotic and highly toxic painkiller. Demerol would cause him hallucinations and paranoid thoughts, but Clift found no other way to deal with the pain. "He was always in agony," remembers Lorenzo James, Clift's live-in secretary and nurse during his last years.[1] Combined with his massive intake of alcohol and sleeping pills, Demerol kept Clift in a confusedly anxious, often semicomatose state; he was also affected by random illnesses, as

EPILOGUE

when between 1962 and 1963 he was hospitalized seven times for issues ranging from hernia to cataracts. Desperate to be working, and terrified that he may never work again, Clift led the life of a hermit, hardly going out and spending whole days crying; most friends had deserted him, unable to cope with his state.[2] In addition, depression and alcoholism had all but destroyed Clift's appetite, and he now subsisted on "a piece of nearly raw meat once a day and some canned baby food."[3] The visible results of Clift's health crisis were horrific: his body looked utterly wasted, almost corpse-like, and the taut skin on his cheekbones evoked the image of a skull. His face was indeed triangular, with no flesh left in it, while his gaze seemed either desperate or vacant; he suggested acute malnutrition and impending death. Each of Clift's public sightings fueled tragic stories about him, as gossip articles described his sensational decline, with the result of further increasing his despair. Yet in all this, Clift could occasionally master the energy to think ahead. In a television interview, in 1963, he talked about his plans for being a film director, sounding perfectly lucid.[4] Somewhere among his devastation, a part of Clift believed his career was not over; in 1965, after three and a half years of unspeakable misery, this belief suddenly appeared justified, as he was offered the lead role in John Huston's *Reflections in a Golden Eye*. This change of fortune was due to Elizabeth Taylor, Clift's costar in the film; she had not only put Clift's casting as her condition for accepting the part but also had placed her whole salary, $1 million, as Clift's insurance. Greatly moved by Taylor's generosity, and ecstatic at the prospect of working again, Clift read the script and immediately agreed to it; his depression seemed to vanish overnight. *Reflections in a Golden Eye* was an ambitious project, an adaptation of a novel by Carson McCullers; it was also peculiarly right for Clift, an apt vehicle for his disquieting appearance and fatigued intensity. Set in postwar Georgia in a remote army post, the film centers on the unhappy Major Weldon Penderton (eventually played by Marlon Brando), secretly gay yet married to the beautiful Leonora (Elizabeth Taylor). The couple move along in a nightmarish plot, surrounded by bizarre and distressed characters, including a woman who cuts off her own nipples (Alison Langdon, played by Julie Harris); the major is haunted by homoerotic desires, while his wife seeks consolation with other officers. Increasingly anxious and finally panicked, the major shoots dead Private Williams (Robert Forster), a young soldier he had been obsessed with; the film ends with this murder, while Leonora's hysterical screams echo in the night. *Reflections in a Golden Eye* would have been ideal for Clift. The major's sparse spoken part, his intense emotional charge, and the eccentric desperation infusing the narrative, would have suited not only Clift's talent but also his very troubled persona. Perhaps most importantly of all, Major Penderton would have been the first explicitly queer role of Clift's career. However, despite the guarantee Elizabeth Taylor provided, the producers were still dubious about Clift's reliability, and the film's schedule was being constantly postponed; frantic at the thought of losing the part, Clift then grabbed the first chance to prove his fitness for work. *The Defector* was a trite, hopelessly mediocre thriller, directed by the undistinguished Raoul Lévy (who was to commit suicide two months after the film's release), yet Clift agreed to do it, for the sole purpose of showing the *Reflections* producers, who included Huston, that he was still capable of working. Indeed, as soon as he was signed up for *The Defector*, the shooting schedule for *Reflections* was magically finalized;[5] aware that his staying power would be under scrutiny, Clift insisted on doing his own stunts in *The Defector*, diving and swimming in icy river waters. The film has a cliché Cold War plot, in which Clift plays an American scientist trapped in communist East Germany; devoid of cinematic interest, it shows Clift as an exhausted man, desperately floating through a worthless script. Difficult to appreciate in critical terms, or to link in any way to Clift's previous films, *The Defector* stands anomalously in his career. Its meaning does not lie in performance, narrative, or style, but in being a visual record of Clift at the end of his life. *The Defector* made Clift sink into another depression, as the film's awfulness filled him with self-loathing.[6] It is a sad irony that it remains the last film he ever made, released after his death. If there is any value to be found in *The Defector*, it is as evidence of Clift's overwhelming need to work, of his self-definition as an actor. It was a passport to the coveted role in *Reflections in a Golden Eye*. It would seem right to see *Reflections*, and not *The Defector*, as the last film that Clift had wanted to make, and to conclude with this consideration the analysis of his career; in a sense, all of Clift's work had led to *Reflections in a Golden Eye*, where sexual difference was finally acknowledged, even if tragically dealt with.

EPILOGUE

On July 23, 1966, in the early hours of the morning, Montgomery Clift died at his home in New York; he was found lying naked on top of his bed, with a book by his side. An autopsy excluded overdose or suicide and declared that he had died of "occlusive coronary heart disease"; he was forty-five years old. He was leaving behind an extraordinary legacy, the record of a dazzling talent expressed through an outstanding range of films; bringing to the screen his own interpretation of difference, in a steady defiance of normative conventions, he had made an indelible mark as an artist, and as a truly queer star.

NOTES

Introduction

1. Quoted in Graham McCann, *Rebel Males: Clift, Brando, and Dean* (London: Hamish Hamilton, 1991), 61.
2. Richard Dyer, *Stars* (London: BFI, 1998), 63.
3. Quoted in Patricia Bosworth, *Montgomery Clift: A Biography* (New York: Limelight Editions, 2007), 138.
4. Quoted in ibid., 144.
5. Montgomery Clift interview on the Hy Gardner Show, WOR-TV, January 13, 1963.
6. Robert LaGuardia, *Monty: A Biography of Montgomery Clift* (New York: Primus, 1977), 68.
7. Bosworth, *Montgomery Clift: A Biography*, 154.

Chapter 1

1. Amy Lawrence, *The Passion of Montgomery Clift* (Berkeley: University of California Press, 2010).
2. Steven Cohan, *Masked Men: Masculinity and the Movies in the Fifties* (Bloomington: Indiana University Press, 1997).
3. Cohan, *Masked Men: Masculinity and the Movies in the Fifties*, 201–37.
4. Ibid., 212.
5. Judith Butler, "Imitation and Gender Insubordination," in *Inside/Out: Lesbian Theories, Gay Theories*, ed. Diana Fuss (New York: Routledge, 1991), 13–31.
6. Marjorie Garber, *Vested Interests: Cross-Dressing and Cultural Anxiety* (New York: Routledge, 1992).
7. Cohan, *Masked Men: Masculinity and the Movies in the Fifties*, 226.
8. Ibid.
9. Thomas Waugh, "Montgomery Clift Biographies: Stars and Sex,"

in *The Fruit Machine: Twenty Years of Writings on Queer Cinema* (Durham, NC: Duke University Press, 2000), 93–100.

10. Dyer, *Stars*, 53.
11. McCann, *Rebel Males: Clift, Brando, and Dean*, 58, 62.
12. Ibid., 58.
13. Kylo-Patrick R. Hart, "Gay Male Spectatorship and the Films of Montgomery Clift," *Popular Culture Review* 10, no. 1 (1999): 69–82.
14. Brett Farmer, "Gay Engagement with the Dephallicized Male Image: The Case of Montgomery Clift," in *Spectacular Passions: Cinema, Fantasy, Gay Male Spectatorships* (Durham, NC: Duke University Press, 2000), 224–46.
15. Ibid., 242.
16. Ibid., 230.
17. Ibid., 245.
18. Michel Foucault, *The History of Sexuality: The Will to Knowledge* (vol. 1), *The Use of Pleasure* (vol. 2), *The Care of the Self* (vol. 3) (London: Penguin, 1990–98).
19. Mark Norris Lance and Alessandra Tanesini, "Identity, Judgements, Queer Politics," in *Queer Theory*, ed. Iain Morland and Annabelle Willox (Houndmills: Palgrave Macmillan, 2005), 179.
20. Annamarie Jagose, *Queer Theory: An Introduction* (New York: New York University Press, 1996), 131.
21. Eve Kosofsky Sedgwick, *Between Men: English Literature and Male Homosocial Desire* (New York: Columbia University Press, 1985).
22. Eve Kosofsky Sedgwick, *Epistemology of the Closet* (Berkeley: University of California Press, 1990).
23. Ibid., 3.
24. Judith Butler, *Gender Trouble* (New York: Routledge, 1990).
25. Ibid., 43.
26. Esther Newton, *Mother Camp: Female Impersonators in America* (Chicago: University of Chicago Press, 1972).
27. Eve Kosofsky Sedgwick, *Tendencies* (Durham, NC: Duke University Press, 1993), 8.
28. Bosworth, *Montgomery Clift: A Biography*, 154.
29. Patrick Califia, "Gay Men, Lesbians, and Sex: Doing It Together," in Morland and Willox, *Queer Theory*, 25.
30. Alexander Doty, *Making Things Perfectly Queer: Interpreting Mass Culture* (Minneapolis: University of Minnesota Press, 1993), 3.
31. Lance and Tanesini, "Identity, Judgements, Queer Politics," 178.
32. Sheila Jeffreys, "Heterosexuality and the Desire for Gender," in *Theorising Heterosexuality: Telling It Straight*, ed. Diane Richardson (Buckingham: Open University Press, 1998), 77.

33. Leo Bersani, *Homos* (Cambridge, MA: Harvard University Press, 1995), 9.

34. Califia, "Gay Men, Lesbians, and Sex: Doing It Together," 189.

35. Doty, *Making Things Perfectly Queer: Interpreting Mass Culture*, xvii.

36. Lynne Segal, *Straight Sex: Rethinking the Politics of Pleasure* (Berkeley: University of California Press, 1994), 260–61.

37. Nikki Sullivan, *A Critical Introduction to Queer Theory* (Edinburgh: Edinburgh University Press, 2003) 134.

38. Clyde Smith, "How I Became a Queer Heterosexual," in *Straight with a Twist: Queer Theory and the Subject of Heterosexuality*, ed. Calvin Thomas (Urbana: University of Illinois Press, 2000), 66.

39. Calvin Thomas, "Straight with a Twist: Queer Theory and the Subject of Heterosexuality," in *Straight with a Twist: Queer Theory and the Subject of Heterosexuality* (Urbana: University of Illinois Press, 2000), 30.

40. Carrie Sandahl, "Queering the Crip or Cripping the Queer? Intersections of Queer and Crip Identities in Solo Autobiographical Performance," *JLQ: A Journal of Lesbian and Gay Studies* 9, no. 1–2 (2003): 37.

41. Eli Clare, *Exile and Pride: Disability, Queerness, and Liberation* (New York: South End Press, 1999), 112.

42. Robert McRuer, "As Good as It Gets: Queer Theory and Critical Disability," *JLQ: A Journal of Lesbian and Gay Studies* 9 (2003): 97.

43. Butler, *Gender Trouble*, xxv.

44. Marjorie Garber, "The Return to Biology," in Morland and Willox, *Queer Theory*, 56.

45. Anne Fausto-Sterling, "The Five Sexes," *The Sciences* (March–April 1993): 22.

46. Sedgwick, *Epistemology of the Closet*, 43.

47. Ellen Cole, "Is Sex a Natural Function?," in *Boston Marriages: Romantic but Asexual Relationships among Contemporary Lesbians*, ed. Esther D. Rothblum and Kathleen A. Brehony (Amherst: University of Massachusetts Press, 1993), 92.

48. Leslie Raymer, "What's Sex Got to Do with It?," in Rothblum and Brehony, *Boston Marriages*, 99.

49. Lisa Isherwood, *The Power of Erotic Celibacy* (London: T & T Clark, 2006).

50. Marny Hall, "Why Limit Me to Ecstasy? Towards a Positive Model of Genital Incidentalism among Friends and Other Lovers," in Rothblum and Brehony, *Boston Marriages*, 47.

51. Kathleen A. Brehony, "Coming to Consciousness: Some Reflections on the Boston Marriage," in Rothblum and Brehony, *Boston Marriages*, 20.

52. Sedgwick, *Tendencies*, 8.

NOTES TO CHAPTER 2

53. Ben Davies and Jana Funke, eds., *Sex, Gender, and Time in Fiction and Culture* (Houndmills: Palgrave Macmillan, 2011), 3.

54. Elizabeth Freeman, *Time Binds: Queer Temporalities, Queer Histories* (Durham, NC: Duke University Press, 2011).

55. David Halperin, *Saint Foucault: Towards a Gay Hagiography* (Oxford: Oxford University Press, 1995), 62.

Chapter 2

1. Cohan, *Masked Men: Masculinity and Movies in the Fifties*, 208.

2. Lawrence, *The Passion of Montgomery Clift*, 46.

3. Barry Keith Grant, *Shadows of Doubt: Negotiations of Masculinity in American Genre Films* (Detroit: Wayne State University Press, 2011), 67.

4. Farmer, *Spectacular Passions: Cinema, Fantasy, Gay Male Spectatorships*, 234.

5. Howard Hawks interviewed by Peter Bogdanovich, in Scott Breivold, ed., *Howard Hawks Interviews* (Jackson: University Press of Mississippi, 2006), 17.

6. Sidney Skolsky, "The New Look in Hollywood Men," *Photoplay* (July 1967): 111.

7. Sedgwick, *Between Men: English Literature and Male Homosocial Desire*, 1–2.

8. Sedgwick, *Epistemology of the Closet*, 15.

9. Sedgwick, *Between Men: English Literature and Male Homosocial Desire*, 21.

10. Ibid., 2.

11. Quoted in Bosworth, *Montgomery Clift: A Biography*, 121.

12. Elisa Glick, "The Dialectics of Dandyism," *Cultural Critique* 48 (Spring 2001): 144.

13. Sedgwick, *Epistemology of the Closet*, 73.

14. McCann, *Rebel Males: Clift, Brando, and Dean*, 58.

15. Lawrence Shaffer, "Reflections on the Face in Film," *Film Quarterly* 31, no. 2 (1977–78): 7–8.

16. Glick, "The Dialectics of Dandyism," 129–34.

17. Quoted in Neil Sinyard, *Fred Zinnemann: Films of Character and Conscience* (Jefferson, NC: McFarland, 2003), 80.

18. Sedgwick, *Tendencies*, 64.

19. Ibid.

20. Ibid.

21. Kathryn Bond Stockton, *The Queer Child: or, Growing Sideways in the Twentieth Century* (Durham, NC: Duke University Press, 2009), 62.

22. LaGuardia, *Monty: A Biography of Montgomery Clift*, 65.

23. Stockton, *The Queer Child: or, Growing Sideways in the Twentieth Century*, 252.

24. Hart, "Gay Male Spectatorship and the Films of Montgomery Clift," 76.

25. Butler, "Imitation and Gender Insubordination," 13–31.

26. Ralph Stern, "*The Big Lift* (1950): Image and Identity in Blockaded Berlin," *Cinema Journal* 46, no. 2 (2007): 66–90.

Chapter 3

1. Cohan, *Masked Men: Masculinity and the Movies in the Fifties*, 235.

2. Hart, "Gay Male Spectatorship and the Films of Montgomery Clift," 70.

3. Sedgwick, *Epistemology of the Closet*, 204.

4. Cohan, *Masked Men: Masculinity and the Movies in the Fifties*, 233.

5. Bosworth, *Montgomery Clift: A Biography*, 184.

6. Sedgwick, *Epistemology of the Closet*, 159.

7. Bersani, *Homos*, 146.

8. Bosworth, *Montgomery Clift: A Biography*, 214.

9. Sedgwick, *Epistemology of the Closet*, 204.

10. Ibid., 222–23.

11. Judith M. Kass, *The Films of Montgomery Clift* (Secaucus, NJ: Citadel Press, 1979), 131.

12. Quoted in Bosworth, *Montgomery Clift: A Biography*, 182.

13. Alfred Hitchcock interviewed by Pia Langstrom in *Masters of Cinema*, 1972, WCBS-TV.

14. Sedgwick, *Epistemology of the Closet*, 3.

15. Ibid., 202–12.

16. Montgomery Clift Papers, New York Public Library, Billy Rose Theater Division, Final Script, box 11A, folder 2, final script 8/9/52.

17. Sedgwick, *Epistemology of the Closet*, 73.

18. Butler, "Imitation and Gender Insubordination," 16.

19. Amy Lawrence, "Constructing a Priest, Silencing a Saint: The PCA and *I Confess*," *Film History: An International Journal* 19, no. 1 (2007): 68.

20. Montgomery Clift Papers, Final Script, box 11A, folder 2, 8/9/52.

21. Ibid.

22. Lawrence, *The Passion of Montgomery Clift*, 196.

23. Montgomery Clift Papers, box 11, folder 1, First Estimating Draft, 15/12/1952.

24. Bosworth, *Montgomery Clift: A Biography*, 252; and Fred Zinnemann, *An Autobiography* (London: Bloomsbury, 1992), 130–31.

25. Judith Butler, "Contagious Word: Paranoia and 'Homosexuality'

NOTES TO CHAPTER 4

in the Military," in Morland and Willox, *Queer Theory*, 142–57.

26. "Don't Ask, Don't Tell" is the specific name given to the 1993 reincarnation of preexistent US laws against gay soldiers, whose persecution dates back to 1778. In 1941, the year in which *From Here to Eternity* is set, current laws were strengthened to include "homosexual proclivities" as a disqualifying condition for inclusion in the military draft. DADT was finally repealed by President Barack Obama on December 22, 2010, and the repeal came into effect on September 20, 2011. The cultural and social impact of this recent legislative step has yet to be assessed.

27. Sigmund Freud, *Civilization and Its Discontents* (London: Penguin, 2002).

28. Butler, "Contagious Word: Paranoia and 'Homosexuality' in the Military," 150.

29. Montgomery Clift Papers, box 11, folder 1, First Estimating Draft, 15/12/52.

30. Zinnemann, *An Autobiography*, 131.

31. Montgomery Clift Papers, box 11, folder 3, Revised Final Draft, 24/2/53.

32. Montgomery Clift Papers, box 11, folder 1, First Estimating Draft, 15/12/52.

33. Quoted in Bosworth, *Montgomery Clift: A Biography*, 248.

Chapter 4

1. Bosworth, *Montgomery Clift: A Biography*, 291–92; and LaGuardia, *Monty: A Biography of Montgomery Clift*, 135.

2. Montgomery Clift interview on the Hy Gardner Show, WOR-TV, January 13, 1963.

3. Bosworth, *Montgomery Clift: A Biography*, 295–97.

4. Quoted in ibid., 298.

5. LaGuardia, *Monty: A Biography of Montgomery Clift*, 144.

6. Lawrence, *The Passion of Montgomery Clift*, 178.

7. LaGuardia, *Monty: A Biography of Montgomery Clift*, 145.

8. Bosworth, *Montgomery Clift: A Biography*, 310.

9. Ibid., 313.

10. Quoted in ibid., 310.

11. Quoted in ibid., 314.

12. LaGuardia, *Monty: A Biography of Montgomery Clift*, 164.

13. Ibid.

14. Bosworth, *Montgomery Clift: A Biography*, 314.

15. Ibid., 313.

16. LaGuardia, *Monty: A Biography of Montgomery Clift*, 146–47.

17. Dyer, *Stars*, 163–64.
18. Ibid., 64.
19. LaGuardia, *Monty: A Biography of Montgomery Clift*, 153.
20. Quoted in Bosworth, *Montgomery Clift: A Biography*, 305.
21. Quoted in ibid.
22. LaGuardia, *Monty: A Biography of Montgomery Clift*, 153.
23. Quoted in Bosworth, *Montgomery Clift: A Biography*, 340.
24. LaGuardia, *Monty: A Biography of Montgomery Clift*, 151.
25. Bosworth, *Montgomery Clift: A Biography*, 300.
26. Quoted in ibid., 313.
27. Quoted in LaGuardia, *Monty: A Biography of Montgomery Clift*, 150.
28. LaGuardia, *Monty: A Biography of Montgomery Clift*, 165.
29. Quoted in Kass, *The Films of Montgomery Clift*, 164–65.
30. *Variety*, October 4, 1957, 3.
31. *Los Angeles Examiner*, October 9, 1957, 8.
32. Quoted in Bosworth, *Montgomery Clift: A Biography*, 314.
33. Montgomery Clift Papers, box 14, folder 3, 23/9/55.
34. Bosworth, *Montgomery Clift: A Biography*, 327.
35. Quoted in Bosworth, *Montgomery Clift: A Biography*, 328.
36. Quoted in Kass, *The Films of Montgomery Clift*, 171.
37. Bosworth, *Montgomery Clift: A Biography*, 319.
38. Montgomery Clift Papers, box 17, folders 1–6.
39. LaGuardia, *Monty: A Biography of Montgomery Clift*, 172.
40. Quoted in LaGuardia, *Monty: A Biography of Montgomery Clift*, 170.
41. LaGuardia, *Monty: A Biography of Montgomery Clift*, 170.
42. Bosworth, *Montgomery Clift: A Biography*, 319.
43. Sedgwick, *Tendencies*, 9.
44. Ibid.
45. LaGuardia, *Monty: A Biography of Montgomery Clift*, 75.
46. Bosworth, *Montgomery Clift: A Biography*, 135.
47. Montgomery Clift Papers, First Draft Continuity, box 17, folder 4, 25/4/57.
48. Montgomery Clift Papers. This is a separate note inserted in the First Draft, box 17, folder 4, 25/4/57; the press quote is typed and the comment is written under it in Clift's handwriting.
49. Robert McRuer, *Crip Theory: Cultural Signs of Queerness and Disability* (New York: New York University Press, 2006).
50. Ibid., 2.
51. Montgomery Clift interview on the Hy Gardner Show, WOR-TV, January 13, 1963.
52. McRuer, *Crip Theory: Cultural Signs of Queerness and Disability*, 9.
53. Montgomery Clift Papers, box 17, folder 6, 23/05/57.

NOTES TO CHAPTER 4

54. Sandahl, "Queering the Crip or Cripping the Queer? Intersections of Queer and Crip Identities in Solo Autobiographical Performance," 26.
55. Montgomery Clift Papers, First Continuity Draft, box 17, folder 4, 25/4/57.
56. Ibid.
57. Montgomery Clift Papers, no date, box 17, folder 6.
58. Bosworth, *Montgomery Clift: A Biography*, 321.
59. Sally R. Munt, *Queer Attachments: The Cultural Politics of Shame* (Aldershot: Ashgate, 2008).
60. Ibid., 23.
61. Bosworth, *Montgomery Clift: A Biography*, 332.
62. LaGuardia, *Monty: A Biography of Montgomery Clift*, 189–91.
63. Gavin Lambert, "Lonelyhearts," *Film Quarterly* 12, no. 3 (1959): 48.
64. Patricia MacCormack, "Queer Posthumanism: Cyborgs, Animals, Monsters, Perverts," in *The Ashgate Research Companion to Queer Theory*, ed. Norren Giffney and Michael O'Rourke (Farnham: Ashgate, 2009), 115.
65. Munt, *Queer Attachments: The Cultural Politics of Shame*, 4.
66. Charles Darwin, *The Expression of Emotions in Man and Animals* (London: Harper Collins, 1999), 319.
67. Montgomery Clift Papers, Final Revised Script, box 12, folder 8, 30/6/58.
68. Munt, *Queer Attachments: The Cultural Politics of Shame*, 4.
69. Montgomery Clift Papers. The first version is in the Final Revised Script, box 12, folder 8, 30/6/58; the latter, which features in the film's final cut, is in the leather-bound script bearing Dore Schary's dedication to Clift, box 13, folder 2.
70. Munt, *Queer Attachments: The Cultural Politics of Shame*, 4.
71. Bosworth, *Montgomery Clift: A Biography*, 334.
72. Marcia Lawrence, "Suddenly, Last Summer," *Screen Stories* (February 1960): 29.
73. LaGuardia, *Monty: A Biography of Montgomery Clift*, 200–201.
74. Montgomery Clift Papers, First Draft, box 15, folder 5, no date.
75. Montgomery Clift Papers, Final Draft, box 15, folder 6, 24/4/59.
76. D. A. Miller, "Visual Pleasure in 1959," in *Outtakes: Essays on Queer Theory and Film*, ed. Ellis Hanson (Durham, NC: Duke University Press, 1999), 121.
77. Michelangelo Capua, *Montgomery Clift: A Biography* (Jefferson, NC: McFarland, 2002), 122; and LaGuardia, *Monty: A Biography of Montgomery Clift*, 205.
78. This is retrospectively fascinating in the light of Taylor's real-life devotion to various queer men, from Clift himself to Rock Hudson, and in relation to her tireless dedication to fight AIDS and its associated stigma.

79. LaGuardia, *Monty: A Biography of Montgomery Clift*, 203.

80. Kevin Ohi, "Devouring Creation: Cannibalism, Sodomy, and the Scene of Analysis in 'Suddenly, Last Summer,'" *Cinema Journal* 38, no. 3 (1999): 40.

81. Miller, "Visual Pleasure in 1959," 110.

82. Ohi, "Devouring Creation: Cannibalism, Sodomy, and the Scene of Analysis in 'Suddenly, Last Summer,'" 40.

83. Leo Bersani, "Is the Rectum a Grave?," in *Is the Rectum a Grave? and Other Essays* (Chicago: University of Chicago Press, 2010), 3–30.

84. Ibid., 29.

85. Ibid.

Chapter 5

1. Thomas, "Straight with a Twist: Queer Theory and the Subject of Heterosexuality," 32.

2. Bosworth, *Montgomery Clift: A Biography*, 134–35.

3. Ibid., 342.

4. LaGuardia, *Monty: A Biography of Montgomery Clift*, 267.

5. McCann, *Rebel Males: Clift, Brando, and Dean*, 74.

6. Lawrence Grobel, *The Hustons* (New York: Charles Scribner's Sons, 1989), 506.

7. Ellen Cole, "Is Sex a Natural Function?," 192.

8. Elia Kazan, *A Life* (New York: Alfred A. Knopf, 1988), 597.

9. Bosworth, *Montgomery Clift: A Biography*, 345.

10. Kazan, *A Life*, 600.

11. Judy White, "Sympathy for the Devil: Elia Kazan Looks at the Dark Side of Technological Progress in *Wild River*," *Literature Film Quarterly* 22, no. 4 (1994): 229.

12. Kazan, *A Life*, 599.

13. Quoted in Michael Ciment, *Kazan on Kazan* (London: Secker and Warburg, 1974), 134.

14. *Films in Review* (1960): 356.

15. Quoted in Kass, *The Films of Montgomery Clift*, 80.

16. LaGuardia, *Monty: A Biography of Montgomery Clift*, 207.

17. Montgomery Clift Papers, box 17, folder 2, no date.

18. Raymer, "What's Sex Got to Do with It?," 108.

19. Adrienne Rich, "Compulsory Heterosexuality and Lesbian Existence," *Signs* 5, no. 4 (1980): 632–60.

20. Kazan, *A Life*, 597.

21. Serge Toubiana, "Black Desert, White Desert," in *The Misfits: Story of a Shoot*, by Arthur Miller and Serge Toubiana (London: Phaidon, 2011), 65.

NOTES TO CHAPTER 5

22. Arthur Miller, *Timebends* (New York: Harper and Row, 1988), 462.
23. Serge Toubiana. "Something Burning Up: An Interview with Arthur Miller," in Miller and Toubiana, *The Misfits: Story of a Shoot*, 37.
24. Montgomery Clift Papers, Revised Screenplay, box 13, folder 4, March 1960.
25. Quoted in Bosworth, *Montgomery Clift: A Biography*, 354.
26. Both quotes from LaGuardia, *Monty: A Biography of Montgomery Clift*, 213–14.
27. LaGuardia, *Monty: A Biography of Montgomery Clift*, 215.
28. Quoted in Grobel, *The Hustons*, 496.
29. Quoted in Miller and Toubiana, *The Misfits: Story of a Shoot*, 147.
30. Bersani, *Homos*, 146.
31. Quoted in LaGuardia, *Monty: A Biography of Montgomery Clift*, 215.
32. Freeman, *Time Binds: Queer Temporalities, Queer Histories*, 9.
33. Ibid., 96.
34. Quoted in LaGuardia, *Monty: A Biography of Montgomery Clift*, 53.
35. Montgomery Clift Papers, box 7, folders 1–6, and box 8, folders 1–9.
36. Jeanne Green recounts this in the documentary *Hollywood Rebels: Montgomery Clift* (Claudio Masenza, 1983, Ciak Studio).
37. LaGuardia, *Monty: A Biography of Montgomery Clift*, 182.
38. Ibid., 199–200.
39. Freeman, *Time Binds: Queer Temporalities, Queer Histories*, 4.
40. Ibid., 8.
41. The Jewish Virtual Library, a division of the American-Israeli Cooperative Enterprise, at http://www.jewishvirtuallibrary.org/jsource/Holocaust/disabled.html.
42. Farmer, "Gay Engagement with the Dephallicized Male Image: The Case of Montgomery Clift," 231; LaGuardia, *Monty: A Biography of Montgomery Clift*, 216; Lawrence, *The Passion of Montgomery Clift*, 216–17.
43. Kass, *The Films of Montgomery Clift*, 198.
44. Thomas Doherty, "Judgment at Nuremberg," *Cineaste* (Spring 2005): 58.
45. Philip K. Scheuer, *Los Angeles Times*, December 22, 1961, 39.
46. Freeman, *Time Binds: Queer Temporalities, Queer Histories*, 5.
47. Montgomery Clift Papers, no date, box 12, folder 2.
48. Montgomery Clift Papers, box 12, folder 2, 1/9/60 and 20/1/60.
49. Montgomery Clift Papers, Revised Final Script, box 12, folder 3, 9/1/61.
50. Montgomery Clift Papers, box 9, folder 6, 14/9/61.

Epilogue

1. Quoted in Bosworth, *Montgomery Clift: A Biography*, 405.
2. LaGuardia, *Monty: A Biography of Montgomery Clift*, 260–61.
3. Jack Larson quoted in LaGuardia, *Monty: A Biography of Montgomery Clift*, 271.
4. Montgomery Clift interview on the Hy Gardner Show, WOR-TV, January 13, 1963.
5. Bosworth, *Montgomery Clift: A Biography*, 407.
6. LaGuardia, *Monty: A Biography of Montgomery Clift*, 278.

FILMOGRAPHY

Red River (Howard Hawks, 1948)
The Search (Fred Zinnemann, 1948)
The Heiress (William Wyler, 1949)
The Big Lift (George Seaton, 1950)
A Place in the Sun (George Stevens, 1951)
I Confess (Alfred Hitchcock, 1953)
Stazione Termini (Vittorio De Sica, 1953)
From Here to Eternity (Fred Zinnemann, 1953)
Raintree County (Edward Dmytryk, 1957)
The Young Lions (Edward Dmytryk, 1958)
Lonelyhearts (Vincent Donehue, 1958)
Suddenly, Last Summer (Joseph Mankiewicz, 1959)
Wild River (Elia Kazan, 1960)
The Misfits (John Huston, 1961)
Judgment at Nuremberg (Stanley Kramer, 1961)
Freud (John Huston, 1962)
The Defector (Raoul Lévy, 1966)

BIBLIOGRAPHY

Bersani, Leo. *Homos*. Cambridge, MA: Harvard University Press, 1995.
———. *Is the Rectum a Grave? and Other Essays*. Chicago: University of Chicago Press, 2010.
Bosworth, Patricia. *Montgomery Clift: A Biography*. New York: Limelight Editions, 2007.
Brehony, Kathleen A. "Coming to Consciousness: Some Reflections on the Boston Marriage." In Rothblum and Brehony, *Boston Marriages*, 19–28.
Butler, Judith. "Contagious Word: Paranoia and 'Homosexuality' in the Military." In Morland and Willox, *Queer Theory*, 142–57.
———. *Gender Trouble*. New York: Routledge, 1990.
———. "Imitation and Gender Insubordination." In *Inside/Out: Lesbian Theories, Gay Theories*, edited by Diana Fuss, 13–31. New York: Routledge, 1991.
Califia, Patrick. "Gay Men, Lesbians, and Sex: Doing It Together." In Morland and Willox, *Queer Theory*, 22–26.
Capua, Michelangelo. *Montgomery Clift: A Biography*. Jefferson, NC: McFarland, 2002.
Ciment, Michael. *Kazan on Kazan*. London: Secker and Warburg, 1974.
Clare, Eli. *Exile and Pride: Disability, Queerness, and Liberation*. New York: South End Press, 1999.
Clift, Montgomery, Papers. New York Public Library, Billy Rose Theater Division.
Cohan, Steven. *Masked Men: Masculinity and the Movies in the Fifties*. Bloomington: Indiana University Press, 1997.
Cole, Ellen. "Is Sex a Natural Function?" In Rothblum and Brehony, *Boston Marriages*, 187–93.
Darwin, Charles. *The Expression of Emotions in Man and Animals*. London: Harper Collins, 1999.
Davies, Ben, and Jana Funke, eds. *Sex, Gender, and Time in Fiction and Culture*. Houndmills: Palgrave Macmillan, 2011.
Doherty, Thomas. "Judgment at Nuremberg." *Cineaste* (Spring 2005): 58.

BIBLIOGRAPHY

Doty, Alexander. *Making Things Perfectly Queer: Interpreting Mass Culture.* Minneapolis: University of Minnesota Press, 1993.

Dyer, Richard. *Stars.* London: BFI, 1998.

Farmer, Brett. "Gay Engagement with the Dephallicized Male Image: The Case of Montgomery Clift." In *Spectacular Passions: Cinema, Fantasy, Gay Male Spectatorships,* 224–46. Durham, NC: Duke University Press, 2000.

Fausto-Sterling, Anne. "The Five Sexes." *The Sciences* (March–April 1993): 20–24.

Foucault, Michel. *The History of Sexuality: The Will to Knowledge* (vol. 1), *The Use of Pleasure* (vol. 2), *The Care of the Self* (vol. 3). London: Penguin, 1990–98.

Freeman, Elizabeth. *Time Binds: Queer Temporalities, Queer Histories.* Durham, NC: Duke University Press, 2011.

Freud, Sigmund. *Civilization and Its Discontents.* London: Penguin, 2002.

Garber, Marjorie. "The Return to Biology." In Morland and Willox, *Queer Theory,* 54–69.

———. *Vested Interests: Cross-Dressing and Cultural Anxiety.* New York: Routledge, 1992.

Glick, Elisa. "The Dialectics of Dandyism." *Cultural Critique* 48 (Spring 2001): 129–63.

Grant, Barry Keith. *Shadows of Doubt: Negotiations of Masculinity in American Genre Films.* Detroit: Wayne State University Press, 2011.

Grobel, Lawrence. *The Hustons.* New York: Charles Scribner's Sons, 1989.

Hall, Marny. "Why Limit Me to Ecstasy? Towards a Positive Model of Genital Incidentalism among Friends and Other Lovers." In Rothblum and Brehony, *Boston Marriages,* 43–61.

Halperin, David. *Saint Foucault: Towards A Gay Hagiography.* Oxford: Oxford University Press, 1995.

Hart, Kylo-Patrick R. "Gay Male Spectatorship and the Films of Montgomery Clift." *Popular Culture Review* 10, no. 1 (1999): 69–82.

Isherwood, Lisa. *The Power of Erotic Celibacy.* London: T & T Clark, 2006.

Jagose, Annamarie. *Queer Theory: An Introduction.* New York: New York University Press, 1996.

Jeffreys, Sheila. "Heterosexuality and the Desire for Gender." In *Theorising Heterosexuality: Telling It Straight,* edited by Diane Richardson, 75–90. Buckingham: Open University Press, 1998.

Jewish Virtual Library, a division of the American-Israeli Cooperative Enterprise, at www.jewishvirtuallibrary.org/jsource/Holocaust/disabled.html.

Kass, Judith M. *The Films of Montgomery Clift.* Secaucus, NJ: Citadel Press, 1979.

Kazan, Elia. *A Life.* New York: Alfred A. Knopf, 1988.

LaGuardia, Robert. *Monty: A Biography of Montgomery Clift.* New York: Primus, 1977.

Lambert, Gavin. "Lonelyhearts." *Film Quarterly* 12, no. 3 (1959): 46–48.

Lance, Mark Norris, and Alessandra Tanesini. "Identity, Judgements, Queer Politics." In Morland and Willox, *Queer Theory*, 171–86.

Lawrence, Amy. "Constructing a Priest, Silencing a Saint: The PCA and *I Confess*." *Film History: An International Journal* 19, no. 1 (2007): 58–72.

———. *The Passion of Montgomery Clift*. Berkeley: University of California Press, 2010.

Lawrence, Marcia. "Suddenly, Last Summer." *Screen Stories* (February 1960): 29.

MacCormack, Patricia. "Queer Posthumanism: Cyborgs, Animals, Monsters, Perverts." In *The Ashgate Research Companion to Queer Theory*, edited by Noreen Giffney and Michael O'Rourke, 111–28. Farnham: Ashgate, 2009.

McCann, Graham. *Rebel Males: Clift, Brando, and Dean*. London: Hamish Hamilton, 1991.

McRuer, Robert. "As Good as It Gets: Queer Theory and Critical Disability." *JLQ: A Journal of Lesbian and Gay Studies* 9, no. 1–2 (2003): 79–106.

———. *Crip Theory: Cultural Signs of Queerness and Disability*. New York: New York University Press, 2006.

Miller, Arthur. *Timebends*. New York: Harper and Row, 1988.

Miller, Arthur, and Serge Toubiana. *The Misfits: Story of a Shoot*. London: Phaidon, 2011.

Miller, D. A. "Visual Pleasure in 1959." In *Outtakes: Essays on Queer Theory and Film*, edited by Ellis Hanson, 97–125. Durham, NC: Duke University Press, 1999.

Morland, Iain, and Annabelle Willox. *Queer Theory*. Houndmills: Palgrave Macmillan, 2005.

Munt, Sally R. *Queer Attachments: The Cultural Politics of Shame*. Aldershot: Ashgate, 2008.

Newton, Esther. *Mother Camp: Female Impersonators in America*. Chicago: University of Chicago Press, 1972.

Ohi, Kevin. "Devouring Creation: Cannibalism, Sodomy, and the Scene of Analysis in 'Suddenly, Last Summer.'" *Cinema Journal* 38, no. 3 (1999): 27–49.

Raymer, Leslie. "What's Sex Got to Do with It?" In Rothblum and Brehony, *Boston Marriages*, 99–108.

Rich, Adrienne. "Compulsory Heterosexuality and Lesbian Existence." *Signs* 5, no. 4 (1980): 632–60.

Rothblum, Esther D., and Kathleen A. Brehony. *Boston Marriages: Romantic but Asexual Relationships among Contemporary Lesbians*. Amherst: University of Massachusetts Press, 1993.

Sandhal, Carrie. "Queering the Crip or Cripping the Queer? Intersections of Queer and Crip Identities in Solo Autobiographical Performance." *JLQ: A*

Journal of Lesbian and Gay Studies 9, no. 1–2 (2003): 25–56.

Scheuer, Philip K. "Judgment at Nuremberg." *Los Angeles Times*, December 22, 1961, 39.

Sedgwick, Eve Kosofsky. *Between Men: English Literature and Male Homosocial Desire*. New York: Columbia University Press, 1985.

———. *Epistemology of the Closet*. Berkeley: University of California Press, 1990.

———. *Tendencies*. Durham, NC: Duke University Press, 1993.

Segal, Lynne. *Straight Sex: Rethinking the Politics of Pleasure*. Berkeley: University of California Press, 1994.

Shaffer, Lawrence. "Reflections on the Face in Film." *Film Quarterly* 31, no. 2 (1977–78): 7–8.

Sinyard, Neil. *Fred Zinnemann: Films of Character and Conscience*. Jefferson, NC: McFarland, 2003.

Skolsky, Sidney. "The New Look in Hollywood Men." *Photoplay* 41, no. 43 (1967): 111–12.

Smith, Clyde. "How I Became a Queer Heterosexual." In Thomas, *Straight with a Twist*, 60–67.

Stern, Ralph. "*The Big Lift* (1950): Image and Identity in Blockaded Berlin." *Cinema Journal* 46, no. 2 (2007): 66–90.

Stockton, Kathryn Bond. *The Queer Child: or, Growing Sideways in the Twentieth Century*. Durham, NC: Duke University Press, 2009.

Sullivan, Nikki. *A Critical Introduction to Queer Theory*. Edinburgh: Edinburgh University Press, 2003.

Thomas, Calvin. "Straight with a Twist: Queer Theory and the Subject of Heterosexuality." In Thomas, *Straight with a Twist*, 11–44.

Thomas, Calvin, ed. *Straight with a Twist: Queer Theory and the Subject of Heterosexuality*. Urbana: University of Illinois Press, 2000.

Toubiana, Serge. "Black Desert, White Desert." In Miller and Toubiana, *The Misfits: Story of a Shoot*, 48–97.

———. "Something Burning Up: An Interview with Arthur Miller." In Miller and Toubiana, *The Misfits: Story of a Shoot*, 6–47.

Warner, Michael. Introduction to *Fear of a Queer Planet: Queer Politics and Social Theory*. Minneapolis: University of Minnesota Press, 1993.

Waugh, Thomas. "Montgomery Clift Biographies: Stars and Sex (1979–80)." In *The Fruit Machine: Twenty Years of Writings on Queer Cinema*, 93–100. Durham, NC: Duke University Press, 2000.

White, Judy. "Sympathy for the Devil: Elia Kazan Looks at the Dark Side of Technological Progress in *Wild River*." *Literature Film Quarterly* 22, no. 4 (1994): 227–31.

Zinnemann, Fred. *An Autobiography*. London: Bloomsbury, 1992.

INDEX

Note: Italicized page numbers indicate photographs.

AIDS and HIV crisis, 21–22
alienation and self-alienizing, Clift's: in *The Big Lift*, 74; following car accident, 2, 6, 126; in *Freud*, 218; in *The Misfits*, 186–87, 190, 198; in *Young Lions*, 9, 136–39, 141–45, 148
Americanness: in *The Big Lift*, 7–8, 54–55, 67–68, 70–71, 74, 76; disruptive portrayals by Clift, 104; in *From Here to Eternity*, 8; in *The Search*, 7–8, 54–58, 62, 65–66
An American Tragedy (Dreiser), 78
asexuality: in Clift's life, 6; in Clift's performances, 14, 19, 115, 125, 212; in Clift's screen persona following car accident, 134; nonactive sexuality vs., 29, 184; pathologizing drive of heteronormativity and, 19
Avedon, Richard, 3

Baxter, Anne, 101–2
Berlin Blockade, in *The Big Lift*, 66
Bersani, Leo, 9, 25–26, 88, 171–72, 197
Big Lift, The (film), *73*; Berlin Blockade as setting for, 66; central strand of narrative, 67; Clift's role and performance in, 4–5, 70, 74–75; gendered Americanness destabilized in, 7–8, 54–55, 72–74; plot description and analysis, 66–74, 76; as propaganda effort, 67–68, 70–71
bisexuality, in Cohan's text, 14
Bosworth, Patricia, 177

"boy," concept of, 13
Brando, Marlon, 16–17, 137, 140–41, 145, 147
Butler, Judith, 8, 23–24, 28, 71, 96, 108–9

Califa, Patrick, 24–25
Capote, Truman, 102
car accident (1956): circumstances of, 121–22; and Clift's departure from normative time, 200–201; in Cohan's study, 15–16; effects of, 2, 5–6, 28–30, 122–30; response of fans to, 127
Catholic Legion of Decency, 173
Celluloid Closet, The (documentary film), 170–71
chrononormativity and heteronormativity, 30, 203
Clare, Eli, 27
Clareman, Jack, 124
Clift, Montgomery: addictions, 6, 105, 126, 138; ambiguous sexuality of, 3, 5, 9, 12–14, 18–19, 75–76; audience response to, 127, 129–30, 136–37; audio recordings and narrations by, 221; Brando's script changes and, 140–41; celibacy, 29; childlike behaviors of, 202; as closeted subject, 7; complaints of his marketing as sex symbol, 176; death of, 223; disruptive presence of, 6, 13; emotional expressiveness, 52; as Hollywood outcast, 221–23; as icon of youthful rebellion, 16; legacy as film star, 1–2;

INDEX

Clift, Montgomery (*continued*)
multiplicity of, 77; perfectionist approach to acting, 6, 30–31; physical and mental health, 153, 177, 180, 198–99, 221–23; physical appearance, 3, 125, 198–99; relationships with men and older women, 201; reshooting of scene in *The Search*, 63–64; resistance to categorization, 25; response to machismo, 42–43; return to Broadway, 121; script interventions by, 4, 33, 90, 99–100, 160, 207–8; stunt work in *The Defector*, 223; subversive function of, 4–5, 11–12, 199–200; Taylor's relationship with, 5, 8, 82–83, 86–87, 222–23; Taylor's screen interaction with, 173–74, 197. *See also* alienation and self-alienizing, Clift's; car accident (1956); persona of Clift

Clift, Montgomery, movie stills and photographs: *The Big Lift*, 73; *Freud*, 214; *The Heiress*, 51; *From Here to Eternity*, 110, 117; *I Confess*, 100; *Judgment at Nuremberg*, 208; *Lonelyhearts*, 158; Monroe and, 195; *A Place in the Sun*, 7, 87; *Raintree County*, 133; *Red River*, 39; *The Search*, 59, 64; *Suddenly, Last Summer*, 168; Taylor and, 83; *Wild River*, 183; *Young Lions*, 138

closet, idea of: Butler on, 96; Clift and, 7; in *Freud*, 212–14; in *The Heiress*, 80; in *I Confess*, 92–94; in *A Place in the Sun*, 8, 14–15, 49, 80–81, 88; Sedgwick on, 23, 51, 80, 89–90, 92, 96

Cohan, Steven, 13–16, 33, 79
Cold War, in *The Big Lift*, 66
crip theory, 9, 142–45, 150

dance trope, in *The Misfits*, 191–92
Dandy, the, 50, 53–54
Darwin, Charles, 155
Dean, James, 17
Defector, The (film), 6, 126–27, 199, 223
De Sica, Vittorio, 102
deviant temporality, 30, 199–203, 208–9, 212

disability studies, 27, 142
discourse, notion of, 20
Dmytryk, Edward, 128–29
Don't Ask, Don't Tell (DADT) policy of US military, 107–9, 112, 230n26
Doty, Alexander, 25–26
Dreiser, Theodore, 78
Dyer, Richard, 16, 125–26

erotic celibacy, 29
erotohistoriography, 200, 212

fame, basis of, 3
fan literature, 3
Farmer, Brett, 17–18, 34
Fausto-Sterling, Anne, 28
film critics: on Clift in *Raintree County*, 129–30; on Clift in *Red River*, 3; on Clift in *Wild River*, 183; on *A Place in the Sun*, 77–78; on *The Search*, 3, 34, 54
Fiore, Carlo, 138
Foucault, Michel, 20
Freeman, Elizabeth, 200
Freud (film), 214; Clift's assertion of sexually and temporally hybrid identity, 9; as Clift's last big role, 6, 209–10; Clift's role and performance in, 211–12, 214–19; representation of the closet in, 212–14; snake image in narrative of, 213; temporal deviance in, 212
Freud, Sigmund, 17, 20, 108, 212, 214
From Here to Eternity (film): analyzed as a queer text, 8; Clift's erotic attachments in, 19; Clift's role and performance in, 104–5, 113; Jones's novel and Taradash's script, differences in, 107; plot description and analysis, 105–7, 109–19

Garber, Marjorie, 28
gay activism model, 21
gay spectatorship, 17
gender formation. *See* performative gender formation theory

244

INDEX

gender normativity, 28
gender roles, in *The Misfits*, 188–89
Glass Menagerie, The (Williams), 221
Glick, Elisa, 50, 53
Grant, Barry Keith, 33
Green, Jeanne and Fred, 202
guilt transference theme, in *I Confess*, 93

Hart, Kylo-Patrick R., 17, 79
Hawks, Howard, 34
hegemonic normality, 27
Heiress, The (film): Clift's motivation for role in, 45; Clift's role and performance, 7, 48–54; the closet in, 80; Morris/Clift as embodiment of the Dandy, 50, 53–54; Morris/Clift as object of desire and sexual enigma, 7, 46–47, 50–51; plot description and analysis, 45–46; tension between erotic object and controlling subject, 47–49
Hepburn, Katharine, 161–62
heteronormativity: in *The Big Lift*, 69–70; chronological structure and, 199–203; chrononormativity and, 30, 203; Clift's disruptive relation to, 166, 182; compulsory sex and, 184; cultural hegemony of able-bodied, 27; defiance of, in *I Confess*, 95; pathologizing drive of, 29
heterosexuality, 15, 43–44, 184
History of Sexuality (Foucault), 20
Hitchcock, Alfred, 90, 98
Hollywood studios, 4, 6, 124–25, 198, 222–23
Holman, Libby, 5, 127, 201
homoerotic subtext, in *Wild River*, 181
homo-ness, theorization of, 25–26, 88
homosexuality: homo-style, 87–88; queering of, 25; US military and, 107–9
homosocial courtship, 43
homosocial desire theory, 7, 40–41
Hopper, Hedda, 5, 127
hospitalizations, 221–22
Hudson, Rock, 122

Hughes, Howard, 34
Huston, John, 177, 222–23
hybridity: queer seduction and, 154–55; temporal, 200–203, 209, 212

I Confess (film), 100; Clift's interventions in, 90, 99–100; Clift's role and performance in, 92–93, 97–102; plot description and analysis, 91–99
identity: creation of, 20–21; gender and national, in *The Big Lift*, 71; hybrid, in *Wild River* and *Freud*, 9; male, Clift's portrayal of, 1, 4, 17–18, 33; queer, 25
Indrisano, Johnny, 148
institutionalized temporality, 202
Isherwood, Lisa, 29
Is the Rectum a Grave? (Bersani), 9, 171–72

Jagose, Annamarie, 22
James, Lorenzo, 221
Jeffreys, Sheila, 25
Jones, James, 106–7
Jones, Jennifer, 102
Judgment at Nuremberg (film), 208; Clift's looks in, 199; Clift's role and performance in, 203–9; Clift's script revisions, 207–8; display of deviant temporality in, 208–9; narrative structure of, 203

Kafka, Franz, 136–37
Kass, Judith M., 90
Kazan, Elia, 179–80, 182–83, 185
Kerr, Deborah, 117
Kinsey reports on sexual behavior, 4

LaGuardia, Robert, 124, 177
Lancaster, Burt, 117, *117*
Lance, Mark Norris, 22, 25
Lange, Hope, 147
language, as constitutive of reality, 20
Larson, Jack, 123
Lawrence, Amy, 12–13, 33, 98, 103, 122
Lévy, Raoul, 223
Life magazine cover, 3
Lockridge, Ross, 131

245

INDEX

Lonelyhearts (film), *158;* Clift's role and performance in, 153–55, 157–61; Clift's script interventions, 160; focus on social and sexual perversion, 9; plot description and analysis, 151–53; as queer discourse on subversive reclamation of shame, 150–51; Schary's script compared to West's novel, 152–53
Loy, Myrna, 201

MacCormack, Patricia, 154–55
male identity, Clift's portrayal of, 1, 4, 17–18, 33, 88–89. *See also* masculinity, subversion of
male-to-male desire: Freud and, 108; in scholarship on Clift, 15, 37; in *Wild River*, 181, 185
man-boy love narrative, in *The Search*, 61–64, 66
Mankiewicz, Joseph, 162, 202
Martin, Dean, 137–39, 145
Marxist criticsm, 20
masculinity, subversion of: in *The Big Lift*, 72–74, 76; in *The Heiress*, 48–50; in *The Misfits*, 189–91
Masked Men (Cohan), 13–16
masochism, 17
McCann, Graham, 16, 53
McCarthy, Kevin, 122
McCarthy era, 4
McCullers, Carson, 222
McRuer, Robert, 9, 27, 142, 144
Method school of acting, 4
MGM studios, 124–25, 127
military draft, 230n26
Miller, Arthur, 191, 194–95
Misfits, The (film): Clift's "straight queer" presence in, 9, 188–91; dancing trope in, 191–92; discourse of alienation in, 198; off-screen personas of Clift and Monroe, 194–97; patriarchal virility acknowledged and questioned in, 189; plot description and analysis, 185–87, 191–94, 198; publicity for, 186

Monroe, Marilyn, *195;* Clift's affinity with, 5, 9, 177, 188, 194–97
Munt, Sally R., 9, 150–51, 155, 159, 161

near-sameness concept, 9, 88, 188, 194, 197
Newton, Esther, 24
nonsexual relationships, 184–85
normative temporality, 206

Ohi, Kevin, 171

Paramount studios, 4
Parsons, Louella, 3
Passion of Montgomery Clift (Lawrence), 12–13
performative gender formation theory, 8, 23–24, 28, 71
persona of Clift: ambiguity in, 14, 70, 85; blueprint for, 13; critical analyses of, 11–19; crystallization of, 8; erotic, 49, 61; key elements in, 3, 7; military roles and, 103–4; off-screen, 194–97; in *A Place in the Sun*, 77, 90; in *Red River*, 43; star, 24, 34–35, 42, 44; temporal incongruity in, 201; variances in, 19; in *Wild River*, 179
Place in the Sun, A (film), 7, 87; Clift's role and performance, 77, 79, 90; the closet in, 8, 14–15, 49, 80, 88; Cohan's reading of closeted gay subtext in, 15; critical discussion of, 77–78, 90; double life of George/Clift, 81–82; George-Alice affair in, 79; narrative of, 82–83; plot description and analysis, 78–90
politics of difference, 22
polysemy, structured, 125–26, 134
popular press, 5, 127
poststructuralism, 19–20
post–World War II era, 3–4
press, 5, 127
preterition, in *I Confess*, 93

queer, as term and practice, 21–22
queer identity, 25
queering of "homosexual," 25

246

INDEX

queerness, function of concept, 141–42
queerness, straight, 9, 26–27, 175–76, 181–83, 186, 188–89
queer reclamation of shame, 9, 150–51
queer scholarship, 23, 28
queer temporality, 9, 30, 199–202, 220
queer theory: antiheteronormative project of, 28; expansion of notions of sameness, 88; fluidity in scope and boundaries of, 19; and idea of the closet, 23; and interrogation of time, 30; introduction to, 7; poststructuralism and, 20; recent developments in, 6

Raintree County (film), 39, 133; Clift's motives in making of, 121; Clift's presence in, following car accident, 128–30; Clift's role and performance in, 130, 132–36; critical response and public reaction to Clift in, 129–30; as document of Clift's fragmentation, 9, 128; plot description and analysis, 131–33; press speculation about Clift during filming of, 127
Raymer, Leslie, 29, 184–85
Red River (film), 39; Clift's erotic self-display in, 7, 34–35, 38–40; Clift's intervention in screen representations of male identity, 33; Clift's role and performance in, 7, 34–35, 37–40; contiguity of heterosexuality and homosexuality in, 15, 43–44; film critics on Clift in, 3; homophobic patriarchal order challenged in, 42; plot description and analysis, 35–37; Sedgwick's concept of homosocial desire applied to, 40–41
Reflections in a Golden Eye (film), 222
Remick, Lee, 180, 182–83, 183, 183–84
reviews. See film critics
Rich, Adrienne, 184
Rivers, Caryl, 3
Roosevelt, Franklin D., 55
Rush, Barbara, 147
sameness and near-sameness, 9, 25, 87–88, 188, 194, 197
Sandahl, Carrie, 144
Saussure, Ferdinand de, 20
Schaffer, Lawrence, 53
Schary, Dore, 152–53
Schell, Maximilian, 148–49
Schofield Barracks, Hawaii, 112
scholarship on Clift, 6–7, 11–13, 15–17
Seagull, The (Chekhov), 121
Search, The (film), 59, 64; Americanness destabilized in, 7–8, 54–56, 65–66; binary structure of, 55–56; Clift's role and performance, 54, 60, 62–65; desire introduced, 58–61; Karel's story and persona, 57–58; man-boy love narrative, 61–64, 66; plot description and analysis, 7–8, 54–56, 55–66; reviews of, 3, 34, 54
Sedgwick, Eve Kosofsky: on discourses of bodies and sexuality, 28; homosocial desire theory, 7, 40–41; on homo-style homosexuality, 87–88; on idea of the closet, 51, 80, 89–90, 92, 96; on queerness concept, function of, 141–42; on queer theory, 61; on queer theory and idea of the closet, 23; on straight queerness, 26–27
Selznick, David O., 102
sexual activity, in post–World War II era, 4
sexual categories, oppressiveness of, 20–21
sexual delay, 61
sexuality, Clift's: decrease in activity, 177
sexual orientation, nature of, 25
shame: cultural politics of, 150–51; disruptive potential of, 155; in Lonely Hearts, 154, 157, 159–61; queer reclamation of, 9; in Suddenly, Last Summer, 162, 165–66, 173
Shaw, Irwin, 139, 141
Sinatra, Frank, 118
Smith, Clyde, 26
societal normativity, Clift's challenge of, 31

247

INDEX

Springer, John, 196
Stapleton, Jean, 158
stardom, 2, 125–26, 134
Stazione Termini (Indiscretion of an American Wife) (film), 102–3
Stevens, George, 79
Stockton, Kathryn Bond, 61, 64
straight queerness concept, 9, 26–27, 175–76, 181–83, 186, 188–89
Suddenly, Last Summer (film), 168; Clift's role and performance in, 162, 165–68; focus on social and sexual perversion, 9; plot description and analysis of, 163–70, 173; publicity for, 161; scholarship on, 171–72
Sullivan, Nikki, 26
Surtees, Bob, 129

Tanesini, Alessandra, 22, 25
Taradash, Daniel, 107
Taylor, Elizabeth, 83, 133, 168; Clift's car accident and, 122; Clift's relationship with, 5, 8, 82–83, 86–87, 222–23; Clift's screen interaction with, 173–74, 197; friendships with queer men and fight against AIDS, 232n78; in *A Place in the Sun*, 77, 87; in *Raintree County*, 121, 131, 134–35; in *Suddenly, Last Summer*, 161, 163, 167–69, 171, 173
Taylor, Frank, 196
temporal hybridity, 9, 30, 200–203, 209, 214
temporality, deviant, 30, 199–203, 208–9, 212
temporal queer theory, 199–202
temporal theory, 214

Thomas, Calvin, 26
Todd, Mike, 170

unconscious, theory of the, 20
United Nationas Relief and Rehabilitation Administration (UNRRA), 55, 56

Vidal, Gore, 161–62

Wayne, John, 33–34
West, Nathanael, 151
Wilding, Michael, 122
Wild River (film), 183; Clift's role and performance in, 9, 175–76, 178–82, 184–85; heterosexuality's queer potential in, 9, 176, 180–82; homoerotic subtext in, 181; nature of male desire queered in, 182, 184–85; plot description and analysis, 176–79; proposal and wedding scenes, 183–84
Williams, Tennessee, 161, 221

York, Susannah, 217–18
Young Lions, The (film), 138; audience response to Clift in, 136–37; Clift's physical appearance in, 136–37, 145–50; Clift's role and performance in, 136–38, 141–49; crip concept in, 142–44; early version of script, 144; fight scenes, 148; script changes to gain Pentagon approval, 140; self-alienizing move by Clift in, 9

Zinnemann, Fred, 54, 63, 112

www.ingramcontent.com/pod-product-compliance
Lightning Source LLC
Chambersburg PA
CBHW051539230426
43669CB00015B/2650